The
Process
of
Science

ANTHONY CARPI | ANNE E EGGER

a Visionlearning publication

The Process of Science
by Anthony Carpi, PhD and Anne E. Egger, PhD
ISBN: 978-1-257-96132-0

Printed in the United States of America.
Text and cover design by Heather Falconer.
Cover images: cell and DNA images © jscreationzs / FreeDigitalPhotos.net; earth image © Salvatore Vuono / FreeDigitalPhotos.net

Published by Visionlearning, Inc., New Canaan, CT.
www.visionlearning.com

Image credits: page 2, from GWS – The Great War: The Standard History of All European Conflict (1915); page 5 © D.K. Demcheck, courtesy of the USGS; page 9, Earthrise © NASA; page 13 © Epogee, Ltd.; page 16 Andromeda galaxy © NASA; page 18 Hubble Diagram © Huntington Library; page 19 © WMAP/NASA; page 26 (bottom) © David B. Fankhauser, Ph.D.; page 29, courtesy of Oxford Museum of Natural History; page 42 © NSF; page 60 © Geo ExPro; page 64 © Palmen; page 66 © NASA; page 68 © ISI Web of Science; page 91, from http://www.webexhibits.org/calendars/year-text-Copernicus.html; page 96 © TOMS science team & and the Scientific Visualization Studio, NASA GSFC; page 110, Deep Impact © NASA/JPL-Caltech/UMB; page 117 © NASA; page 120, Image courtesy of Ian Parker, http://parkerlab.bio.uci.edu/; pages 121 and 122 © CB Hunt; page 124 © Michael Ernst, Woods Hole Research (www.whrc.org); page 129 © Corel Corporation; page 135, courtesy of Good Housekeeping magazine; page 139, graphic courtesy of NASA's Earth Observatory; page 144, image courtesy the National Center for Earth-surface Dynamics Data Repository http://www.nced.umn.edu/Data_Repository.html [accessed September, 2008] © National Center for Earth-surface Dynamics Data Repository; page 149 © Brian Hayes, American Scientist; page 152, image courtesy NOAA Geophysical Fluid Dynamics Laboratory; page 163 © University of Wisconsin – Madison Space Science and Engineering Center; page 166 © IPCC; page 173 © Marc Schuelper; page 178 © Hannes Grobe; page 195 © Tomasz Sienicki; page 205 © Commonwealth of Australia 2006; page 206, courtesy of the Daily Telegraph; page 207 (bottom) © USGS Landsat Project; page 214 © Macmillan Publishers Ltd., used with permission from Nature; page 215 © American Association for the Advancement of Science/ Cornell Lab of Ornithology; page 218 © Science; page 220 © NASA; page 226, courtesy of XX; pages 229 and 231 © Anne Egger; page 236 © American Association for the Advancement of Science/Deanne Fitzmaurice; page 244 © Elsevier (2008); page 246 © American Association for the Advancement of Science; page 254 © US Coast Guard, Visual Information Gallery; page 256 © Gordon Research Conferences; page 259 © Climate Progress Fund, Center for American Progress Action Fund; page 260 © Deb Agarwal.

All other artwork © Visionlearning, Inc., or available in the public domain through Wikipedia/Creative Commons.

*For John, Carina,
and all of our students.*

Table of Contents

Foreword

Scientific literacy continues to be the primary goal for pre- and post-secondary science education in the United States and throughout the world. Although current reform documents developed by various stakeholders (e.g. scientists, educators, industry, policy makers) have echoed the importance of achieving a literate citizenry, the goal is not new. Scientific literacy has been prized as an educational goal for at least four decades, and actually much longer; often referred to using different names. Although definitions of scientific literacy have varied over the years, the focus is commonly the development of citizens who can use their scientific knowledge to make informed decisions about scientifically-based societal and personal issues.

In contrast to the decision-making goal of scientific literacy, science instruction in pre- and post-secondary schools has focused almost exclusively on helping students "understand" the foundational concepts, theories, laws, and principles in the particular science under study. I have placed quotation marks around the word understand because this is typically a euphemism for *memorize*. All of us recognize that memorized knowledge does not lend itself to the informed decision making envisioned in the goal of scientific literacy. In response to our dissatisfaction there has been an emphasis on having students develop in-depth understandings of scientific knowledge, understandings that can be applied to make sense of the natural world. During our quest to search for ways to develop in-depth understandings, the very definition of what it means to understand scientific knowledge has been transformed.

The importance of having students understand how scientific knowledge is developed (i.e. scientific inquiry) and the characteristics of the knowledge that are necessarily derived from the manner in which the knowledge was developed (i.e. nature of science) has been recognized. That is, for students to really understand a scientific concept it is important for them to have an understanding of how the concept was developed as well as the ontological and epistemological status of the concept. For example, does a student really understand what an atom is if they can only draw the picture that is portrayed in books, or do they also need to know that what is pictured in books is a representation, of something that has never been seen, derived from experimental results? The latter is the case and it is only with such an understanding that pre- and post-secondary students can approximate what is desired in the scientifically literate individual.

Unfortunately, instruction in science rarely addresses scientific inquiry and nature of science. Further, few textbooks address these issues and simply focus on the knowledge in its "final" form. What is provided in the pages of *The Process of Science* can certainly change this scenario. Carpi and Egger have provided an engaging text that college science faculty (actually, I believe the chapteres would be effective at the high school level, as well) can insert into their existing courses to insure that scientific inquiry and nature of science are emphasized. The chapters will help students develop a much more in-depth understanding of the scientific concepts, laws, and theories they are being asked to learn and will better equip students to make the informed decisions that the goal of scientific literacy advocates.

The introduction of the book clearly delineates 12 understandings *about* science and the scientific process that students should know. These understandings extend beyond just knowing foundational scientific concepts, laws, theories, etc. and the doing of science. For example, this text stresses the idea that "scientists use multiple research methods" as opposed to a single set and sequence of steps, typically known as the Scientific Method. It is also stressed that "scientific knowledge evolves with new evidence and perspectives." In short, scientific knowledge is not absolute and it changes based on additional knowledge and/or viewing the same knowledge from a different perspective. The view of science advocated by Carpi and Egger's text, and consistent with recent reforms, is that science is a human endeavor and the knowledge it develops is impacted and enriched by human characteristics. It is important to note that the 12 understandings, or Key Concepts as described by the authors, are discussed in much more detail and give rise to many subcomponents within the context of the provided instructional materials.

The text is appropriately divided into general areas of concern such as research design, scientific data, scientific communication, and a general overview of science as a human endeavor. The historical examples provided in the individual chapters do an excellent job of highlighting the understandings of science targeted and they are engaging to read. Although Carpi and Egger's scientific areas of expertise are primarily in the chemical and geological sciences, they have been extremely careful in the development of the modules so that they give adequate attention to all of the commonly taught science areas in college. I have personally used some of these materials with science teachers in a Masters degree program and they thoroughly enjoyed the readings, but more importantly the readings enhanced their understandings of science.

Carpi and Egger's approach clearly considers the constraints of college teaching. The instructional materials can be used as a complete and cohesive set to provide students with the most comprehensive overarching view of science. However, they can also be selectively used to highlight certain aspects of the process of science. This provides instructors with the freedom to "cherry pick" those chapters that can best be integrated into the existing course curriculum. Personally, I would strongly recommend the inclusion of all the chapters, however the reality of classroom life requires some flexibility when one adds to his/her curriculum. Carpi and Egger are advocating an important enrichment to the current state of college level science, rather then completely revising all the good work that already exists. Interestingly, their approach is quite similar to what I have found to be enormously successful with secondary level science students.

Overall, this text and collection of online instructional modules is an excellent addition to the resources used by the college level science instructor. Their format and use is quite flexible, but most importantly the book as a whole addresses areas of knowledge all too often ignored in college level instruction. If we truly want our college graduates to develop the ability to make informed decisions with respect to scientifically-based social and personal issues, these graduates must know more than foundational science. They must know how the knowledge was developed and what characteristics the knowledge has (e.g. tentative) have been engendered by the process of knowledge development (i.e. scientific inquiry). This knowledge set is certainly consistent with the overall goal of scientific literacy. The text provided by Carpi and Egger was an ambitious undertaking, but it represents a significant step toward the improvement of college level science teaching; a step that will provide students with a more accurate and informed conception of science as a way of knowing.

Norman G. Lederman
Professor and Chair
Mathematics and Science Education
Illinois Institute of Technology

December 15, 2010

Preface

The origins of this book lie in our combined teaching and advising experiences at diverse institutions, from a community college to a large, multi-campus city university to a world-renowned research university. Each of us has had encounters where we felt that otherwise capable students were simply missing the point of how science works. When we turned to society as a whole, we saw the same issues reflected back at us: public perception of socio-scientific issues such as climate change (today) and the health hazards associated with smoking (in the past) were clouded by a lack of understanding about how science really works. In response, we felt a need to emphasize in our teaching not what we know, but how we know what we know in our disciplines.

Unfortunately, few resources were available to support this kind of teaching and learning. As a result, we submitted a proposal to the U.S. Department of Education to develop such a resource, and we were funded to do so. In conversation with our students and with an array of science educators, we uncovered many misconceptions that students hold about the process of science. Subsequently, we began to write materials to address those misconceptions and to demystify the process of science and the work of scientists themselves.

The result is collected in this book, aimed primarily at undergraduate students at an introductory science level. The book can stand alone as a resource for students preparing to do research for the first time or for anyone who might be interested in learning more about the process of science, but we also envision the readings here being integrated into introductory courses in biology, chemistry, Earth science, and physics, and the examples we use to illustrate the process of science are drawn from all of these disciplines. The materials in this book are also freely available online at www.visionlearning.com. On the website, you will find all of the chapters as individual modules with several additional features:

- An integrated glossary, where definitions appear on mouse-over;

- A series of targeted links for further exploration, biographies, and classic papers related to the module text;

- Online, customizable quizzes that cover the main topics in the modules;

- Large, high-resolution versions of the images in the book; and

- Many more modules that cover topics in introductory biology, chemistry, Earth science, and physics.

We encourage you to visit the website to take advantage of these additional resources.

Acknowledgements

Detailing the methods and process of science is not a simple task. There are no user guides or handbooks for the uninitiated; the practices, methods and nuances of one's field are commonly learned through a multi-year apprenticeship with a senior scientist. Even then, scientists often take the art of their work for granted – designing research studies, evaluating and interpreting data, working with colleagues and publishing or otherwise sharing their work without explicitly calling out the sets of skills used to do so.

This book is a culmination of four years of research and self-exploration in which we called on the expertise of others to help us better understand the practices that we and other scientists engage in as we actually do science. As such, we are deeply indebted to a number of individuals who helped shape the concepts explored in this book and also reviewed and provided comments on the chapters as they were completed. Our sincere thanks to Heather Boyd at the University of Notre Dame; Mark Connolly, Nancy Ruggeri and Basil Tikoff at the University of Wisconsin; Kaatja Kraft at Mesa Community College; Natalie Kuldell at the Massachusetts Institute of Technology; Norman Lederman at the Illinois Institute of Technology; Nathan Lents and Sandra Swenson at John Jay College; Cathy Manduca at Carleton College; Alfie Rosenberger at Brooklyn College; Judy Scotchmoor and Anna Thanukos at the University of California at Berkeley; and Kimberly Tanner at San Francisco State University. Thanks also to Allan Frei for comments and suggestions, and to Heather Falconer, Alice Letcher, and Yana Mikhailova for technical support.

We are also grateful for the support we received to produce these materials, a portion of the content of this book was developed under grant #P116B06-0183 from the Fund for the Improvement of Postsecondary Education (FIPSE), U.S. Department of Education. However, this does not necessarily represent the policy of the Department of Education, and you should not assume endorsement by the Federal Government. Special thanks to Bette Dow at FIPSE who not only served as our Program Officer but also provided invaluable help and guidance along the way.

Finally, we would like to especially thank our family and friends who supported us during these four years and helped us see this work to completion.

Introduction to
the Process of Science

"In essence, science is a perpetual search for an intelligent and integrated comprehension of the world we live in."
                                    ~ Cornelius Bernardus van Neil

Several years ago, a student working on an undergraduate research project in my (Anthony's) laboratory approached me with concern. "I'm doing something wrong," she exclaimed. I had seen her research results and knew she was making good progress, so I was surprised to hear that she was having a problem. Over the next several days we went through her experimental procedure, we reviewed her instrumental methods, and we examined her results; yet I could not find a problem with her work. Finally, I asked her the obvious question, "Why do you think you're doing something wrong?"

"Because I'm not getting what you said I should get," she replied with some frustration.

Her response startled me. After discussing it with her, I realized that she was mistaking an hypothesis for a foregone conclusion. I had not told her what she "should get," but I was familiar with the existing literature and research in the area and we had discussed some published hypotheses several weeks earlier. When faced with valid research data that did not fit these predictions, I recognized that she had a novel finding and came to change my hypothesis. But she was interpreting her results as a mistake.

Why was I startled by her response? Because despite almost four years of an intensive college science major behind her and several years of high school science experience, this student still subscribed to the common misconception that science is a rigid exercise in proving a pre-conceived point. That there is little creativity or discovery in science, but rather it is a tedious exercise in proving something we already know to be true. I was also startled because I realized that, although I spend many hours with my students, teaching them about scientific research procedures, experimental design, instrument operation, and the scientific literature, I was still not teaching them about science.

But how can this happen? This was an excellent student who had a near perfect "A" grade average, and I was trying to be conscientious in my teaching and advising. Why was there still such a difference between the way she and I perceived her results? The root of the problem goes far deeper than our interaction over the course of the year. Throughout school, science is often portrayed in textbooks and even in the classroom as a series of "known" facts and figures: electrons are negatively charged, DNA is a double helix, earthquakes occur at plate boundaries, etc. Unfortunately, the process by which these discoveries were made and how they fit into scientific progress is often ignored in the classroom. Even when material is added to science lectures about the discovery of these concepts, they are often presented as an obvious and inevitable conclusion. For example, J.J. Thomson's experiments with a cathode ray tube are commonly discussed in chemistry classes (Figure 1). Few teachers present the critical components of the process that humanize Thomson, however, like the fact that when Thomson first presented his ideas on electron charge to the scientific community, a colleague asked him if he was joking! These details help illustrate the nature of scientific discoveries, the skepticism that accompanies new discoveries, and the process of review and validation they undergo before they are accepted. Yet this is rarely conveyed in the classroom along with the content, so it's no wonder these ideas seem like inevitable conclusions.

Figure 1: J.J. Thomson (1856–1940), a British physicist and Nobel laureate credited for discovering the electron.

So where do we learn about how science is practiced? Those fortunate enough to be exposed to scientific research begin to understand because they are engaging in the process of science. After my experience with this student, we discussed the idea that science is not just a collection of known facts, but a process by which we come to know things about the natural world. We discussed the purpose of experimentation, the role of reviewing the existing literature to identify possible research hypotheses, and the need to remain open to various interpretations of the data. Participating in mentored research is one way to learn how science is practiced.

This student went on to complete and publish her research, enroll in a PhD program, and become a qualified scientist in her own right (Mauclair, Layshock, and Carpi, 2008). When asked recently, she did not recall this specific interaction, but she did recall that despite having "The Scientific Method" drilled into her in many science classes, she had little understanding of what science entailed before her undergraduate research experience.

So scientists need to understand how science is done; but why would this matter to anyone not interested in becoming a scientist? Because science and a scientific way of thinking impact more aspects of our daily lives than you might think. Scientific advances in nutrition and medicine have helped raise life expectancy in the United States by more than 20 years in the last century alone. On a personal level, a scientific way of thinking can help you weed through conflicting reports about nutrition and make better choices about healthy eating. Advances in chemistry, physics, and materials science have led to faster computers and smaller cell phones – letting you take pictures with your phone and send them to your friends. And advances in modeling and meteorology have helped us better predict and plan for natural disasters like floods and hurricanes – something we all hope never to encounter, but can now be better prepared for when they do occur.

Understanding science is more than memorizing that the electron has a negative charge. It is understanding how scientific advances are made, validated, and interpreted. It is being able to interpret an elected official's position on stem cell research, climate change, or space exploration. And it is to have the ability to take in new information on diet, exercise, or disease and apply it to our own lives. Understanding the process of science and scientific problem solving can help us make better decisions every day.
SCIENCE IS THE PROCESS, NOT JUST THE RESULT.

What is the process of science?

The process of science refers to the practices employed in science to uncover knowledge and interpret the meaning of those discoveries. Textbooks often simplify and misrepresent this process as a single "Scientific Method" in which a lone scientist moves from observation through questioning to experimentation, but the process of science is much more robust, dynamic, and diverse. At the same time, however, there are core principles that unite the diverse disciplines within science. Biologists, chemists, geologists, physicists and all scientists objectively gather data about the natural world using multiple research methods, employ similar techniques to analyze these data, form hypotheses based on this data, and work within a global community of individuals and organizations contributing to science (Figure 2). These core principles and methods have evolved over time and distinguish science from other disciplines.

This book contains a series of chapters that detail these different aspects of the process of science by highlighting examples from history and connecting those stories to current research. These chapters can be read together to create a comprehensive answer to the question, "What is science and how does it work?" But they can also be used individually to better understand, say, how a scientist works, what an experiment exactly is, or how a scientific theory is developed. Twelve Key Concepts were used to guide the development of these chapters, and these Key Concepts provide a framework for understanding the material in this series.

Key Concepts in the Process of Science

1. Science is a process of investigation into the natural world and the knowledge generated through that process.

2. Scientists use multiple research methods to study the natural world.

3. Data collected through scientific research must be analyzed and interpreted to be used as evidence.

4. Scientific theories are testable explanations supported by multiple lines of evidence.

5. Scientific knowledge evolves with new evidence and perspectives.

6. Science benefits from the creativity, curiosity, diversity, and diligence of individuals.

7. Science is subject to human bias and error.

8. The community of science engages in debate and mitigates human errors.

9. Uncertainty is inherent in nature, but scientists work to minimize and quantify it in data collection and analysis.

10. Scientists value open and honest communication in reporting research.

11. Science both influences and is influenced by the societies and cultures in which it operates.

12. Science is valuable to individuals and to society.

Figure 2: *Sampling water on Lake Pontchartrain. These scientists must not only collect data, but analyze and interpret it as well. The broader scientific community will then validate these interpretations through established procedures.*

Each chapter includes 2 to 5 additional Key Concepts that add detail to the twelve broad ideas listed above; you'll see these at the end of every chapter. The material contained in these chapters is not presented as a distinct discipline within science, but rather as a web that links all scientific disciplines together. Through reading these chapters, we hope you'll see that science is not a simple set of facts and terms to be memorized. It is a robust process that helps us to better understand our surroundings and place in the universe. It is also accessible to anyone, both as way of thinking that you can use everyday, and as a career path where diverse backgrounds and perspectives are an advantage. Whether you become a scientist or a banker or a novelist, understanding the process of science is critical to your participation in society as a citizen.

The Culture of Science

The Nature of
Scientific Knowledge

*"Science is the process of separating the probably true
from the demonstrably false."*
~ E.P. Hubble to V.M. Slipher,
March 6, 1953, LOA.

It seems preposterous to us today that people once thought that the earth
was flat. Who could have possibly thought of our planet as a giant disk
with the stars and heavens above, and boulders, tree roots, and other
things below? But this was the dominant view of Earth in much of the world
before the 2nd century BCE, though the details differed from culture to culture. And it was not explorers who sailed around the world that finally laid
the idea to rest, but an accumulation of evidence long before this. Greek philosophers referred to a spherical Earth as early as the 6th century BCE: they
observed that the moon appeared to be a sphere and therefore inferred that
Earth might also be spherical. Two hundred years later, in the 4th century
BCE, the Greek philosopher Aristotle observed that the shadow of the earth
on the moon during a lunar eclipse is always curved, thus providing some
of the first evidence that the earth is spherical. In the 3rd century BCE, the
mathematician Eratosthenes observed that, at noon on the summer solstice
in the ancient Egyptian city of Syene, the sun was directly overhead as objects did not cast a shadow. Eratosthenes was from Alexandria, Egypt, some
500 miles to the north, and he knew that a tall tower cast a shadow in that
city at the same time on the summer solstice. Using these observations and
measurements of shadow length and distance, he inferred that the surface
of the earth is curved and he calculated a remarkably accurate estimate of
the circumference of the planet (Figure 1). Some years later, the Greek ge-
ographer Strabo added to this evidence when he observed that sailors saw
distant objects move downward on the horizon and disappear as they sailed

away from them. He proposed that this was because the earth was curved and those sailors were not simply moving further away from the objects but also curving around the planet as they sailed.

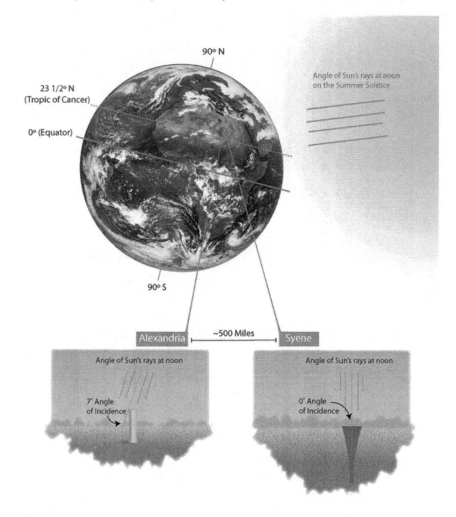

Figure 1: *Representation of Eratosthenes' studies demonstrating the curvature of Earth and the geometry used to calculate the circumference of the planet.*

Aristotle, Eratosthenes, and Strabo didn't call themselves scientists, yet they were using the process of science by making observations and providing explanations for those observations. Thus, we knew that Earth was a sphere long before Ferdinand Magellan's men sailed all the way around it in 1522 or before Apollo 8 astronauts sent back pictures of Earth from space in 1968 (Figure 2), documenting its spherical shape. In fact, those astronauts had to be absolutely confident that the earth was a rotating sphere, orbiting the sun, or they would never have been able to get into orbit. It is the nature of science and scientific knowledge that gave them that confidence, and understanding the difference between scientific knowledge and other types of knowledge is critical to understanding science itself.

Figure 2: Earthrise taken on December 24, 1968 from the Apollo 8 mission.

What is science?

Science consists of two things: a body of knowledge and the process by which that knowledge is produced. This second component of science provides us with a way of thinking and knowing about the world. Commonly, we only see the "body of knowledge" component of science. We are presented with scientific concepts in statement form—the earth is round, electrons are negatively charged, our genetic code is contained in our DNA, the universe is 13.7 billion years old—with little background about the process that led to that knowledge and why we can trust it. But there are a number of things that distinguish the scientific process and give us confidence in the knowledge produced through it.

So then, what is the scientific process? The scientific process is a way of building knowledge and making predictions about the world in such a way that they are testable. The question of whether the earth is flat or round could be put to the test, it could be studied through multiple lines of research, and the evidence evaluated to determine whether it supported a round or flat planet. Different scientific disciplines typically use different methods and approaches to investigate the natural world, but testing lies at the core of scientific inquiry for all scientists.

As scientists analyze and interpret their data, they generate hypotheses, theories, or laws (see our Ideas in Science: Theories, Hypotheses, and Laws chapter), which help explain their results and place them in context of the larger body of scientific knowledge. These different kinds of explanations are tested by scientists through additional experiments, observations, modeling, and theoretical studies. Thus, the body of scientific knowledge builds on previous ideas and is constantly growing. It is deliberately shared with colleagues through the process of peer review (see our Peer Review chapter), where scientists comment on each other's work, and then through publication in the scientific literature (see Utilizing the Scientific Literature) where it can be evaluated and integrated into the body of scientific knowledge by the larger community. And this is not the end: one of the hallmarks of scientific knowledge is that it is subject to change, as new data are collected and reinterpretations of existing data are made. Major theories, which are supported by multiple lines of evidence, are rarely completely changed, but new data and tested explanations add nuance and detail.

A scientific way of thinking is something that anyone can use, at any time, whether or not they are in the process of developing new knowledge and explanations. Thinking scientifically involves asking questions that can be answered analytically by collecting data or creating a model and then testing one's ideas. A scientific way of thinking inherently includes creativity in approaching explanations while staying within the confines of the data. Thinking scientifically does not mean rejecting your culture and background, but recognizing the role that they play in your way of thinking. While testable explanations are a critical component of thinking scientifically, there are other valid ways of thinking about the world around us that do not always yield testable explanations. These different ways of thinking are complimentary — not in competition — as they address different aspects of the human experience.

It's easy to be confident in the scientific process and our knowledge when we can provide irrefutable evidence, as we were able to do by orbiting around the earth in a spaceship and taking pictures of an obviously round planet. But most scientific investigations do not lead to results that are so easily supported, and yet we still rely on and trust the knowledge produced through the process of science. Why do we trust it? Because it works. Science has a long history of creating knowledge that is useful and that gives us more insight into our surroundings. Take one of the statements above: the universe is 13.7 billion years old. Why should we have confidence in this statement?

The age of the universe

How old is the universe? How can we possibly know the age of something that was created not simply before human history, but before our planet came into being? This is a difficult question to address scientifically, so much so that through the early 20th century many scientists assumed that the universe was infinite and eternal, existing for all of time.

Machines and Entropy

The first indication that the universe may not have existed for all of time came from an unlikely source: the study of engines. In the 1820s, Sadi Carnot was a young officer on leave from the French military. While taking classes at various institutions in Paris, he became interested in industrial problems, and was surprised to see that no scientific studies had been undertaken on the steam engine, a relatively new invention at the time and a poorly understood one. Carnot believed that engines could be better understood; a characteristic common to scientists is that they work to better understand things, and so he studied the transfer of energy in engines. He recognized that no engine could be 100% efficient because some energy is always lost from the system as heat (Figure 3). He published his ideas in a book titled *Reflections on the Motive Power of Fire and on Machines Fitted to Develop that Power*, which presented a mathematical description of the amount of work that could be generated by an engine, called the Carnot Cycle (Carnot, 1824).

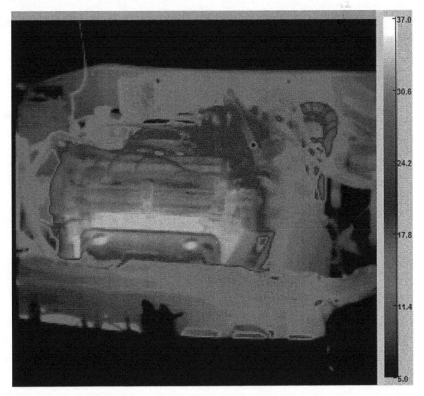

Figure 3: An infrared image of a running engine showing the temperature of various parts of the engine. Higher temperatures (lighter portions of the image) indicate greater heat loss. The loss of heat represents a loss of efficiency in the engine, and a contribution to the increasing entropy of the universe.

Carnot's work didn't receive much attention during his lifetime; he died of cholera in 1832, when he was only 36 years old. But others began to realize the importance of his work and built upon it. One of those scientists was Rudolf Clausius, a German physicist who showed that Carnot's principle was not limited to engines, but in fact applied to all systems in which there was a transfer of energy. Clausius' application of an explanation for one phenomenon to many others is also characteristic of science, which assumes that processes are universal. In 1850, Clausius published a paper in which he developed the Second Law of Thermodynamics, which states that energy always flows from a high energy state (for example, a system that is hot) to a low energy state (one that is cold) (Clausius, 1850). In later work, Clausius coined the term entropy to describe the energy lost from a system when it is transferred, and as an acknowledgement of the pioneering work of Sadi Carnot in providing the foundation for his discoveries, Clausius used the symbol S to refer to the entropy of a system.

But how do engines and entropy relate to the age of the universe? In 1865, Clausius published another paper that restated the second law of thermodynamics as "the entropy of the universe tends to a maximum." If the universe was infinite and existed for all time, the Second Law of Thermodynamics says that all of the energy within the universe would have all been lost to entropy by now. In other words, the stars themselves would have burned out long ago, dissipating their heat into surrounding space. The fact that there are still active stars must mean that the universe has existed for a finite amount of time, and was created at some specific point in time. Perhaps the age of that point in time could be determined?

Redshift and the Doppler Effect

At about the same time, an Austrian physicist by the name of Christian Doppler was studying astronomy and mathematics. Doppler knew that light behaved like a wave, and so began to think about how the movement of stars might affect the light emitted from those stars. In a paper published in 1842, Doppler proposed that the observed frequency of a wave would depend on the relative speed of the wave's source in relation to the observer, a phenomenon he called a "frequency shift" (Doppler, 1842). He made an analogy to a ship at sail on the ocean, describing how the ship would encounter waves on the surface of the water at a faster rate (and thus higher frequency) if it were sailing into the waves than if it were traveling in the same direction as the waves. You might be familiar with the frequency shift, which we now call the Doppler Effect in his honor, if you have ever listened to the sound of traffic while standing on the side of the road. The familiar high-to-low pitch change is an example of the effect – the actual frequency of the waves emitted is not changing, but the speed of the passing vehicle affects how quickly those waves reach you. Doppler proposed that we would see the same effect on any stars that were moving: their color would shift towards the red end of the spectrum if they were moving away from the earth (called a redshift) and towards the blue end of the spectrum if they were moving closer (called a blueshift) (see Figure 4). He expected to be able to see this shift in binary stars, or pairs of stars that orbit around each other. Eventually, Doppler's 1842 paper, entitled "On the coloured light of the double stars and certain other stars of the heavens," would change the very way we look at the universe. However, at the time, telescopes were not sensitive enough to confirm the shift he proposed.

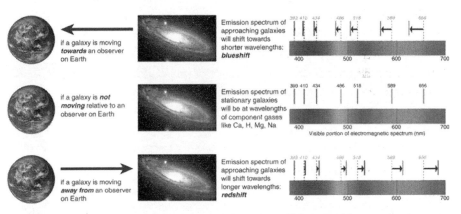

Figure 4: *A representation of how the perceived spectrum of light emitted from a galaxy is affected by its motion.*

Doppler's ideas became part of the scientific literature and by that means, they became known to other scientists. By the early 1900s, technology finally caught up with Doppler and more powerful telescopes could be used to test his ideas. In September of 1901, an American named Vesto Slipher had just completed his undergraduate degree in mechanics and astronomy at Indiana University. He got a job as a temporary assistant at the Lowell Observatory in Flagstaff, Arizona, while continuing his graduate work at Indiana. Shortly after his arrival, the observatory obtained a three-prism spectrograph, and Slipher's job was to mount it to the 24-inch telescope at the observatory and learn to use it to study the rotation of the planets in the solar system. After a few months of problems and trouble-shooting, Slipher was able to take spectrograms of Mars, Jupiter, and Saturn. But Slipher's personal research interests were much farther away than the planets of the solar system. Like Doppler, he was interested in studying the spectra of binary stars, and he began to do so in his spare time at the observatory.

Over the next decade, Slipher completed a Masters degree and a PhD at Indiana University, while continuing his work at Lowell Observatory measuring the spectra and Doppler shift of stars. In particular, Slipher focused his attention on stars within spiral nebulae (Figure 5), expecting to find that the shift seen in the spectra of the stars would indicate that the galaxies those stars belonged to were rotating. Indeed, he is credited with determining that galaxies rotate, and was able to determine the velocities at which they rotate. But in 1914, having studied 15 different nebulae, he announced a curious discovery at a meeting of the American Astronomical Society in August, "In the great majority of cases the nebulae are receding; the largest velocities are all positive....The striking preponderance of the positive sign indicates a general fleeing from us or the Milky Way." Slipher had found that most galaxies showed a redshift in their spectrum, indicating that they were all moving away from us in space, or receding (Slipher, 1915). By measuring the magnitude of the redshift, he was able to determine the recessional velocity or the speed at which objects were "fleeing." Slipher had made an interpretation from his observations that put a new perspective on the universe, and in response, he received a standing ovation for his presentation.

Slipher continued his work with redshift and galaxies and published another paper in 1917, having now examined 25 nebulae and seeing a redshift in 21 of them. Georges Lemaître, a Belgian physicist and astronomer, built on Slipher's work while completing his PhD at the Massachusetts Institute

Figure 5: The Andromeda galaxy, one of the spiral nebulae studied by Vesto Slipher, as seen in infrared light by NASA's Wide-field Infrared Survey Explorer.

of Technology. He extended Slipher's measurements to the entire universe, and calculated mathematically that the universe must be expanding in order to explain Slipher's observation. He published his ideas in a 1927 paper called "A homogeneous Universe of constant mass and growing radius accounting for the radial velocity of extragalactic nebulae" (Lemaître, 1927), but his paper met with widespread criticism from the scientific community. The English astronomer Fred Hoyle ridiculed the work, and coined the term "Big Bang" theory as a disparaging nickname for Lemaître's idea. And none other than Albert Einstein criticized Lemaître, writing to him "Your math is correct, but your physics is abominable" (Deprit, 1984).

Einstein's criticism had a personal and cultural component, two things we often overlook in terms of their influence on science. Several years earlier, Einstein had published his general theory of relativity (Einstein, 1916). In formulating the theory, Einstein had encountered one significant problem: general relativity predicted that the universe had to be either contracting or expanding – it did not allow for a static universe. But a contracting or expanding universe could not be eternal, while a static, non-moving universe could, and the prevailing cultural belief at the time was that the universe was eternal. Einstein was strongly influenced by his cultural surroundings, and, as a result, he invented a "fudge factor," which he called the cosmological constant, that would allow the theory of general relativity to be consistent with a static universe. But science is not a democracy or plutocracy; it is neither the most common or most popular conclusion that becomes accepted, but rather the conclusion that stands up to the test of evidence over time. Einstein's cosmological constant was being challenged by new evidence.

The expanding universe

In 1929, an American astronomer working at the Mt. Wilson Observatory in southern California made an important contribution to the discussion of the nature of the universe. Edwin Hubble had been at Mt. Wilson for 10 years measuring the distances to galaxies, among other things. In the 1920s, he was working with Milton Humason, a high school dropout and assistant at the observatory. Hubble and Humason plotted the distances they had calculated for 46 different galaxies against Slipher's recession velocity and found a linear relationship (see Figure 6) (Hubble, 1929).

In other words, their graph showed that more distant galaxies were receding faster than closer ones, confirming the idea that the universe was indeed expanding. This relationship, now referred to as Hubble's Law, allowed them to calculate the rate of expansion as a function of distance from

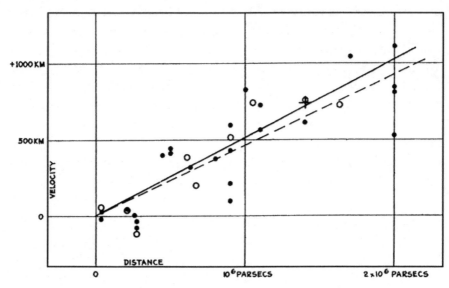

Figure 6: The original Hubble diagram, labeled as "Figure 1" in his 1929 publication. The relative velocity of galaxies (in km/sec) is plotted against distance to that galaxy (in parsecs; a parsec is 3.26 light years). The slope of the line drawn through the points gives the rate of expansion of the universe (the Hubble Constant).

the slope of the line in the graph. This rate term is now referred to as the Hubble Constant. Hubble's initial value for the expansion rate was 500 km/ sec/Megaparsec, or about 160 km/sec per million-light-years.

Knowing the rate at which the universe is expanding, one can calculate the age of the universe by in essence "tracing back" the most distant objects in the universe to their point of origin. Using his initial value for the expansion rate and the measured distance of the galaxies, Hubble and Humason calculated the age of the universe to be approximately 2 billion years. Unfortunately, the calculation was inconsistent with lines of evidence from other investigations. By the time Hubble made his discovery, geologists had used radioactive dating techniques to calculate the age of the earth at about 3 billion years (Rutherford, 1929) – or older than the universe itself! Hubble had followed the process of science, so what was the problem?

Even laws and constants are subject to revision in science. It soon became clear that there was a problem in the way that Hubble had calculated his constant. In the 1940s, a German astronomer named Walter Baade took advantage of the blackouts that were ordered in response to potential attacks during World War II and used the Mt. Wilson Observatory in Arizona to look at several objects that Hubble had interpreted as single stars. With darker surrounding skies, Baade realized that these objects were, in fact, groups of stars, and each was fainter, and thus more distant, than Hubble had calculated. Baade doubled the distance to these objects, and in turn halved the Hubble constant and doubled the age of the universe. In 1953, the American astronomer Allan Sandage, who had studied under Baade, looked in more detail at the brightness of stars and how that varied with distance. Sandage further revised the constant, and his estimate of 75 km/sec/ Megaparsec is close to our modern day estimate of the Hubble constant of 72 km/sec/Megaparsec, which places the age of the universe at 12 to 14 billion years old. The new estimates developed by Baade and Sandage did not negate what Hubble had done (it is still called the Hubble constant, after all), but they revised it based on new knowledge. The lasting knowledge of science is rarely the work of an individual, as building on the work of others is a critical component of the process of science. Hubble's findings would have been limited to some interesting data on the distance to various stars had it not also built on, and incorporated the work of Slipher. Similarly, Baade and Sandage's contribution were no less significant because they "simply" refined Hubble's earlier work.

Since the 1950s, other means of calculating the age of the universe have been developed. For example, there are now methods for dating the age of the stars, and the oldest stars date to approximately 13.2 billion years ago (Frebel *et al.*, 2007). The Wilkinson Microwave Anisotropy Probe is collecting data on cosmic microwave background radiation (Figure 7), and using

Figure 7: Visual representation of the cosmic microwave background radiation of the universe. Differences in shades of gray represent temperature differences of the background radiation of less than 1/1000th of one degree, suggesting that the background radiation throughout the universe is relatively uniform. Data collected by the Wilkinson Microwave Anisotropy Probe, a satellite launched into orbit by NASA in 2001. For more information, see the WMAP Further Exploration link on our website.

this data in conjunction with Einstein's theory of general relativity, scientists have calculated the age of the universe at 13.7 ± 0.2 billion years old (Spergel *et al.*, 2003). The convergence of multiple lines of evidence on a single explanation is what creates the solid foundation of scientific knowledge.

Why should we trust science?

Why should we believe what scientists say about the age of the universe? We have no written records of its creation, and no one has been able to "step outside" of the system, as astronauts did when they took pictures of the earth from space, to measure its age. Yet the nature of the scientific process allows us to accurately state the age of the observable universe. These predictions were developed by multiple researchers and tested through multiple research methods. They have been presented to the scientific community through publications and public presentations. And they have been confirmed and verified by many different studies. New studies, or new research methods, may be developed that might possibly cause us to refine our estimate of the age of the universe upward or downward – this is how the process of science works, it is subject to change as more information and new technologies become available. But it is not tenuous – our age estimate may be refined, but the idea of an expanding universe is unlikely to be overturned. As evidence builds to support an idea, our confidence in that idea builds.

Upon seeing Hubble's work, even Albert Einstein changed his opinion of a static universe and called his insertion of the cosmological constant the "biggest blunder" of his professional career. Hubble's discovery actually confirmed Einstein's theory of general relativity, which predicts that the universe must be expanding or contracting. Einstein refused to accept this idea because of his cultural biases. His work had not predicted a static universe, but he assumed this must be the case given what he had grown up believing. When confronted with the data, he recognized that his earlier beliefs were flawed, and came to accept the findings of the science behind the idea. This is a hallmark of the science, while an individual's beliefs may be biased by personal experience, the scientific enterprise works to collect data to allow for a more objective conclusion to be identified. Incorrect ideas may be upheld for some amount of time, but eventually the preponderance of evidence helps to lead us to correct these ideas. Once used as a term of disparagement, the "Big Bang" theory is now the leading explanation for the origin of the universe as we know it.

There are other questions we can ask about the origin of the universe, not all of which can be answered by science. Scientists can answer when and how the universe began, but cannot calculate the reason why it began, for example. That type of question must be explored through philosophy, religion, and other ways of thinking. The questions that scientists ask must be testable. Scientists have provided answers to testable questions that have helped us calculate the age of the universe:, like how distant are certain stars and how fast are they receding from us. Whether or not we can get a definitive answer, we can be confident in the process by which the explanations were developed, allowing us to rely on the knowledge that is produced through the process of science. Someday we may find evidence to help us understand why the universe was created, but for the time being science will limit itself to the last 13.7 or so billion years of phenomenon to investigate.

Key Concepts for this chapter

► Science consists of a body of knowledge and the process by which that knowledge is developed.

► The core of the process of science is generating testable explanations, and the methods and approaches to generating knowledge are shared publicly so that they can be evaluated by the community of scientists.

► Scientists build on the work of others to create scientific knowledge.

► Scientific knowledge is subject to revision and refinement as new data, or new ways to interpret existing data, are found.

References

Carnot, S. (1824). *Réflexions sur la puissance motrice du feu, et sur les machines propres à développer oette puissance:* Gauthier-Villars.

Clausius, R. (1850). Ueber die bewegende Kraft der Wärme und die Gesetze, welche sich daraus für die Wärmelehre selbst ableiten lassen. *Annalen der Physik,* 155(3), 368-397.

Deprit, A. (1984, 1984). *Monsignor Georges Lemaitre.* Paper presented at the Big-Bang Cosmology Symposium in honour of G. Lemaitre.

Doppler, C. (1842). Uber das farbige Licht der Doppelsterne und einiger anderer Gestirne des Himmels (On the colored light of the double stars and certain other stars of the heavens). *Abh. Kniglich Bhmischen Ges. Wiss,* 2, 467-482.

Einstein, A. (1916). Die grundlage der allgemeinen relativitätstheorie. *Annalen der Physik,* 354(7), 769-822.

Frebel, A., Christlieb, N., Norris, J. E., Thom, C., Beers, T. C., & Rhee, J. (2007). Discovery of HE 1523–0901, a Strongly r-Process-enhanced Metal-poor Star with Detected Uranium. *The Astrophysical Journal Letters,* 660, L117.

Hubble, E. (1929). A relation between distance and radial velocity among extra-galactic nebulae. *Proceedings of the National Academy of Sciences of the United States of America,* 15(3), 168.

Lemaître, G. (1927). Un univers homogène de masse constante et de rayon croissant rendant compte de la vitesse radiale des nébuleuses extra-galactiques. Annales de la Societe Scietifique de Bruxelles, 47, 49-59.

Rutherford, E. (1929). Origin of actinium and age of the Earth. *Nature,* 123, 313-314.

Slipher, V. M. (1915). Spectrographic observations of nebulae. *Popular Astronomy,* 23, 21-24.

Spergel, D. N., Verde, L., Peiris, H. V., Komatsu, E., Nolta, M. R., Bennett, C. L., . . . Kogut, A. (2003). First-year Wilkinson Microwave Anisotropy Probe (WMAP) observations: determination of cosmological parameters. *The Astrophysical Journal Supplement Series,* 148, 175.

Scientists and the
Scientific Community

"I am neither especially clever nor especially gifted. I am only very, very curious."

~ Albert Einstein

O n July 7, 2007, the Live Earth concerts took place on all continents. The global event was meant to promote awareness of a "climate in crisis" and featured a range of musical performers, from the Police and Madonna to Kanye West and the Black Eyed Peas, playing at venues around the world. Perhaps the least heralded performance was by the indie rock band Nunatak, who played to a sold-out crowd of 17 people – all of the current residents at the Rothera Research Station on Adelaide Island, Antarctica, one of the most remote places on the planet (Figure 1). The performance was taped and later broadcast to millions of people.

What does this have to do with science? Actually, it has everything to do with science. The band Nunatak consists entirely of scientists and researchers stationed at Rothera: Matt Balmer, an electronics engineer and the lead vocalist; Alison Massey, a marine biologist and saxophonist; Rob Webster, a

Figure 1: *The Rothera Research Station on Adelaide Island.*

meteorologist and drummer; Tris Thorne, a communications engineer and violinist; and Roger Stilwell, a polar guide and bass guitarist. As scientists, they were each conducting research on Adelaide Island in 2007. As people who happen to be scientists, however, they are also musicians, and musicians with an interest in promoting awareness of climate change. Participating in Live Earth was a natural outgrowth of their personal and professional interests.

We often forget the human side of scientists, that they are people who, in addition to their professional labels like professor, physicist, or researcher, also have personal labels, like musician, cook, hiker, or parent. At first glance, these personal pursuits may seem irrelevant to the process of science. In fact, the opposite is true – science benefits from the creativity and interests of a diverse group of individuals who bring many different points of view to the table. Individual scientists bring all of the strengths and weaknesses of humans to their profession, from creativity in problem solving to the failures of judgment that create problems. But science could not exist without these unique contributions. Individual scientists are influenced by their personal experiences, mentoring and collaboration, chance events, their diverse perspectives, and their personal judgment. The role of each of these influences is explored in more detail here.

The influence of personal experience

We often think of scientists as people who must be completely removed from emotion in order to perform their work. Indeed, scientists try to remain objective to the outcomes of the research they undertake, but their personal experiences, interests and background often contribute to the research topics that they pursue. For example, in 2007, Dr. Stefanie Raymond-Whish and several of her colleagues at Northern Arizona University published a paper entitled, "Drinking Water with Uranium below the U.S. EPA Water Standard Causes Estrogen Receptor–Dependent Responses in Female Mice." In the paper, they describe a series of experiments in which female mice were exposed to elevated levels of uranium in their drinking water. They found that the mice experienced physical changes similar to those they undergo in response to the hormone estrogen. Raymond-Whish's personal interest in this topic had nothing to do with mice. She was motivated to conduct this research for other reasons: as a member of the Navajo tribe and resident of the Four Corners region of the Navajo reservation, she and her family had long experienced elevated levels of uranium in their drinking water due to the presence of numerous unreclaimed uranium mines and mills. Her grandmother had died of breast cancer, and her mother had been diagnosed with the disease and survived. She knew that some forms of breast cancer had been linked with high doses of estrogen. Raymond-Whish began her work on mice in order to test the hypothesis that higher-than-normal breast cancer rates among residents of the Four Corners were related to uranium in the drinking water – a hypothesis intimately connected to her personal experiences.

Other scientists come to investigate research questions as new experiences present themselves. For example, Dr. Adam Sylvester is an anthropologist whose research focuses on the origins of bipedalism in hominids, or how humans came to walk upright (Sylvester, 2006). While working on his PhD dissertation, he attended a meeting of the American Association of Physical Anthropologists, and was interested in a research poster he saw there. The authors compared the thickness of cortical bone (the dense, outer layer of all bones that gives them strength) in the hands and fingers of the great apes and humans, and found that apes have thicker cortical bone in their hands than humans, possibly a result of the mechanical stress associated with knuckle-walking and tree climbing. Sylvester, an avid rock climber in addition to an anthropologist, began to wonder if climbers might also have thicker cortical bone in their fingers as a result of the mechanical stress put on them. He knew that there was a tremendous amount of research on the response of bone to mechanical stress, but the mechanisms causing this response were not well understood. From this poster, he was inspired to initiate a study of the hand bones of recreational rock climbers as compared to non-climbers, the factors that might contribute to changes in cortical thickness and strength, and whether these changes had any negative impacts on the hand joints (Sylvester, Christensen, and Kramer, 2006). Through measuring bone strength and width of 4 bones in the hands of 27 recreational rock climbers and 35 non-climbers, they found that the climbers did have larger hand bones with greater cortical thickness than non-climbers, but they are at no greater risk of joint problems like osteoarthritis. Sylvester's combination of personal and professional interests led him to think creatively about his research, resulting in a study that contributed to our understanding of stress response in athletes.

Even those scientists whose personal experiences do not consciously affect their choice of research are influenced by their background and upbringing. For example, most school children learn that Gregor Mendel was an Austrian monk who studied heredity in pea plants (Figure 2). However, few of us learn any details of Mendel's life, resulting in a common misconception of Mendel as an isolated monk and scientist who happened upon pea plants as a research subject by chance. But this is far from true. Gregor Mendel was born in 1822 in a small village named Hyncice in what is now the Czech Republic. His father was a peasant farmer who raised crops to feed his family and sell for a small profit. As the only son, Gregor was expected to take up his father's profession in farming. However, Mendel demonstrated an early interest and aptitude in school, particularly in natural history.

Figure 2: Gregor Mendel

So instead of farming, he went on to study physics, mathematics and logic at the Philosophical Institute at Olomouc, a prominent college at one of the oldest universities in the Czech Republic. Mendel's family could not afford to pay for his tuition, and financial hardship eventually forced him to withdraw from university.

Several of Mendel's teachers recognized potential in the young man and suggested he apply to the Augustinian monastery of St. Thomas at Brno to continue his studies (Figure 3). He was not a particularly religious man, but the monastery was well-known as a center for learning in the natural sciences and agriculture due in part to the influence of a scholarly abbot named Cyrill Napp, the monastery's administrator. Abbot Napp was fascinated with understanding breeding better, particularly the role of inheritance in economically important farm animals and plants, and he quickly recognized Mendel's potential as a scholar. Mendel brought an aptitude for science and experience in farming to the monastery, where he had access to land, greenhouses, and guidance from a mentor interested in making farming more profitable. Napp even provided financial support for Mendel's education, at one point commenting, "I shall not grudge any requisite expense for the furtherance of his training" (Orel and Wood, 2000). When viewed in the

Figure 3: The monastery of St. Thomas at Brno with a picture of Mendel's gardens.

context of events and circumstances in his life, Mendel's work on heredity in pea plants (a crop of enormous economic importance then as well as today) is more than just an intellectual exercise – it was fundamentally influenced by his background, culture, and the economics of the time.

The influence of mentoring and collaboration

Mendel could not have done his work without the guidance and mentorship of Abbott Napp. In fact, an essential part of graduate education in the sciences (and an increasingly important part of undergraduate education in science) is strongly mentored research. Students work with an established scientist for a period of time, learning how to collect reliable data in their discipline, training in specialized laboratory or computer analysis procedures, studying data analysis techniques, and gaining experience in many other aspects of science. These skills are difficult to convey in a classroom, and science relies on the personal interaction between mentor and student for passing on not only knowledge, but skills and techniques. In fact, scientists often speak of the scientific "families" in the same way they refer to their real families – students who work with an advisor at the same time are like siblings, their advisor is like a parent.

Mentoring has always been a part of science. While this might be easy to imagine now, we often have a hard time thinking about the mentoring process when looking back at famous scientists. In addition to Abbott Napp, Mendel worked with a number of scientists at the nearby Brno Philosophical Institute who played a significant role in mentoring him and collaborating with him. He studied under Franz Diebl, a respected expert in agriculture and a teacher of natural science who published several manuscripts on plant breeding. Diebl described a technique for the artificial fertilization of plants, which Mendel read about and later utilized: the technique involved using a small paintbrush to cross-pollinate plants while snipping off the anthers of the plants to prevent natural pollination.

Mendel also worked closely with F. Matthew Klácel, a fellow Augustinian monk who held an appointment as a professor of philosophy and managed the experimental garden at the monastery. Klácel recognized that new plant and animal species that resulted from agricultural (in other words, artificial) crosses were evidence for the concept of change in organisms. This idea contradicted a then-popular view called Fixity of Species, which stated that organisms were unchanging and had appeared on earth in their current form at the time of creation. The concept of change in organisms was in its infancy when Mendel began his work with peas in 1856; in fact, Charles Darwin's landmark book *The Origin of Species* would not be published until 1859 (see the Charles Darwin I: The Origin of Species module on our website for more information). If organisms did not change over time, as the Fixity of Species idea held, there would be no reason to look at patterns of inheritance in organisms. Thus, the unconventional views of Klácel and others strongly influenced Mendel's work.

Collaboration remains a critical aspect of science today, maybe even more so than in Mendel's day because of the complexity and scope of questions scientists study. When Adam Sylvester, the physical anthropologist, became interested in the effects of rock climbing on bone size, he knew he needed some additional expertise and knowledge, so he turned to two colleagues for collaboration. One was Dr. Angi Christensen, an FBI scientist who had been a fellow graduate student at the University of Tennessee – they shared the same mentor. Dr. Christensen was also a friend and forensic anthropologist with expertise in comparing X-rays of human bones to individualize skeletal remains. Thus, in their study, the data that was collected from subjects was X-rays of their hands, from which the authors measured and compared bone size. The two also sought out Dr. Patricia Kramer, an anthropologist who studies macaque monkeys as a model to understand the origins and progression of osteoarthritis in humans. The addition of her expertise to the team allowed the researchers to make predictions about the effect of the bone changes they observed on the development of joint diseases in these individuals. Their combined areas of expertise made for a productive collaboration that resulted in the publication of a peer-reviewed journal article.

Though we tend to laud individual scientists for their achievements, it is the rare case that individuals make great achievements without collaborating with other sciences. Scientists constantly work with collaborators at their own institutions and with fellow researchers across the world. In fact, one of the roles of scientific societies is to foster collaboration and improve communication between scientists to facilitate scientific progress (see our Scientific Institutions and Societies chapter later in this book).

The influence of chance and luck

Because we only see the final results of scientific research, it is easy to believe that scientists pursue their research along well-planned and precise pathways. In reality, however, most scientists' paths are constantly changing based on their evolving interests, the data they collect, their interactions with others, and even serendipity. In 1997, Mark Erdmann, a marine biology graduate student, was wandering through an Indonesian fish market with his wife on their honeymoon. She pointed out a strange-looking fish that she had never seen before, and Mark immediately recognized it as a coelacanth – a rare fish that closely resembles fossils from 400 million years ago (Figure 4). Their fish market find proved an important scientific discovery as it was only the second time a known, living population of coelacanths was identified.

Figure 4: A model of a coelacanth from the Oxford Museum of Natural History.

While chance played a big role in this discovery, it was not random or haphazard. Erdmann's interest in marine biology was one of the reasons he was at the fish market in the first place. Louis Pasteur, the French microbiologist, notoriously said, "Chance favors the prepared mind," and he could not have been more correct. Erdmann recognized data that was relevant to his interests when he saw it, even though it may not have been obvious to someone else without the expertise.

Likewise, most scientists understand that unexpected outcomes can be significant discoveries in and of themselves and they are prepared to accept and investigate these occurrences. In 1981, Brian MacMahon, an epidemiologist at Harvard University, came across one such unexpected outcome. He and his colleagues had set out to determine if alcohol or tobacco increased the risk of pancreatic cancer. They asked 369 patients with pancreatic cancer and 644 control patients to complete a survey about their lifestyle habits. The researchers did not find any significant relationships between drinking or smoking and pancreatic cancer; however, their results indicated that survey respondents who had pancreatic cancer were more likely to drink coffee – a relationship they weren't even investigating (MacMahon at al., 1981). MacMahon pursued the potential link between coffee and pancreatic cancer for many years, and he even stated in an interview that he had given up drinking coffee (Schmeck, 1981). But just because a scientist pursues a research question does not mean that the results will be significant. After more than 2 decades and 25 published studies of research on the connections between coffee-drinking and pancreatic cancer, the question was resolved. Dominique Michaud, a researcher at the National Cancer Institute, and her colleagues showed that there is in fact no causative link between coffee consumption and pancreatic cancer (Michaud at el., 2001). The correlation that MacMahon and colleagues had originally seen was likely due to confounding factors, such as diet, for which they had not controlled in their original study.

The influence of diversity

You might be discouraged looking at a list of famous scientists – Nobel Prize winners, for example, or members of the National Academy of Sciences. These groups are dominated by men, mostly European and American, mostly white. But look at the membership of any scientific society today, and you will see something much different, and much more diverse. Gender, race, and culture all influence a person as a scientist, but they don't have to stand in the way of anyone becoming a scientist.

In fact, science benefits from a diversity of backgrounds and perspectives. One of the disciplines where gender has played a big role is primate anthropology. Through the 1960s, the family groups of several species of primates were described in the literature as male-dominated, and females of the species were passive and dependent on their more aggressive male counterparts. The authors of these journal articles were all men: in fact, not a single woman received a PhD in the United States in anthropology in the 1960s. In 1973, Jane Lancaster, an anthropologist who received her PhD at the University of California at Berkeley while studying primate communication, published the article "In praise of the achieving female monkey" (Lancaster, 1973). The piece proposed a radical notion at the time: that female monkeys could do anything that male monkeys could. Thelma Rowell, a primate biologist, would show that it was female baboons – not males – that determined the route that groups took in their day-to-day foraging (Rowell, 1972). The biological anthropologist Shirley Strum showed that a male baboon's investment in developing relationships with females was more important in terms of reproductive success than the male's rank in the group (Strum, 1974). As more and more women entered the field of anthropology, they continued to challenge the traditional stereotypes of primate behavior (Schiebinger, 2000). Today, largely as a result of the contribution of women in the field, scientists recognize that females provide the social stability in baboon culture while males move from group to group.

The influence of mistakes and misjudgment

Of course, with all the benefits of individuals – our creativity, our diversity, and our ability to capitalize on serendipity – come our downfalls. We can make mistakes. In the mid-1960s, Nikolai Fedyakin, a Soviet physicist working at a laboratory in Kostroma, Russia observed that water that had condensed in narrow quartz tubes appeared to exhibit peculiar properties, including a very high viscosity similar to that of syrup. Other Soviet scientists heard of the work and reproduced the strange fluid, publishing their findings in science journals (Lippincott, Stromberg, Grant, and Cessac, 1969). The strange form of water was thought to be a rare, polymerized form in which individual molecules bonded together to form long chains that impeded flow, and the new substance was thus nicknamed polywater. By the late 1960s, polywater had ignited a scientific uproar – while some scientists were able to reproduce the results, others could not.

In the early 1970s, Denis Rousseau, a research scientist who was working at the Bell Laboratories at the time, used infrared spectroscopy to show that polywater was not a new form of water. It was just plain water that was contaminated because of dirty glassware and was similar in composition to human sweat (Rousseau and Porto, 1970). Fedyakin made an honest, and very human, mistake – his observations were real, and he was able to reproduce the results; however, he came to the wrong conclusions about his findings. While individuals can make mistakes, the collective community of scientists corrects those mistakes by repeating experiments and looking further into reported phenomenon, as Rousseau did. This review and replication is an essential component of the process of science that ensures that scientific knowledge is reliable.

In addition to making mistakes, scientists are also capable of outright deception. For example, Woo Suk Hwang, a researcher at Seoul National University, and a group of South Korean and American collaborators published a paper in 2004 stating that they had created the first-ever human embryonic stem cell lines that matched the DNA of patients (Hwang et al., 2004). The work was hailed a landmark triumph, and the journal that published the paper, Science, considered naming the research one of their "Breakthroughs of the Year" for 2005. However, after anonymous allegations of data irregularities appeared on a South Korean website, the paper underwent intense scrutiny and was later discredited and withdrawn from the journal. Follow-up investigation has suggested that the researchers participated in fraud by fabricating much of the data that was reported in the manuscript.

Very few scientists perpetrate fraud; just as few people engage in fraudulent behavior in their lives and careers. But as with mistakes, the scientific community helps discover and correct fraud through the processes of replication, open publication, collaboration, and peer review (see our Peer Review chapter).

Creativity and the scientist

Christopher Edwards, in an article entitled "The right stuff: What distinguishes great scientists," argues that it is not genius that distinguishes great scientists, but open-mindedness and creativity (Edwards, 2000). Many of the examples above highlight that sentiment – none of these scientists are necessarily smarter than others. Instead, they are pursuing their interests creatively and diligently. And progress in science itself depends on the experiences and creativity that individuals bring to their work in seeking answers to research questions. If you would like to read more about the day-to-day operations of a scientist, visit our series titled *The Penguin Diaries* on the Visionlearning website, which chronicles the daily tasks of a researcher studying the diet of Gentoo and Chinstrap penguins in the Antarctic.

Key Concepts for this chapter

▶ Science is a human endeavor. It benefits from the creativity, curiosity, and diligence of individual scientists, and is also subject to human error.

▶ Scientists are diverse in many ways, and their personal experiences – including cultures, backgrounds, and chance – influence the paths they follow.

▶ Scientists benefit from mentoring and collaboration, working in communities within, or across, institutions and disciplines.

References

Allen, G. (2003) *Mendel and Modern Genetics: The Legacy for Today*. Endeavor. 27(2):63-68.

Cho, M.K., McGee, G., Magnus, D. (2006). Research Conduct: Lessons of the Stem Cell Scandal. *Science* 311 (5761): 614.

Edwards, C. G. (2000). The right stuff: What distinguishes great scientists. *HMS Beagle: The BioMedNet Magazine.*

Eisenhaber, F., Schleiffer, A. (2007) Gregor Mendel: The Beginning of Biomathematics. Retrieved September 10, 2007, from the IMP Bioinformatics Group, http://mendel.imp. ac.at/mendeljsp/biography/biography.jsp.

Hwang, W.S., Ryu, Y.J., Park, J.H., Park, E.S., Lee, E.G., Koo, J.M., Jeon, H.Y., Lee, B.C., Kang, S.K., Kim, S.J., Ahn, C., Hwang, J.H., Park, K.Y., Cibelli, J.B., Moon, S.Y. (2004) Evidence of a Pluripotent Human Embryonic Stem Cell Line Derived from a Cloned Blastocyst. *Science* 303 (5664):1669.

Kemp, M. (2002) Peas without pictures: Gregor Mendel and the mathematical birth of modern genetics. *Nature* 417:490.

Lancaster, J. B. (1973). In praise of the achieving female monkey. *Psychology Today,* 7, 30-32.

Lippincott, E. R., Stromberg, R. R., Grant, W. H., & Cessac, G. L. (1969). Polywater. *Science,* 164(3887), 1482-1487.

MacMahon, B., Yen, S., Trichopoulos, D., Warren, K., & Nardi, G. (1981). Coffee and cancer of the pancreas (Vol. 304, pp. 630-633).

Mendel, G. (1866). Versuche über Pflanzen-Hybriden. Verh. Naturforsch. Ver. Brünn, 4, 3-47 (in English in Mendel, G. (1901) Experiments in Plant Hybridization. *J. R. Hortic. Soc.* 26, 1-32).

Michaud, D. S., Giovannucci, E., Willett, W. C., Colditz, G. A., & Fuchs, C. S. (2001). Coffee and Alcohol Consumption and the Risk of Pancreatic Cancer in Two Prospective United States Cohorts 1. *Cancer Epidemiology Biomarkers & Prevention,* 10(5), 429-437.

Nagda, B.A., Gregerman, S.R., Jonides, J., von Hippel, W., Lerner, J.S. (1998). Undergraduate Student-Faculty Research Partnerships Affect Student Retention *Rev. Higher Ed.* 22(1):55-72

Orel, V. (1996). Heredity before Mendel. In Orel, V., *Gregor Mendel: The First Geneticist.* Oxford University Press.

Orel, V., Wood, R. J. (2000) Essence and Origin of Mendel's Discovery. *C. R. Acad. Sci. Paris Sciences de la Vie.* 323:1037-1041.

Peasleea, M.H., Orel, V. (2007). The evolutionary ideas of F. M. (Ladimir) Klacel, teacher of Gregor Mendel. *Biomed Pap Med Fac Univ Palacky Olomouc Czech Repub.* 151(1):151–156

Rousseau, D. L., & Porto, S. P. S. (1970). Polywater: Polymer or Artifact? *Science,* 167(3926), 1715-1719.

Rowell, T. (1972). *The social behaviour of monkeys.* Penguin Books Harmondsworth.

Schiebinger, L. (2000). Has feminism changed science? *Signs,* 1171-1175.

Schmeck, H. M. (1981, March 12). Study links coffee use to pancreas cancer. *New York Times*

Strandberg, M.W.P. (2007). The Setting of the Drama: What Mendel Set Out To Do; Determining The Rules of the Game of Hybridization. Retrieved on September 22, 2007, from Malcolm Stradnberg's website, the Massachusetts Institute of Technology, http://web.mit.edu/mwpstr/www/mend/node3.html.

Strum, S. C. (1974). Life with the Pumphouse Gang: New insights into baboon behavior. *Natn. Geogr,* 147, 672–691.

Sylvester, A. D. (2006). Locomotor decoupling and the origin of hominin bipedalism. *Journal of Theoretical Biology,* 242(3), 581-590.

Sylvester, A. D., Christensen, A. M., & Kramer, P. A. (2006). Factors influencing osteological changes in the hands and fingers of rock climbers. *Journal of Anatomy,* 209(5), 597.

von Tschermak-Seysenegg, E. (1951) The Rediscovery of Gregor Mendel's Work: An Historical Retrospect. *The Journal of Heredity.* 42:163-171.

Westerlund, J., Fairbanks, D. (2004). Gregor Mendel and "myth-conceptions." *Science Education,* 88(5):754-758.

Scientific Institutions and Societies

"As long as [research institutions] are vigorous and healthy and their scientists are free to pursue the truth wherever it may lead, there will be a flow of new scientific knowledge to those who can apply it to practical problems in Government, in industry, or elsewhere."

~ Vannevar Bush

We all make use of different types of institutions. Banks provide us credit to make the process of buying and selling things easier. Telephone companies provide us with access to vast wireless and wired networks that allow us to speak with friends by simply dialing their telephone number. And colleges and universities allow us to learn from experienced teachers and mentors that we might not otherwise meet in the course of our lives. You may not have thought of it this way before, but as part of an academic institution, you not only have access to the resources of that institution – professors, buildings, classes – but you are part of a community of people with shared interests and goals. Within that setting, there are clubs that one can join depending on one's specific interests – sports teams, student groups, different living communities, even study groups – all of which are smaller collections of individuals with similar interests and/or skills. To each of these groups, we all bring our own interests and skills, and we benefit from the interactions with others.

Scientists also have institutions that support them, and they work within a community of individuals with whom they share ideas. For example, academic institutions support research by scientists and other scholars as part of their broader educational missions, federal agencies and private foundations often provide funding to support researchers, and scientific societies support and promote communication and collaboration between scientists. And yet, it is easy to forget the role of these support structures and focus just on the scientists that make discoveries. For example, we picture Galileo Galilei looking through his telescope in a remote Italian village or Gregor Mendel counting peas in the isolation of an Augustinian monastery – both alone, working. But Galileo had a position at the University of Pisa starting in 1588, which provided him with a stipend; in return, he tutored students and taught classes there. He sought funding for his work from the wealthy and influential Medici family. And he was member of the Lyncean Academy, a small group of European scientists who met regularly to discuss science and who published several of Galileo's works. These various institutions with which he was involved were crucial to his career as a scientist and led to widespread recognition of some of his most fundamental research.

Galileo was one of the first scientists to take on the many roles that are common among scientists today. As in any other human endeavor, individual scientists rely on the support of several institutions, and the nature of those institutions varies widely. A high-school teacher is an individual who possesses knowledge to teach students, but that teacher is part of a school and a school district, and may belong to other professional organizations that help support him or her as a teacher. Science is no different: scientists are individuals with particular knowledge and understanding, but they cannot act alone. Scientists are supported by at least three different kinds of institutions: research institutions, funding institutions, and professional societies. Research institutions physically house scientists and provide research facilities; they include many colleges and universities, government organizations like the U.S. Geological Survey, and corporations like DuPont or Exxon-Mobil. Professional societies facilitate the communication of the

Figure 1: Undergraduate students presenting their research at a poster session.

results of scientific research and foster the development of scientific communities, hosting meetings like the one shown in Figure 1. These societies may be specific to a discipline, such as the Society of Vertebrate Paleontology, or broad and all-encompassing, such as the American Association for the Advancement of Science. Funding institutions, like the National Science Foundation and National Institutes of Health, provide grant money to scientists through a competitive process so that they can conduct research. An individual scientist may work at one or more research institutions, belong to several professional societies, and receive funding from multiple sources – all of which can influence a scientist's research. Likewise, the institutions are influenced by the communities of scientists that make up their membership.

The role of the research institution

We now consider it normal that many scientists are professors at universities, teaching classes while conducting research and advising students, but this has not always been the case. When Cambridge University was established in England in the 1200s, there were no professors; the men who taught courses of study (and they were, indeed, all men) had completed the same course of study themselves and were considered Masters. These men did not conduct any sort of research, and teaching was a matter of handing down the same information that they themselves had been taught.

During the 1500s and 1600s, the make-up of universities began to change when members of the English royalty endowed several professorships at Cambridge and Oxford, providing stipends for the recipients. Attaining one of these coveted positions meant going beyond the given course of study and conducting original research; as a result, the university became a place where new knowledge was generated. One of the most famous of the endowed professorships, the Lucasian Chair of Mathematics, was established in 1663 at Cambridge University by Henry Lucas, a Member of Parliament (Bruen, 1995). The fame of this position derives from its second holder: Sir Isaac Newton. Newton was appointed Lucasian Chair in 1669 and held the position until 1702, during which time he produced his most important works like the *Principia*. The support offered through the position at Cambridge gave Newton the freedom to pursue research that was of interest to him, without which we may not have seen Newton's Laws of Motion when we did. The Lucasian Chair still exists today, and the current holder of the position is another very well-known scientist: theoretical physicist Stephen Hawking.

The establishment of funds to support individual scientists within the university was a critical step in creating the scientific research institution, but universities are not the only place where scientific research occurs. Many major research institutions are part of the government: in the United States, for example, government-run research institutions include the U.S. Geological Survey (USGS), Los Alamos National Laboratory (LANL), and NASA. The establishment of these research institutions was often in response to a broad initiative within the government, such as the exploration of the western territories in the 1860s that led to the consolidation of several different groups of surveyors into the USGS. Similarly, World War II strongly influenced the development of scientific institutions. In response to a series of letters in 1939 and 1940 from Albert Einstein (available on our website at www.visionlearning.com) warning of the possibility of the development of nuclear weapons by Germany, President Franklin Roosevelt ordered the War Department to begin work on an atomic bomb. His order led to the establishment of a number of national laboratories in 1943, including LANL in New Mexico and Oak Ridge National Laboratory in Tennessee. Scientists hired to work at these new national labs were not completely free to focus on the research that interested them (like Newton at Cambridge); instead they were asked by the government to focus on specific problems that fostered the development of nuclear weapons. The focus of research at LANL remained the development and testing of weapons until 1992, when the Nuclear Test Ban Treaty was signed by President George H.W. Bush. Since then, LANL's mission has changed to focus on the science behind national security, which includes everything from securing nuclear weapons stockpiles to studying the possible effects of global warming.

Additionally, scientific research takes place at commercial corporations, where it is often described as "research and development," or R&D. In 1970, for example, the Xerox Corporation established its Palo Alto Research Center, known as Xerox PARC, to bring together researchers in information science, physical science, and engineering to create the "architecture of information." In this venue, fundamental scientific research was supported to the extent that it could contribute to the development of new technologies or products that could contribute to the overall theme of the architecture of information. The effort led to the development of photocopiers, initially, but the research branch of Xerox is perhaps most famous for its development of the mouse, first used with the personal computer by Apple in the early 1980s.

The role of the professional society

Research institutions are important support networks for most scientists. When those scientists are ready to share the results of their research with the broader scientific community, however, they often seek feedback and review from their peers through additional means – by presenting their work at meetings of societies like the American Geophysical Union (AGU), a professional scientific society with over 45,000 members from 140 countries. Part of the mission of the AGU is to "advance the various geophysical disciplines through scientific discussion, publication, and dissemination of information," accomplished through sponsoring meetings that bring members together and publishing journals of peer-reviewed work. Professional societies in other disciplines share similar missions, such as the Ecological Society of America, American Institute of Physics, and the American Chemical Society, to name only a few.

Professional societies play a critical role in fostering scientific progress. One of the longest-lived professional societies developed during the Scientific Revolution of the mid-1600s, when the concept of rigorous, observation- and experiment-based science began to take hold in England. The Royal Society of London originated in the ideas of Francis Bacon. Bacon was not a scientist himself, but an English statesman and philosopher who published a book in 1620 entitled *Instauratio Magna* about the application of what we now might call the scientific research method. In it, he described the process of inductive reasoning, in which facts are collected and a theory is developed to explain those facts. This method stands in stark contrast to the Aristotelian process, known as deductive reasoning, in which reason was used instead of observation to determine explanations. Importantly, Bacon also viewed the scientific process as a community endeavor that required financial and philosophical support from institutions like governments and universities.

Bacon died in 1626, but his philosophy lived well beyond him and spread. In 1648, a group of scientists at Oxford University in England formed what they called an "experimental science club," and began to hold regular meetings at which they would conduct experiments and discuss the results. By including the word "experimental" in their title, this group acknowledged their adherence to Bacon's ideas about science rather than Aristotle's (see Figure 2). In November of 1660, the group became a more formal entity, drawing up a charter and naming themselves the Royal Society of London. The original twelve fellows of the Society included Christopher

Wren and Robert Boyle, the scientist immortalized in Boyle's Law, which relates the pressure and temperature of a given mass of gas to its volume (eventually leading to the Ideal Gas Law). The fellows paid annual dues and met weekly to conduct scientific research largely through experiments or descriptive method (see our Experimentation chapter). This was a radical notion at the time – though several clubs existed where men would assemble to discuss science, the discussions at these clubs were not centered on developing new knowledge by actually conducting research (Gribbin, 2007). The Fellows rotated responsibility for the weekly meetings, which soon proved challenging to coordinate. So in 1662, the Royal Society hired Boyle's as-

Figure 2: Frontispiece from the 1667 History of the Royal Society by Thomas Sprat. The figure on the right is Francis Bacon; Lord Brouncker, the first president is to the left of the bust of Charles II, the first patron of the society. Bacon is pointing to Boyle's apparatus for his gas experiments.

sistant, Robert Hooke, as the Curator of Experiments, in which role he was responsible for devising and running the weekly research experiences. In 1665, the Society began publishing its journal, *Philosophical Transactions of the Royal Society of London*, which described not only the events at the weekly meetings but the results of scientific investigations of its members outside the weekly meetings.

The Royal Society set the stage for the modern professional society, officially recognizing the importance of the community in building scientific knowledge. Within the sciences, math, and engineering fields, there are many thousands of professional societies all over the world. An individual scientist may belong to one or many, depending on his or her field, the variety of their interests, and the length of time they have been working as a scientist. For all scientists who wish to practice science, becoming a member of a professional society is an important step that gives them access to a community of peers from whom they can both learn and seek feedback on their own work.

In addition, many professional societies give awards to members to recognize achievement in scientific research. The American Chemical Society, for example, solicits nominations for 58 national awards in chemistry ranging from the Priestley Medal (in honor of Joseph Priestley) given to recognize distinguished services to chemistry to the Paul J. Flory Education Award, which recognizes outstanding achievement by an individual in promoting undergraduate or graduate polymer education. As in any other profession, these awards recognize individuals who excel in their work and they are considered significant achievements for a scientist.

The role of the funding institution

Research institutions and professional societies are essential to scientific progress and to the individual scientist, but most scientists need to seek additional financial support from outside sources. Historically, funding was sought through personal relationships with wealthy patrons; for example, the Medici family funded the work of a number of famous scientists including Galileo, and in turn, Galileo named the four largest moons of Jupiter that he discovered *Medicea Sidera* (the Medician stars). More recently, governments have played a large role in funding scientific research. In the United States, the federal government is the largest single supporter of scientific research. Although the federal government has always supported research in the U.S. (such as the scientific surveys of the West described in our chapter on Description), there were no federal agencies dedicated specifically to funding scientific research prior to World War II. In a way, WWII acted as a kind of "scientific revolution" in the United States, laying the foundations for the establishment of federal funding agencies such as the National Science Foundation (NSF).

During WWII, Vannevar Bush led the Office of Scientific Research and Development (OSRD), established at the onset of the war to financially support research that had immediate application to wartime activities. Although the OSRD's mission was to focus on research with "immediate application" to the war effort, Bush realized that many of these applications relied on basic scientific research into materials science, physics, and many other disciplines; as a result, government support for so-called "basic" research nearly tripled over the war period. As the war ended and this office was destined to disappear, Bush wrote an influential essay in 1945 entitled "Science – The Endless Frontier" which advocated the development of a National Research Foundation (Bush, 1945). Bush believed that, "The Government should accept new responsibilities for promoting the flow of new scientific knowledge and the development of scientific talent in our youth. These responsibilities are the proper concern of the Government, for they vitally affect our health, our jobs, and our national security."

Throughout history, many governments have supported research in development of national defense. But Bush strongly advocated for government support for basic scientific research that may not result in immediate applications, and he suggested that funding be disbursed to scientists through a competitive grant process rather than through favor. Over the next five years, his proposal underwent criticism, revisions, and political dealings (Mazuzan, 1994). Finally, in 1950, Congress approved the establishment of the National Science Foundation (NSF) (Figure 3) with an initial budget of $15 million, most of which would go to scientists to conduct research. Today, the NSF is one of the major funding institutions in the United States. In 2006, the NSF received 40,000 proposals, funded approximately 11,000 of them, and had a total agency budget of almost $5.6 billion, of which $4.3 billion went to scientific research.

Figure 3: *The logo of the National Science Foundation.*

Many other U.S. government agencies provide funding for scientific research, including the Department of Energy, the National Institutes of Health, and the Department of Defense. In fact, the development of this text that you are now reading was funded by the U.S. Department of Education, and part of that money went to bringing experts together to discuss what should be included in a series of readings about the process of science and the role of scientific institutions in the scientific process. In 1997, total government spending on science and scientific research in the United States was estimated at 2.5% of the total gross domestic product, or approximately $300 billion (May, 1997). Federal research funding proposals are commonly judged based on both their relevance to a funding agency's priorities and the scientific merit of the proposal as determined by peer review, so proposals that are submitted to most agencies are reviewed internally as well as sent out to other scientists to be reviewed (see our Peer Review chapter).

Private foundations and corporations offer another means of financial support for many scientists. The Howard Hughes Medical Institute, for example, is a private, non-profit organization that grants as much as $700 million dollars a year, primarily for biomedical research, and about $80 million dollars a year towards science education. You may be more familiar with the Bill and Melinda Gates Foundation, started by the founder of Microsoft, which awards grants in global health and development projects.

The influence of scientific institutions

Together, these scientific institutions – research institutions, professional societies, and funding institutions – form a large part of the community of science. Through them, scientists interact with one another, share ideas, conduct peer reviews, secure funding for research, and obtain access to space and facilities – all of which facilitate the research process and lead to scientific progress.

Each of these institutions is also capable of influencing the direction of scientific progress in its own way. Governments are strongly influenced by political and social motivating factors: clearly, the United States' participation in World War II led to focused scientific research into harnessing nuclear energy to make weapons. Without the motivating factor of a world war, this research may never have been deemed critical by the government, and the scientific research may never have been pursued. Federal funding agencies continue to set research priorities and solicit grant applications from scientists that address these priorities. Similarly, universities can influence the direction that scientific research takes in their institutions. The institution's administration or faculty choose the research areas in which they hire new faculty – these decisions may come at the behest of a donor or they may reflect a desire to maintain existing strengths or develop new ones.

Professional societies generally have less influence over the direction that research takes, though they are often responsible for promoting particular research areas through publications. In addition, they may release position statements to the government and the public concerning their conclusions regarding how the scientific research their members have conducted affects the general public. For example, the American Geophysical Union's position statement on global climate change begins:

> Human activities are increasingly altering the Earth's climate. These effects add to natural influences that have been present over Earth's history. Scientific evidence strongly indicates that natural influences cannot explain the rapid increase in global near-surface temperatures observed during the second half of the 20th century. (AGU, 2003)

Such position statements are meant to emphasize the importance of scientific knowledge to policy decisions, and to be considered legitimate they must fall within the realm of research facilitated by the professional society and be approved by a majority of its members. The development of such statements by institutions within the community of science should emphasize to the general public that issues such as climate change are strongly supported by multiple lines of evidence.

Unfortunately, the influence that institutions have on the process of science is not always positive. Recent stories in the media have loudly decried the possible bias that pharmaceutical companies exert on research at medical institutions; and the tobacco industry's negative impacts on research regarding the health impacts of cigarette smoke is now widely accepted (see the Comparison chapter). Space exploration is another controversial area of scientific research. President George W. Bush's announcement in 2005 of his initiative to send humans to Mars and return to the Moon met with criticism from institutions like the American Institute for Physics, whose members note that funding the Space Exploration Initiative has diverted funds from other programs, like maintenance and replacement of satellites that collect data on weather and climate – data that helps communities prepare for severe weather events like hurricanes. While we would like to imagine that scientists are driven purely by their curiosity and interest in research questions, the reality is that the availability of funding can often be one of the driving forces behind research, and these funding priorities change over time.

The biggest influence that all scientific institutions have, however, is on scientific progress. Consider again being a student – while it's not impossible to learn on your own, outside of the academic institution, it would be more difficult to find knowledgeable people to help you when you needed it, to determine which books and resources are useful, and to work with a group of peers. The same is true for science. While a lot of scientific thinking can go on anywhere, our scientific institutions provide an important mechanism for supporting and communicating that work in order to build our scientific knowledge over time.

Key Concepts for this chapter

▶ The community of science includes institutions and professional societies that support scientists physically, financially, and intellectually.

▶ Research institutions include universities, national laboratories, government agencies, and corporations that all provide physical space and support for scientific research.

▶ Professional societies promote interactions between individuals across institutions by organizing meetings and publications.

▶ Governments, private industry, and other institutions provide financial support for scientific research through grants and research contracts.

▶ All of these institutions affect the direction of scientific research, and may even bias it, by setting research priorities.

References

AGU (2003). Human Impacts on Climate [Electronic Version] from http://www.agu.org/sci_soc/policy/positions/climate_change.shtml

Bruen, R. (1995). Lucasian Chair [Electronic Version], 2007 from http://www.lucasianchair.org/prof.html.

Bush, V. (1945). *Science - The Endless Frontier: A Report to the President*. Retrieved from http://nsf.gov/about/history/nsf50/vbush1945.jsp.

Gribbin, J. (2007). *The Fellowship: Gilbert, Bacon, Harvey, Wren, Newton, and the Story of a Scientific Revolution*. London: Overlook Hardcover.

May, R. M. (1997). The Scientific Wealth of Nations. *Science*, 275(5301), 793-796.

Mazuzan, G. T. (1994). The National Science Foundation: A Brief History. Retrieved from http://nsf.gov/about/history/nsf50/nsf8816.jsp.

Ideas in Science:
Theories, Hypotheses, and Laws

"It is a capital mistake to theorize before one has data."

~ Sir Arthur Conan Doyle

Imagine yourself shopping in a grocery store with a good friend who happens to be a chemist. Struggling to choose between the many different types of tomatoes in front of you, you pick one up, turn to your friend and ask her if she thinks the tomato is organic. Your friend simply chuckles and replies, "Of course it's organic!" without even looking at how the fruit was grown. Why the amused reaction? Your friend is highlighting a simple difference in vocabulary. To a chemist, the term "organic" refers to any compound in which hydrogen is bonded to carbon. Tomatoes (like all plants) are abundant in organic compounds – thus your friend's laughter. In modern agriculture, however, the term "organic" has come to mean food items grown or raised without the use of chemical fertilizers, pesticides, or other additives.

So who is correct? You both are. Both uses of the word are correct, though they mean different things in different contexts. There are, of course, lots of words that have more than one meaning (like "bat," for example), but multiple meanings can be especially confusing when two meanings convey very different ideas and are specific to one field of study.

Scientific theories

The term "theory" also has two meanings, and this double meaning often leads to confusion. In common language, the term theory generally refers to speculation or a hunch or guess. You might have a theory about why your favorite sports team isn't playing well, or who ate the last cookie from the cookie jar. But these theories do not fit the scientific use of the term.

In science, a theory is a well-substantiated and comprehensive set of ideas that explains a phenomenon in nature. A scientific theory is based on large amounts of data and observations that have been collected over time. Scientific theories can be tested and refined by additional research, and they allow scientists to make predictions. Though you may be correct in your hunch, your cookie jar conjecture doesn't fit this more rigorous definition.

All scientific disciplines have well-established, fundamental theories. For example, atomic theory describes the nature of matter and is supported by multiple lines of evidence from the way substances behave and react in the world around us (see our website's series on Atomic Theory). Plate tectonic theory describes the large scale movement of the outer layer of the earth and is supported by evidence from studies about earthquakes, magnetic properties of the rocks that make up the seafloor, and the distribution of volcanoes on earth (see our series on Plate Tectonic Theory). The theory of evolution by natural selection, which describes the mechanism by which inherited traits that affect survivability or reproductive success can cause changes in living organisms over generations, is supported by extensive studies of DNA, fossils and other types of scientific evidence (see our Charles Darwin series for more information). Each of these major theories guides and informs modern research in those fields, integrating a broad, comprehensive set of ideas.

So how are these fundamental theories developed, and why are they considered so well-supported? Let's take a closer look at some of the data and research supporting the theory of natural selection to better see how a theory develops.

The development of a scientific theory:
Evolution and natural selection

The theory of evolution by natural selection is sometimes maligned as Charles Darwin's speculation on the origin of modern life forms. However, evolutionary theory is not speculation, and while Darwin is rightly credited with first articulating the theory of natural selection, his ideas built on more than a century of scientific research that came before him, and are supported by over a century and a half of research since.

Research about the origins and diversity of life proliferated in the 18th and 19th centuries. Carolus Linnaeus, a Swedish botanist and the father of modern taxonomy was a devout Christian who believed in the concept of Fixity of Species, an idea based on the biblical story of creation. The Fixity of Species concept said that each species is based on an ideal form that has

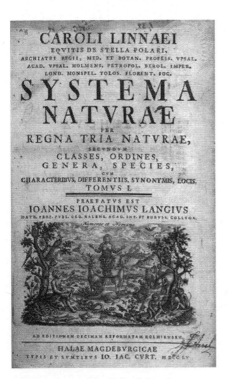

Figure 1: Cover of the 1760 edition of Systema Naturae.

not changed over time. In the early stages of his career, Linnaeus traveled extensively and collected data on the structural similarities and differences between different species of plants. Noting that some very different plants had similar structures, he began to piece together his landmark work *Systema Naturae* in 1735 (Figure 1). In *Systema*, Linnaeus classified organisms into related groups based on similarities in their physical features. He developed a hierarchical classification system, even drawing relationships between seemingly disparate species (for example, humans, orangutans, and chimpanzees) based on the physical similarities that he observed between these organisms. Linnaeus did not explicitly discuss change in organisms or propose a reason for his hierarchy, but by grouping organisms based on physical characteristics, he suggested that species are related, unintentionally challenging the Fixity notion that each species is created in a unique, ideal form.

Also in the early 1700s, Georges-Louis Leclerc, a French naturalist, and James Hutton, a Scottish geologist, began to develop new ideas about the age of the earth. At the time, many people thought of the earth as 6,000 years old, based on a strict interpretation of the events detailed in the Christian Old Testament by the influential Scottish Archbishop Ussher. By observing other planets and comets in the solar system, Leclerc hypothesized that earth began as a hot, fiery ball of molten rock, mostly consisting of iron. Using the cooling rate of iron, Leclerc calculated that earth must therefore be at least 70,000 years old in order to have reached its present temperature. Hutton approached the same topic from a different perspective, gathering observations of the relationships between different rock formations and the rates of modern geological processes near his home in Scotland. He recognized that the relatively slow processes of erosion and sedimentation could not create all of the exposed rock layers in only a few thousand years (see our Rock Cyle module online). Based on his extensive collection of data (just one of his many publications ran to 2,138 pages), Hutton suggested that the earth was far older than human history – hundreds of millions of years old. While we now know that both Leclerc and Hutton significantly underestimated the age of the earth (by about 4 billion years), their work shattered long-held beliefs and opened a window into research on how life can change over these very long timescales.

With the age of the earth now extended by Leclerc and Hutton, more researchers began to turn their attention to studying past life. Fossils are the main way to study past life forms, and several key studies on fossils helped in the development of a theory of evolution. In 1795, Georges Cuvier began to work at the National Museum in Paris as a naturalist and anatomist. Through his work, Cuvier became interested in fossils found near Paris, which some claimed were the remains of the elephants that Hannibal rode over the Alps when he invaded Rome in 218 BCE. In studying both the fossils and living species, Cuvier documented different patterns in the dental structure and number of teeth between the fossils and modern elephants (Figure 2) (Horner, 1843). Based on this data, Cu-

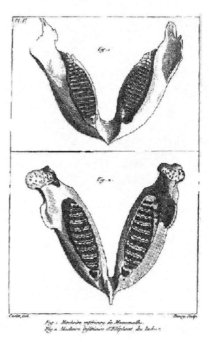

Figure 2: Illustration of an Indian elephant jaw and a mammoth jaw from Cuvier's 1796 paper.

vier hypothesized that the fossil remains were not left by Hannibal, but were from a distinct species of animal that once roamed through Europe and had gone extinct thousands of years earlier: the mammoth. The concept of species extinction had been discussed by a few individuals before Cuvier, but it was in direct opposition to the Fixity of Species concept – if every organism were based on a perfectly adapted, ideal form, how could any cease to exist? That would suggest it was no longer ideal.

While Cuvier's work provided critical evidence of extinction, a key component of evolution, he was highly critical of the idea that species could change over time. As a result of his extensive studies of animal anatomy, Cuvier had developed a holistic view of organisms, stating that the "number, direction, and shape of the bones that compose each part of an animal's body are always in a necessary relation to all the other parts, in such a way that ... one can infer the whole from any one of them" In other words, Cuvier viewed each part of an organism as a unique, essential component of the whole organism. If one part were to change, he believed, the organism could not survive. His skepticism about the ability of organisms to change led him to criticize the whole idea of evolution, and his prominence in France as a scientist played a large role in discouraging the acceptance of the idea in the scientific community.

Jean Baptiste Lamarck was a contemporary of Cuvier's at the National Museum in Paris who studied invertebrates like insects and worms. As Lamarck worked through the museum's large collection of invertebrates, he was impressed by the number and variety of organisms. He became convinced that organisms could, in fact, change through time, stating that "time and favorable conditions are the two principal means which nature has employed in giving existence to all her productions. We know that for her time has no limit, and that consequently she always has it at her disposal." This was a radical departure from both the fixity concept and Cuvier's ideas, and it built on the long time scale that geologists had recently established. Lamarck proposed that changes that occurred during an organism's lifetime could be passed on to their offspring; suggesting, for example, that a body builder's muscles would be inherited by their children. As it turned out, the mechanism by which Lamarck proposed that organisms change over time was wrong, and he is now often referred to disparagingly for his "inheritance of acquired characteristics" idea. Yet despite the fact that some of his ideas were discredited, Lamarck established a support for evolutionary theory that others would build on and improve.

In the early 1800s, a British geologist and canal surveyor named William Smith added another component to the accumulating evidence for evolution. Smith observed that rock layers exposed in different parts of England bore similarities to one another: these layers (or strata) were arranged in a predictable order, and each layer contained distinct groups of fossils. From this series of observations, he developed a hypothesis that specific groups of animals followed one another in a definite sequence through earth's history, and this sequence could be seen in the rock layers. Smith's hypothesis was based on his knowledge of geological principles, including the Law of Superposition.

The Law of Superposition states that sediments are deposited in a time sequence, with the oldest sediments deposited first, or at the bottom, and newer layers deposited on top. The concept was first expressed by the Persian scientist Avicenna in the 11th century, but was popularized by the Danish scientist Nicolas Steno in the 17th century. Note that the law does not state how sediments are deposited, it simply describes the relationship between the ages of deposited sediments.

Smith backed up his hypothesis with extensive drawings of fossils uncovered during his research (Figure 3) thus allowing other scientists to confirm or dispute his findings. His hypothesis has, in fact, been confirmed by many other scientists and has come to be referred to as the Law of Faunal Succession. His work was critical to the formation of evolutionary theory as it not only confirmed Cuvier's work that organisms have gone extinct, but it also showed that the appearance of life does not date to the birth of the planet. Instead, the fossil record preserves a timeline of the appearance and disappearance of different organisms in the past, and in doing so offers evidence for change in organisms over time.

It was into this world that Charles Darwin entered: Linnaeus had developed a taxonomy of organisms based on their physical relationships, Leclerc and Hutton demonstrated that there was sufficient time in earth's history for organisms to change, Cuvier showed that species of organisms have gone extinct, Lamarck proposed that organisms change over time, and Smith established a timeline of the appearance and disappearance of different organisms in the geological record.

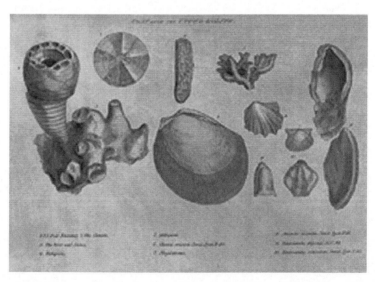

Figure 3: *Engraving from William Smith's 1815 monograph on identifying strata by fossils.*

Charles Darwin collected data during his work as a naturalist on the HMS Beagle starting in 1831. He took extensive notes on the geology of the places he visited; he made a major find of fossils of extinct animals in Patagonia and identified an extinct giant ground sloth named *Megatherium*. He experienced an earthquake in Chile that stranded beds of living mussels above water where they would be preserved for years to come. Perhaps most famously, he conducted extensive studies of animals on the Galápagos Islands, noting subtle differences in species of mockingbird, tortoise, and finch that were isolated on different islands with different environmental conditions. These subtle differences made the animals highly adapted to their environments. This broad spectrum of data led Darwin to propose an idea about how organisms change "by means of natural selection" (Figure 4). But this idea was not based only on his work, it was also based on the accumulation of evidence and ideas of many others before him. Because his proposal encompassed and explained many different lines of evidence and previous work, they formed the basis of a new and robust scientific theory regarding change in organisms – the theory of evolution by natural selection.

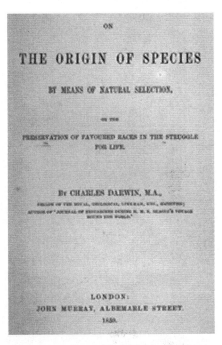

Figure 4: Title page of the 1859 Murray edition of The Origin of Species *by Charles Darwin.*

Darwin's ideas were grounded in evidence and data so compelling that if he had not conceived them, someone else would have. In fact, someone else did. Between 1858 and 1859, Alfred Russel Wallace, a British naturalist, wrote a series of letters to Darwin that independently proposed natural selection as the means for evolutionary change; the letters were presented to the Linnean Society of London, a prominent scientific society at the time. This long chain of research highlights that theories are not just the work of one individual. At the same time, however, it often takes the insight and creativity of individuals to put together all of the pieces and propose a new theory. Both Darwin and Wallace were experienced naturalists who were familiar with the work of others. While all of the work leading up to 1830 contributed to the theory of evolution, Darwin's and Wallace's theory changed the way that future research was focused by presenting a comprehensive, well-substantiated set of ideas, thus becoming a fundamental theory of biological research.

Expanding, testing, and refining scientific theories

Since Darwin and Wallace first published their ideas, extensive research has tested and expanded the theory of evolution by natural selection. Darwin had no concept of genes or DNA or the mechanism by which characteristics were inherited within a species. A contemporary of Darwin's, the Austrian monk Gregor Mendel, first presented his own landmark study *Experiments in Plant Hybridization* in 1865, in which he provided the basic patterns of genetic inheritance, describing which characteristics (and evolutionary changes) can be passed on in organisms. Still, it wasn't until much later that a "gene" was defined as the heritable unit. In 1937, the Ukrainian born geneticist Theodosius Dobzhansky published *Genetics and the Origin of Species*, a seminal work in which he described genes themselves and demonstrated that it is through mutations in genes that change occurs. The work defined evolution as "a change in the frequency of an allele within a gene pool" (Dobzhansky, 1982). These studies and others in the field of genetics have added to Darwin's work, expanding the scope of the theory.

More recently, Dr. Richard Lenski, a scientist at Michigan State University, isolated a single *Escherichia coli* bacterium in 1989 as the first step of the longest running experimental test of evolutionary theory to date – a true test meant to replicate evolution and natural selection in the lab. After the single microbe had multiplied, Lenski isolated the offspring into 12 different strains, each in their own glucose-supplied culture, predicting that the genetic make-up of each strain would change over time to become more adapted to their specific culture as predicted by evolutionary theory. These 12 lines have been nurtured for over 40,000 bacterial generations (luckily bacterial generations are much shorter than human generations) and exposed to different selective pressures such as heat, cold, antibiotics, and infection with other microorganisms. Lenski and colleagues have studied dozens of aspects of evolutionary theory with these genetically isolated populations. In 1999, they published a paper that demonstrated that random genetic mutations were common within the populations and highly diverse across different individual bacteria. However, "pivotal" mutations that are associated with beneficial changes in the group are shared by all descendants in a population and are much rarer than random mutations, as predicted by the theory of evolution by natural selection (Papadopoulos *et al.*, 1999).

While established scientific theories like evolution have a wealth of research and evidence supporting them, this does not mean that they cannot be refined as new information or new perspectives on existing data become available. For example, in 1972, biologist Stephen Jay Gould and paleontologist Niles Eldredge took a fresh look at the existing data regarding the timing by which evolutionary change takes place. Gould and Eldredge did not set out to challenge the theory of evolution; rather they used it as a guiding principle and asked more specific questions to add detail and nuance to the theory. This is true of all theories in science: they provide a framework for additional research. At the time, many biologists viewed evolution as occurring gradually, causing small incremental changes in organisms at a relatively steady rate. The idea is referred to as phyletic gradualism, and is rooted in the geological concept of uniformitarianism. After reexamining the available data, Gould and Eldredge came to a different explanation, suggesting that evolution consists of long periods of stability that are punctuated by occasional instances of dramatic change – a process they called punctuated equilibrium.

Like Darwin before them, their proposal is rooted in evidence and research on evolutionary change, and has been supported by multiple lines of evidence. In fact, punctuated equilibrium is now considered its own theory in evolutionary biology. Punctuated equilibrium is not as broad of a theory as natural selection. In science, some theories are broad and overarching of many concepts, such as the theory of evolution by natural selection, while others focus on concepts at a smaller, or more targeted, scale such as punctuated equilibrium. And punctuated equilibrium does not challenge or weaken the concept of natural selection; rather it represents a change in our understanding of the timing by which change occurs in organisms, and a theory within a theory. The theory of evolution by natural selection now includes both gradualism and punctuated equilibrium to describe the rate at which change proceeds.

Other scientific terms: Hypotheses and laws

One of the challenges in understanding scientific terms like theory is that there is not a precise definition even within the scientific community. Some scientists debate over whether certain proposals merit designation as a hypothesis or theory, and others mistakenly use the terms interchangeably. But there are differences in these terms. A hypothesis is a proposed explanation for an observable phenomenon. Hypotheses, just like theories, are based on observations from research. For example, Leclerc did not hypothesize that the earth had cooled from a molten ball of iron as a random guess; rather he developed this hypothesis based on his observations of information from meteorites.

A scientist often proposes a hypothesis before research confirms it as a way of predicting the outcome of study to help better define the parameters of the research. Leclerc's hypothesis allowed him to use known parameters (the cooling rate of iron) to do additional work. A key component of a formal scientific hypothesis is that it is testable and falsifiable. For example, when Richard Lenski first isolated his 12 strains of bacteria, he likely hypothesized that random mutations would cause differences to appear within a period of time in the different strains of bacteria. But when a hypothesis is generated in science, a scientist will also make an alternative hypothesis, an explanation that explains a study if the data does not support the original hypothesis. If the different strains of bacteria in Lenski's work did not diverge over the indicated period of time, perhaps the rate of mutation was slower than first thought.

So you might ask, if theories are so well supported, do they eventually become laws? The answer is no – not because they aren't well-supported, but because theories and laws are two very different things. Laws describe phenomena, often mathematically. Theories, however, explain phenomena. For example, in 1687 Isaac Newton proposed a Theory of Gravitation, describing gravity as a force of attraction between two objects. As part of this theory, Newton developed a Law of Universal Gravitation that explains how this force operates. This law states that the force of gravity between two objects is inversely proportional to the square of the distance between those objects. Newton's Law does not explain why this is true, but it describes how gravity functions. In 1916, Albert Einstein developed his theory of general relativity to explain the mechanism by which gravity has its effect. Einstein's work challenges Newton's theory, and has been found after extensive testing and research to more accurately describe the phenomenon of gravity. While Einstein's work has replaced Newton's as the dominant explanation of gravity in modern science, Newton's Law of Universal Gravitation is still used as it reasonably (and more simply) describes the force of gravity under many conditions. Similarly the Law of Faunal Succession developed by William Smith does not explain why organisms follow each other in distinct, predictable ways in the rock layers, but it accurately describes the phenomenon.

Theories, hypotheses, and laws are not simply important components of science, they drive scientific progress. For example, evolutionary biology now stands as a distinct field of science that focuses on the origins and descent of species. Geologists now rely on plate tectonics as a conceptual model and guiding theory when they are studying processes at work in the earth's crust. And physicists refer to atomic theory when they are predicting the existence of sub-atomic particles yet to be discovered. This does not mean that science is "finished," or that all of the important theories have been discovered already. Like evolution, progress in science happens both gradually and in short, dramatic bursts. Both types of progress are critical for creating a robust knowledge base with data as the foundation and scientific theories giving structure to that knowledge.

Key Concepts for this chapter

▶ A scientific theory is an explanation inferred from multiple lines of evidence for some broad aspect of the natural world and is logical, testable, and predictive.

▶ As new evidence comes to light, or new interpretations of existing data are proposed, theories may be revised and even change; however, they are not tenuous or speculative.

▶ A scientific hypothesis is an inferred explanation of an observation or research finding; while more exploratory in nature than a theory, it is based on existing scientific knowledge.

▶ A scientific law is an expression of a mathematical or descriptive relationship observed in nature.

References

Cook, H., & Bestman, H. D. (2000). A Persistent View: Lamarckian Thought in Early Evolutionary Theories and in Modern Biology. *Perspectives on Science and Christian Faith,* 52, 86-97.

Dobzhansky, T. G. (1982). *Genetics and the Origin of Species*: Columbia University Press.

Gould, S. J. (2002). *The Structure of Evolutionary Theory*: Belknap Press.

Horner, W. E. (1843). Remarks on the Dental System of the Mastodon, with an Account of Some Lower Jaws in Mr. Koch's Collection, St. Louis, Missouri, Where There Is a Solitary Tusk on the Right Side. *Transactions of the American Philosophical Society,* 8, 53-59.

Johnson, S. (2008). *The invention of air: a story of science, faith, revolution, and the birth of America*. New York: Riverhead Books.

Papadopoulos, D., Schneider, D., Meier-Eiss, J., Arber, W., Lenski, R. E., & Blot, M. (1999). Genomic evolution during a 10,000-generation experiment with bacteria (Vol. 96, pp. 3807-3812): *National Acad Sciences.*

Ideas in Science:
Scientific Controversy

"In science the credit goes to the man who convinces the world, not to the man to whom the idea first occurs."

~ Sir Francis Darwin

The first offshore oil well out-of-sight from land was drilled in 1947 by the Kerr-McGee Corporation, off the coast of Louisiana (see Figure 1). Within a few years, there were a dozen such wells in the Gulf of Mexico, followed by wells drilled off of the coast of California and other locations. In the early 1950s, the United States government passed legislation that gave the federal government jurisdiction over the submerged continental shelf, and allowed the Department of the Interior to lease these areas for mineral development. By the late 1950s, these offshore oil leases were one of the largest revenue generators in the United States, second only to income taxes (Freudenburg and Gramling, 1994).

On January 28, 1969, just as oil workers completed the fifth well on an offshore platform off the coast of Santa Barbara, a blowout occurred that would eventually spill millions of gallons of oils into the water, soil popular beaches and bring the previously out-of-sight drilling practice back into view. A process that had previously seemed to have largely positive effects—revenue generation for the government and a domestic source of energy—now had visible detrimental effects: local beaches were blackened by oil, dead and dying sea birds littered the area, and scores of coastal communities reeked with the stench of oil. On March 21, President Nixon visited the spill and told the assembled crowd of residents and reporters that he would consider a ban on offshore drilling and would convert the area into a permanent ecological preserve. But the ban was lifted on April 1, angering local residents and sparking a controversy over the merits of offshore drilling. Were the benefits worth the risks? Some felt that having a reliable

Figure 1: *The first out-of-sight offshore drilling platform. The platform was located 14 km off the coast of Louisiana in 4 m of water, and operated until 1984.*

source of domestic oil provided security for the country, and outweighed environmental concerns. Others cited the toxic effects of oil spills on fisheries, tourism, and the environment in general as a reason to shut down offshore drilling. The government placed some coastal areas off-limits to drilling, such as the Arctic National Wildlife Refuge, while in other regions, such as the Gulf of Mexico, drilling moved further and further offshore into deeper water. A massive blow-out from one of these wells in April 2010 reinvigorated the controversy over whether or not offshore drilling should be allowed and how it should be regulated. People on all sides of the controversy are using different data as evidence to support their position: a decline in shrimp fishing industry, lax regulation of drilling companies, domestic security and the need for energy resources, the interaction between hurricanes and surface oil. Though it is unlikely that the controversy will ever be resolved to the point where everyone agrees, additional legislation and regulations put in place by the government will determine the future of offshore drilling.

Science is also full of controversy. Similar to the controversy over offshore drilling, scientists appeal to evidence to support their claims, and the nature of the debate changes as new evidence comes to light. But there are some key differences between a scientific controversy and other types of controversy. For example, many people think that the controversy over offshore drilling is holding up progress, whether that progress is economic or environmental or political. In contrast, a controversy in science often creates progress, because it spurs new research and therefore is an essential part of the process of science.

What is scientific controversy?

Scientists can disagree about lots of things, from the mundane (like what is the best kind of analytical instrument to use) to the profound (whether or not string theory is an accurate representation of reality). Two scientists disagreeing over an instrument or string theory — or even the interpretation of data — does not count as a controversy, however. A true scientific controversy involves a sustained debate within the broader scientific community (McMullin, 1987). In other words, a significant number of people must be actively engaged in research that addresses the controversy over time. No matter what the content of the disagreement, the scientists involved all share some fundamental knowledge and agree that the subject matter is worth being concerned about and that the various arguments are legitimate.

What makes the arguments legitimate is that they are based on data. It is not enough for a scientist to simply say, "I don't agree with you": instead, they must conduct the research to garner enough evidence to support their claim. An argument must explain the majority of data available — not just the data collected to support one side. This is not necessarily the case in public controversies such as that over offshore drilling, where a group or individual can decide that some data is more important than other data — the number of birds that died or the economic impact of drilling or the percentage of oil imports. In a scientific controversy, all of the data must be explained and taken into account.

Though controversies are often discussed in informal settings (the same way you might discuss a controversial issue with your friends), the real debate is carried out at research meetings and through the publication of journal articles (see the Understanding Scientific Journals and Articles chapter). It is only through this process that the debate becomes part of the scientific literature (see Utilizing the Scientific Literature) and helps science progress. There is no authoritative body in science that decides what the right answer in a controversy is, nor does it require complete consensus among all scientists. The resolution to a controversy comes when one argument is widely accepted and other arguments fade away. Often, the evidence in favor of one side of the controversy becomes so overwhelming that people simply stop arguing about it. Usually, that happens when multiple lines of evidence coming from multiple different research methods (and perhaps multiple disciplines) all converge.

Controversies are ongoing in every field of science on a regular basis. For example, as of 2010, geophysicists are engaged in a debate about the existence of mantle plumes, thin columns of hot rock that rise from the earth's core to the surface and cause volcanic activity (see, for example, Kerr, 2010). The concept of a mantle plume as a non-moving source of magma for island chains like Hawaii (Figure 2) was first postulated by J. Tuzo Wilson

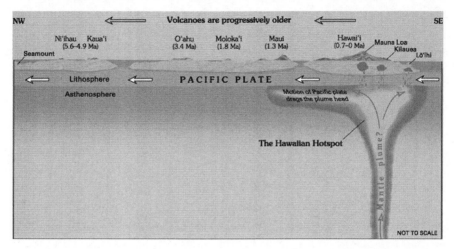

Figure 2: Conceptual cross-section through the earth at the Hawaiian islands, showing the proposed mantle plume. Image courtesy the U.S. Geological Survey, from This Dynamic Planet map (Simkin et al., 2006),

shortly after the development of the theory of plate tectonics (see our on-line module Plate Tectonics I) and was widely accepted over the next thirty years. In 2003, however, a group of scientists led by John Tarduno, a geo-physicist at the University of Rochester, presented strong evidence that the mantle plume thought to be responsible for forming the Hawaiian islands had moved more than 1,000 km over time (Tarduno *et al.*, 2003). That paper launched a multitude of additional studies that began to question the very existence of mantle plumes. The ongoing debate has been heated at times, but has also caused a tremendous leap in our understanding of the volcanic processes associated with mantle plumes, and our scientific knowledge has advanced.

The debate over the existence of mantle plumes is clearly a scientific controversy, and most scientific controversies similarly have little to do with personal, ethical, or political controversies. On the other end of the spectrum, the controversy about the use of stem cells harvested from human embryos in biomedical research is not a scientific controversy – scientists agree about what stem cells are and how they work. Instead, the controversy instead revolves around whether or not it is ethical to use stem cells. Sometimes, however, the lines between scientific controversy and other kinds of controversy get blurred. Scientists are human, after all, and what starts as a scientific controversy may also include personal disagreements (see the chapter on Scientists and the Scientific Community). In other cases, the media may exaggerate a scientific controversy and turn it into a political debate. One example of this kind of blurring of the lines is the study of the relationship between hurricanes and climate change.

Development and resolution of a scientific controversy: Will global warming increase hurricanes?

On his second voyage, the explorer Christopher Columbus encountered a storm while on the island of Hispaniola in 1494: "Eyes never beheld the seas so high, angry, and covered by foam," he wrote in a letter to his benefactor, Queen Isabella. "Never did the sky look more terrible; for one whole day and night it blazed like a furnace. The flashes came with such fury and frightfulness that we all thought the ships would be blasted. All this time, the water never ceased to fall from the sky" (Barnes and Lyons, 2007). Though this was, perhaps, a new experience for Columbus, the storms were well known to the Caribbean locals, who called them *furacano*, a word that became common in English around 1650 as "hurricane." Columbus wrote the first account of a hurricane in the Atlantic (Millás and Pardue, 1968), but there were many more to come.

Throughout the 1800s, hurricanes were observed and described. Early on, several observers noted that these storms were vortices, rotating in a counter-clockwise direction. By the middle part of the century, weather observatories had been established in many locations in North America, and some scientists were recording hurricane tracks. After a major hurricane struck the city of Galveston, Texas, in 1900, killing at least 8,000 people (see Figure 3), analysis of these observations took on a new urgency.

Figure 3: Galveston residents sifting through the wreckage of the 1900 hurricane.

Many of the earliest studies of hurricanes, also called tropical cyclones (or typhoons in the Pacific Ocean), were carried out by scientists who had studied with Vilhelm Bjerknes, a physicist who had determined the equations that govern circulation in the atmosphere (see our chapter on Modeling for more information). In 1917, Bjerknes started the Bergen School of Meteorology in Bergen, Norway, bringing together a group of well-known and accomplished Scandinavian meteorologists (Liljequist, 1980). Their initial research focus was on cyclonic weather systems in the temperate zones, the latitude of most of Europe. By 1928, the group felt that their methods and understanding of these systems were mature, and could be applied to rarer and more complicated storm systems – tropical cyclones (Bergeron, 1954). Erik Palmén, a Finnish meteorologist who moved to Chicago after his time at Bergen, recognized that hurricanes only formed above sea water that was warmer than 26–27° C (~80° F), a critically important observation that he published in 1948 (Palmen, 1948). His publication included a map of sea surface temperature during the warmest part of the year called "hurricane season" with arrows showing the tracks of major hurricanes (see Figure 4). All of the arrows began in a narrow band of the ocean where water temperatures were highest.

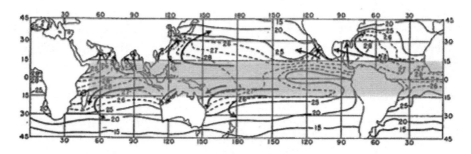

Figure 4: Original Figure 4 from Palmen (1948), with band of higher temperatures shaded in gray.

Sea surface temperature is one manifestation of climate – as global climate changes, the distribution of warmer and colder waters on the sea surface also changes. Tor Bergeron, another member of the Bergen group, went beyond thinking about how sea surface temperature changes annually and considered what happened over longer periods of time, placing hurricanes in the context of long-term climate changes. In a review paper in 1954, Bergeron speculated that the frequency and intensity of hurricanes, as well as where and when they formed, could have changed dramatically over geologic time with small changes in the earth's orbit and solar intensity –

both of which affect global climate (Bergeron, 1954). He urged scientists who studied climate in the past to keep that in mind. At the time, however, the techniques available to assess past climate to the level of detail of individual hurricanes simply didn't exist, and few scientists took up the challenge.

Starting in the 1980s, however, this idea re-emerged as scientists began to see variability in the frequency and intensity of hurricanes that correlated well with short-term climatic cycles that operate on the order of 10–12 years, like the El Niño-Southern Oscillation (ENSO) in the tropical Pacific. El Niño is familiar to many people around the world for its effects on local weather patterns, but evidence became available to show that this cycle in the tropical Pacific affected hurricane generation in the Atlantic Ocean (Gray, 1984). At the same time, more and more scientists began to recognize that global sea surface temperatures were steadily rising as the climate warmed, and they began to explore the links between how global warming would affect both the climatic cycles and hurricane formation (Emanuel, 2003). Most who studied the phenomena found that sea surface temperature changes of the magnitude they were seeing would, indeed, influence hurricane formation, but not nearly as much as natural variability within the climatic cycles.

That general sentiment began to be questioned, however, as more data came in. In June of 2005, Kevin Trenberth, a climate scientist at the National Center for Atmospheric Research (NCAR), published a short article in *Science* entitled "Uncertainty in Hurricanes and Global Warming" (Trenberth, 2005). In it, he stated:

> During the 2004 hurricane season in the North Atlantic, an unprecedented four hurricanes hit Florida; during the same season in the Pacific, 10 tropical cyclones or typhoons hit Japan (the previous record was six). Some scientists say that this increase is related to global warming; others say that it is not. Can a trend in hurricane activity in the North Atlantic be detected? Can any such trend be attributed to human activity? Are we even asking the right questions?

Trenberth was highlighting a controversy that was just beginning to develop at the time, pointing out that we did not yet have enough data or enough theoretical understanding of a process to make valid, reliable interpretations. His questions inspired several other scientists to analyze the available data searching for trends (see Data: Analysis and Interpretation for more information on this process) and to begin new research into the issue. Among those was a group of four atmospheric scientists, three from the Georgia Institute of Technology and one from NCAR. They worked through the early part of the summer and had submitted their work for publication in August 2005.

Prior to publication, however, a dramatic and pertinent event occurred: on Monday, August 29, 2005, Hurricane Katrina made landfall near New Orleans, Louisiana (Figure 5). The hurricane brought with it widespread physical destruction and loss of life, and created a social, political, and economic crisis. Within hours of landfall, however, a question arose in the media: was this particularly destructive hurricane caused by global warming? While this was not a scientific question or one that could be answered through research, it brought the public into the scientific controversy about the relationship between climate change and hurricanes.

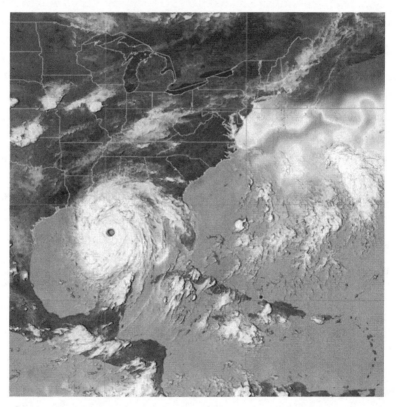

Figure 5: GOES satellite image of Hurricane Katrina on August 29, 2005.

A little over two weeks later, on September 16, the work by the scientists at Georgia Tech and NCAR was published in Science. Their analysis showed that, although the number of total hurricanes had not increased significantly since 1970, the proportion of hurricanes that were category-4 and

-5, the strongest storms, had (Webster *et al.*, 2005). In other words, they concluded that there had been more intense hurricanes, even though the total number had not changed. They correlated these changes with an increase in global sea-surface temperature (SST), which had been steadily rising as global atmospheric temperatures increase. In a very general way, the work by Webster and colleagues implied that there could be more hurricanes like Katrina in the future.

The results of their work had significant social and political implications: if global warming caused more intense hurricanes, there would be additional reason to take action to reduce the magnitude of warming in order to reduce destruction. As a result, the authors of the article received an unusually high number of responses to their work, both responses from scientists that are typical of scientific publications and letters, and personal responses from the general public. In an article published in the *Bulletin of the American Meteorological Society* the following year, three of the original four authors reported on those responses (Curry *et al.*, 2006). Some of the comments they received were valid scientific arguments, but unfortunately, that was not always the case. Many of the comments were based on political and social concerns, and some involved personal attacks on the scientists.

For example, one of the frequent comments that the authors received is that they weren't qualified to analyze the hurricane data, despite the fact that the researchers were all atmospheric scientists that had been working on similar types of climate data for decades (Curry *et al.*, 2006). This type of personal attack can be damaging and create controversy in the media, but it is not a component of the scientific controversy. Of course, scientists are people, and any public debate involves differences in personality and opinion, but those personal differences are not based on the data.

In contrast, some of the points raised in response to the article had a valid scientific basis. For example, one of these more substantial arguments centered on the reliability of the early part of the hurricane record. Accurate, worldwide tracking of hurricanes is a relatively recent phenomenon that only became easy with satellites starting in the 1970s. Aircraft started recording hurricanes in the mid-1940s, but the data were limited to common flight lines over the oceans. Prior to that, the majority of observations about hurricanes were made from land, and even that record only goes back to 1851. Given that hurricanes spend most of their time over the ocean, this meant that the data could be inaccurate and thus difficult to interpret.

Many scientists recognized that much more work was needed in order to make progress in our understanding. As a result, the number of studies addressing the relationship between global warming and hurricanes proliferated over the next few years (see Figure 6). Some scientists used detailed global climate models and found that natural, local climate variability seemed to have a greater effect on hurricane intensity than current global warming (Vecchi and Soden, 2007). Others reanalyzed older hurricane records to correct for systematic bias, removing some storms that were poorly constrained from the record and adding new ones (Landsea *et al.*, 2008). Still others extended the record further back in time by collecting descriptions of independent records that did not rely on human observations (Mann *et al.*, 2009). Throughout this process, scientists disagreed and debated what was really going on with hurricanes as the earth's climate warmed – were they increasing in frequency? Intensity? No change? A NOVA documentary in 2006 pitted MIT scientist Kerry Emanuel against Chris Landsea, a meteorologist at the Miami Hurricane Center, suggesting that the two scientists had a fundamental disagreement about the nature of strong hurricanes (Public Broadcasting System (PBS), 2006).

Within a few years, however, much of the disagreement had subsided. In 2010, the Expert Team on Climate Impacts on Tropical Cycles, a team of scientists assembled by the World Meteorological Organization (WMO),

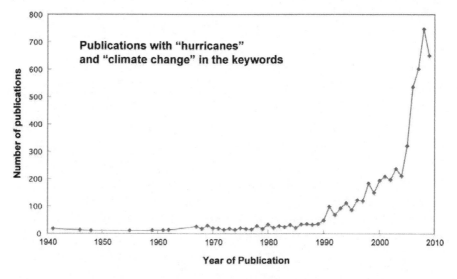

Figure 6: Graph showing the number of scientific publications annually with the words "hurricane" and "climate change" included as keywords. Data is from ISI Web of Science.

attempted to bring all of the new research together and summarize what scientists had learned since 2005. The team, which included both Kerry Emanuel and Chris Landsea, published an article in *Nature Geoscience* entitled "Tropical cyclones and climate change" (Knutson *et al.*, 2010). In the abstract, they summarize the state of the scientific controversy:

> Whether the characteristics of tropical cyclones have changed or will change in a warming climate — and if so, how — has been the subject of considerable investigation, often with conflicting results. Large amplitude fluctuations in the frequency and intensity of tropical cyclones greatly complicate both the detection of long-term trends and their attribution to rising levels of atmospheric greenhouse gases. Trend detection is further impeded by substantial limitations in the availability and quality of global historical records of tropical cyclones. Therefore, it remains uncertain whether past changes in tropical cyclone activity have exceeded the variability expected from natural causes. However, future projections based on theory and high-resolution dynamical models consistently indicate that greenhouse warming will cause the globally averaged intensity of tropical cyclones to shift towards stronger storms, with intensity increases of 2–11% by 2100. Existing modeling studies also consistently project decreases in the globally averaged frequency of tropical cyclones, by 6–34% (Knutson *et al.*, 2010).

In other words, the authors acknowledge the complexity of the issue, noting what aspects make it a difficult subject to study (large natural fluctuations, a limited historical dataset), and that these complexities have caused mixed results from different scientific studies. They also point out, however, where there is agreement: there is consistency in all of the models that predict more strong storms in the future as global climate changes. Their statement also emphasizes that science is a work in progress that relies on the creativity of scientists to overcome problems, and controversy is a natural outcome of that process.

This debate on the relationship between tropical storms and global warming fulfills the requirements for a scientific controversy – it involves a large number of scientists doing active research into the issue, and the debate took place (and continues to take place) in public, through a peer-reviewed process, over a sustained period of time. The nature of the subject under investigation meant that some social and political components were involved, but ultimately the scientific progress that was made was unrelated to a particular storm or situation.

The resolution of controversy

Does the publication of the article by the WMO team mean that the controversy is resolved? Well, yes and no. As stated in the article, most of the current evidence suggests that the occurrence of hurricanes will be affected by climate change, and the number of publications concerning the topic so far seems to have peaked in 2008 (see Figure 5). Other arguments have not faded away completely, however, and there will undoubtedly be more research in this field as new data is collected, the resolution and power of computer models increases, and as warming continues.

More complete resolution is possible; however, such as in the debate over plate tectonic theory that occurred in the 1960's, where the accumulated evidence became overwhelming in support of plate tectonics (see our online module Plate Tectonics I for more information). In other cases, resolution awaits the development of a new technology or technique that can acquire the kind of data that can really address the question. For example, the definition of "race" in humans was the subject of significant study and controversy throughout much of human history, but it wasn't until the sequencing of the human genome that scientists were truly able to examine claims for a genetic basis for race and found none (Jorde and Wooding, 2004).

In most cases, controversy is a sign of health in the scientific endeavor, and the more people that are involved in the controversy, conducting research to address the issues, the more rapidly progress is made. Sometimes the scientists involved in a controversy are portrayed as rivals, similar to the environmentalists vs. the oil companies in the controversy over offshore drilling, but this is not an accurate portrayal. The "winner" in scientific controversies is not one side, but the entire scientific community.

Key Concepts for this chapter

▶ A scientific controversy is a sustained, public debate among the broader scientific community in which arguments are based on evidence.

▶ Controversies cause progress in science by encouraging research on the topic in question.

▶ Controversies are resolved when the evidence overwhelmingly favors one argument.

▶ Scientific controversies are distinct from political, ethical, and personal controversies, though sometimes they overlap or can have complex interactions.

References

Barnes, J., and Lyons, S., 2007, *Florida's hurricane history,* The University of North Carolina Press.

Bergeron, T., 1954, REVIEW OF MODERN METEOROLOGY†-†12. The problem of tropical hurricanes: *Quarterly Journal of the Royal Meteorological Society,* v. 80, p. 131-164.

Curry, J.A., Webster, P.J., and Holland, G.J., 2006, Mixing politics and science in testing the hypothesis that greenhouse warming is causing a global increase in hurricane intensity: *Bulletin of the American Meteorological Society,* v. 87, p. 1025-1037.

Emanuel, K., 2003, Tropical Cyclones: *Annual Review of Earth and Planetary Sciences,* v. 31, p. 75-104.

Freudenburg, W.R., and Gramling, R., 1994, *Oil in troubled waters: Perception, politics, and the battle over offshore drilling:* Albany, State Univ of New York Press, 181 p.

Gray, W.M., 1984, Atlantic Seasonal Hurricane Frequency. Part I: El Niño and 30 mb Quasi-Biennial Oscillation Influences: *Monthly Weather Review,* v. 112, p. 1649-1668.

Jorde, L.B., and Wooding, S.P., 2004, Genetic variation, classification and 'race': *Nat Genet.*

Kerr, R.A., 2010, Another Quarry Sighted in the Great Mantle Plume Hunt?: *Science,* v. 328, p. 1622-a-.

Knutson, T.R., McBride, J.L., Chan, J., Emanuel, K., Holland, G., Landsea, C., Held, I., Kossin, J.P., Srivastava, A.K., and Sugi, M., 2010, Tropical cyclones and climate change: *Nature Geosci,* v. 3, p. 157-163.

Landsea, C.W., Glenn, D.A., Bredemeyer, W., Chenoweth, M., Ellis, R., Gamache, J., Hufstetler, L., Mock, C., Perez, R., Prieto, R., Sánchez-Sesma, J., Thomas, D., and Woolcock, L., 2008, A Reanalysis of the 1911–20 Atlantic Hurricane Database: *Journal of Climate,* v. 21, p. 2138-2168.

Liljequist, G.H., 1980, Tor Bergeron: *Pure and Applied Geophysics,* v. 119, p. 409-442.

Mann, M.E., Woodruff, J.D., Donnelly, J.P., and Zhang, Z., 2009, Atlantic hurricanes and climate over the past 1,500 years: *Nature,* v. 460, p. 880-883.

McMullin, E., 1987, Scientific controversy and its termination, in Jr., H.T.E., and Caplan, A.L., eds., *Scientific controversies: Case studies in resolution and closure of disputes in science and technology:* Cambridge, Cambridge University Press.

Millás, J.C., and Pardue, L., 1968, Hurricanes of the Caribbean and adjacent regions, 1492-1800: Miami, Fla., *Academy of the Arts and Sciences of the Americas.*

Palmen, E., 1948, On the formation and structure of tropical hurricanes: *Geophysica,* v. 3, p. 26-38.

Public Broadcasting System (PBS), 2006, *Stronger Hurricanes,* NOVA, WGBH.

Simkin, T., Tilling, R.I., Vogt, P.R., Kirby, S.H., Kimberley, P., and Stewart, D.B., 2006, This Dynamic Planet, Geological Investigations Map I-2800, U.S. Geological Survey.

Tarduno, J.A., Duncan, R.A., Scholl, D.W., Cottrell, R.D., Steinberger, B., Thordarson, T., Kerr, B.C., Neal, C.R., Frey, F.A., Torii, M., and Carvallo, C., 2003, The Emperor Seamounts: Southward Motion of the Hawaiian Hotspot Plume in Earth's Mantle: *Science,* v. 301, p. 1064-1069.

Trenberth, K., 2005, CLIMATE: Uncertainty in Hurricanes and Global Warming: *Science,* v. 308, p. 1753-1754.

Vecchi, G.A., and Soden, B.J., 2007, Increased tropical Atlantic wind shear in model projections of global warming: *Geophys. Res. Lett.,* v. 34, p. L08702.

Webster, P.J., Holland, G.J., Curry, J.A., and Chang, H.-R., 2005, Changes in Tropical Cyclone Number, Duration, and Intensity in a Warming Environment: *Science,* v. 309, p. 1844-1846.

Scientific Ethics

*"The measure of a man's character is what he would do
if he knew he never would be found out."*

~ Thomas Babington Macaulay

In science, as in all professions, some people try to cheat the system. Charles Dawson (Figure 1) was one of those people – an amateur British archaeologist and paleontologist born in 1864. By the late 19th century, Dawson had made a number of seemingly important fossil discoveries. Not prone to modesty, he named many of his newly discovered species after himself. For example, Dawson found fossil teeth of a previously unknown species of mammal, which he subsequently named *Plagiaulax dawsoni*. He named one of three new species of dinosaur he found *Iguanodon dawsoni* and a new form of fossil plant *Salaginella dawsoni*. His work brought him

Figure 1: *Charles Dawson (right) and Smith Woodward (center) excavating the Piltdown gravels.*

considerable fame: he was elected a fellow of the British Geological Society and appointed to the Society of Antiquaries of London. The British Museum conferred upon him the title of Honorary Collector, and the English newspaper *The Sussex Daily News* dubbed him the "Wizard of Sussex." His most famous discovery, however, came in late 1912, when Dawson showed off parts of a human-looking skull and jawbone to the public and convinced scientists that the fossils were from a new species that represented the missing link between man and ape. Dawson's "Piltdown Man," as the find came to be known, made quite an impact, confounding the scientific community for decades, long after Dawson's death in 1915. Though a few scientists doubted the find from the beginning, it was largely accepted and admired. In 1949, Kenneth Oakley, a professor of anthropology at Oxford University, dated the skull using a newly available fluorine absorption test and found that it was 500 years old rather than 500,000. Yet even Oakley continued to believe that the skull was genuine, but simply dated incorrectly. In 1953, Joseph Weiner, a student in physical anthropology at Oxford University, attended a paleontology conference and began to realize that Piltdown Man simply did not fit with other human ancestor fossils. He communicated his suspicion to his professor at Oxford, Wilfred Edward Le Gros Clark, and they followed up with Oakley. Soon after, the three realized that the skull did not represent the missing link, but rather an elaborate fraud in which the skull of a medieval human was combined with the jawbone of an orangutan and the teeth of a fossilized chimpanzee. The bones were chemically treated to make them look older, and the teeth had even been hand filed to make them fit with the skull. In the wake of this revelation, at least 38 of Dawson's finds have been found to be fakes, created in his pursuit of fame and recognition.

Advances in science depend on the reliability of the research record, so thankfully, hucksters and cheats like Dawson are the exception rather than the norm in the scientific community. But cases like Dawson's play an important role in helping us understand the system of scientific ethics that has evolved to ensure reliability and proper behavior in science. Ethics is a set of moral obligations that define right and wrong in our practices and decisions. Many professions have a formalized system of ethical practices that help guide professionals in the field. For example, doctors commonly take the Hippocratic Oath, which, among other things, states that doctors "do no harm" to their patients. Engineers follow an ethical guide that states that they "hold paramount the safety, health and welfare of the public." Within these professions, as well as within science, the principles become so ingrained that practitioners rarely have to think about adhering to the ethic

– it's part of the way they practice. And a breach of ethics is considered very serious, punishable at least within the profession (by revocation of a license, for example) and sometimes by the law as well.

Scientific ethics calls for honesty and integrity in all stages of scientific practice, from reporting results regardless to properly attributing collaborators. This system of ethics guides the practice of science, from data collection to publication and beyond. As in other professions, the scientific ethic is deeply integrated into the way scientists work, and they are aware that the reliability of their work and scientific knowledge in general depends upon adhering to that ethic. Many of the ethical principles in science relate to the production of unbiased scientific knowledge, which is critical when others try to build upon or extend research findings. The open publication of data, peer review, replication, and collaboration required by the scientific ethic all help to keep science moving forward by validating research findings and confirming or raising questions about results.

Some breaches of the ethical standards, such as fabrication of data, are dealt with by the scientific community through means similar to ethical breaches in other disciplines – removal from a job, for example. But less obvious challenges to the ethical standard occur more frequently, such as giving a scientific competitor a negative peer review. These incidents are more like parking in a no parking zone – they are against the rules and can be unfair, but they often go unpunished. Sometimes scientists simply make mistakes that may appear to be ethical breaches, such as improperly citing a source or giving a misleading reference. And like any other group that shares goals and ideals, the scientific community works together to deal with all of these incidents as best as they can – in some cases with more success than others.

Ethical standards in science

Scientists have long maintained an informal system of ethics and guidelines for conducting research, but documented ethical guidelines did not develop until the mid-20th century, after a series of well-publicized ethical breaches and war crimes. Scientific ethics now refers to a standard of conduct for scientists that is generally delineated into two broad categories (Bolton, 2002). First, standards of methods and process address the design, procedures, data analysis, interpretation, and reporting of research efforts. Second, standards of topics and findings address the use of human and animal subjects in research and the ethical implications of certain research findings. Together, these ethical standards help guide scientific research and ensure that research efforts (and researchers) abide by several core principles (Resnik, 2008), including:

1. Honesty in reporting of scientific data;

2. Careful transcription and analysis of scientific results to avoid error;

3. Independent analysis and interpretation of results that is based on data and not on the influence of external sources;

4. Open sharing of methods, data, and interpretations through publication and presentation;

5. Sufficient validation of results through replication and collaboration with peers;

6. Proper crediting of sources of information, data, and ideas;

7. Moral obligations to society in general, and, in some disciplines, responsibility in weighing the rights of human and animal subjects.

Ethics of methods and process

Scientists are human, and humans don't always abide by the law. Understanding some examples of scientific misconduct will help us to understand the importance and consequences of scientific integrity. In 2001, the German physicist Jan Hendrik Schön briefly rose to prominence for what appeared to be a series of breakthrough discoveries in the area of electronics and nanotechnology. Schön and two co-authors published a paper in the journal *Nature* claiming to have produced a molecular-scale alternative to the transistor (Figure 2) used commonly in consumer devices (Schön *et al.*, 2001). The implications were revolutionary – a molecular transistor could allow the development of computer microchips far smaller than any available at the time. As a result, Schön received a number of outstanding research awards and the work was deemed one of the "breakthroughs of the year" in 2001 by *Science* magazine.

Figure 2: A common transistor, for which Jan Hendrick Schön claimed to have discovered a molecular-scale alternative.

However, problems began to appear very quickly. Scientists that tried to replicate Schön's work were unable to do so. Lydia Sohn, then a nanotechnology researcher at

Princeton University, noticed that two different experiments carried out by Schön at very different temperatures and published in separate papers appeared to have identical patterns of background noise in the graphs used to present the data (Service, 2002). When confronted with the problem, Schön initially claimed that he had mistakenly submitted the same graph with two different manuscripts. However, soon after, Paul McEuen of Cornell University found the same graph in a third paper. As a result of these suspicions, Bell Laboratories, the research institution where Schön worked, launched an investigation into his research in May 2002. When the committee heading the investigation attempted to study Schön's notes and research data, they found that he kept no laboratory notebooks, had erased all of the raw data files from his computer (claiming he needed the additional storage space for new studies), and had either discarded or damaged beyond recognition all of his experimental samples. The committee eventually concluded that Schön had altered or completely fabricated data in at least 16 instances between 1998 and 2001. Schön was fired from Bell Laboratories on September 25, 2002, the same day they received the report from the investigating committee. On October 31, 2002, the journal *Science* retracted eight papers authored by Schön; on December 20, 2002, the journal *Physical Review* retracted six of Schon's papers, and on March 5, 2003, *Nature* retracted seven that they had published.

These actions – retractions and firing – are the means by which the scientific community deals with serious scientific misconduct. In 2004, the University of Konstanz in Germany where Schön received his PhD, took the issue a step further and asked him to return his doctoral papers in an effort to revoke his doctoral degree. As of 2008, the issue was still in the courts. If Schön's degree is revoked (and even if it is not), it is unlikely he will ever be able to get another job as a research scientist. Clearly, the consequences of scientific misconduct can be dire: complete removal from the scientific community.

The Schön incident is often cited as an example of scientific misconduct because he breached many of the core ethical principles of science. Schön admitted to falsifying data to make the evidence of the behavior he observed "more convincing." He also made extensive errors in transcribing and analyzing his data, thus violating the principles of honesty and carefulness. Schön's articles did not present his methodology in a way such that other scientists could repeat the work and he took deliberate steps to obscure his notes and raw data and to prevent the reanalysis of his data and methods. Finally, while the committee reviewing Schön's work exonerated his coauthors of misconduct, a number of questions were raised over whether they exhibited proper oversight of the work in collaborating and co-publishing with Schön. While Schön's motives were never fully identified (he continued to claim that the instances of misconduct could be explained as simple mistakes), it has been proposed that his personal quest for recognition and glory biased his work so much that he focused on supporting specific conclusions instead of objectively analyzing the data he obtained.

Ethics of topics and findings

Despite his egregious breach of scientific ethics, no criminal charges were ever filed against Schön. In other cases, actions that breach the scientific ethic also breach more fundamental moral and legal standards. One instance in particular, the brutality of Nazi scientists in World War II, was so severe and discriminatory that it led to the adoption of an international code governing research ethics.

During World War II, Nazi scientists launched a series of studies: some designed to test the limits of human exposure to the elements in the name of preparing German soldiers fighting the war. Notorious among these efforts were experiments on the effects of hypothermia in humans. During these experiments, concentration camp prisoners were forced to sit in ice water or were left naked outdoors in freezing temperatures for hours at a time. Many victims were left to freeze to death slowly while others were eventually rewarmed with blankets or warm water, or other methods that left them with permanent injuries.

At the end of the war, 23 individuals were tried for war crimes in Nuremberg, Germany in relation to these studies, and 15 were found guilty (Figure 3). The court proceedings led to a set of guidelines, referred to as the Nuremberg Code, which limits research on human subjects. Among other things, the Nuremberg Code requires that individuals be informed of and consent to the research being conducted; the first standard reads: "The voluntary consent of the human subject is absolutely essential." The code also states that the research risks should be weighed in light of the potential benefits, and it requires that scientists

Figure 3: The judges' chamber of the Nuremberg Trials

avoid intentionally inflicting physical or mental suffering for research purposes. Importantly, the code also places the responsibility for adhering to the code on "each individual who initiates, directs or engages in the experiment." This is a critical component of the code that implicates every single scientist involved in an experiment – not just the most senior scientist or first author on a paper. The Nuremberg Code was published in 1949 and is still a fundamental document guiding ethical behavior in research on human subjects that has been supplemented by additional guidelines and standards in most countries.

Other ethical principles also guide the practice of research on human subjects. For example, a number of government funding sources limit or exclude funding for human cloning due to the ethical questions raised by the practice. Another set of ethical guidelines covers studies involving therapeutic drugs and devices. Research investigating the therapeutic properties of medical devices or drugs is stopped ahead of schedule if a treatment is found to have severe negative side effects. Similarly, large-scale therapeutic studies in which a drug or agent is found to be highly beneficial may be concluded early so that the control patients (those not receiving the effective drug or agent) can be given the new, beneficial treatment.

Mistakes versus misconduct

Scientists are fallible and make mistakes – these do not qualify as misconduct. Sometimes, however, the line between mistake and misconduct is not clear. For example, in the late 1980s, a number of research groups were investigating the hypothesis that deuterium atoms could be forced to fuse together at room temperature, releasing tremendous amounts of energy in the process. Nuclear fusion was not a new topic in 1980, but researchers at the time were only able to initiate fusion reactions at very high temperatures, so low temperature fusion held great promise as an energy source. Two scientists at the University of Utah, Stanley Pons and Martin Fleischmann, were among those researching the topic, and they had constructed a system using a palladium electrode and deuterated water to investigate the potential for low temperature fusion reactions. As they worked with their system, they noted excess amounts of heat being generated. Though not all of the data they collected was conclusive, they proposed that the heat was evidence for fusion occurring in their system. Rather than repeat and publish their work so that others could confirm the results, Pons and Fleischmann were worried that another scientist might announce similar results soon and hoped to patent their invention, so they rushed to publicly announce their breakthrough.

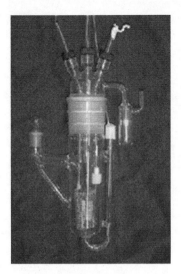

Figure 4: *A cold fusion reactor cell from the naval research center.*

On March 23, 1989, Pons and Fleischmann, with the support of their university, held a press conference to announce their discovery of "an inexhaustible source of energy." The announcement of Pons' and Fleischmann's 'cold fusion' reactor (Figure 4) caused immediate excitement in the press and was covered by major national and international news organizations; among scientists, it was simultaneously hailed and criticized. On April 12, Pons received a standing ovation from about 7,000 chemists at the semi-annual meeting of the American Chemical Society. But many scientists chastised the researchers for announcing their discovery in the popular press rather than through the peer-reviewed literature. Pons and Fleischmann eventually did publish their findings in a scientific article (Fleischmann *et al.*, 1990), but problems had already begun to appear. The researchers had a difficult time showing evidence for the production of neutrons by their system, a characteristic that would have confirmed the occurrence of fusion reactions. On May 1st, 1989, at a dramatic meeting of the American Physical Society less than five weeks after the press conference in Utah, Steven Koonin, Nathan Lewis, and Charles Barnes from Caltech announced that they had replicated Pons and Fleischmann's experimental conditions, found numerous errors in the scientists' conclusions, and further announced that they found no evidence for fusion occurring in the system. Soon after that, the U.S. Department of Energy published a report that stated "the experimental results...reported to date do not present convincing evidence that useful sources of energy will result from the phenomena attributed to cold fusion."

While the conclusions made by Pons and Fleischmann were discredited, the scientists were not accused of fraud – they had not fabricated results or attempted to mislead other scientists, but had made their findings public through unconventional means before going through the process of peer review. They eventually left the University of Utah to work as scientists in the industrial sector. Their mistakes, however, not only affected them, but discredited the whole community of legitimate researchers investigating cold fusion. The phrase 'cold fusion' became synonymous with junk science and federal funding in the field almost completely vanished overnight. It took almost 15 years of legitimate research and the renaming of their field from cold fusion to "low energy nuclear reactions" before the U.S. Department of Energy again considered funding well designed experiments in the field (DOE SC, 2004).

Everyday ethical decisions

Scientists also face ethical decisions in more common ways and everyday circumstances. For example, authorship on research papers can raise questions. Authors on papers are expected to have materially contributed to the work in some way and have a responsibility to be familiar with and provide oversight of the work. Jan Hendrik Schön's coauthors clearly failed in this responsibility. Sometimes newcomers to a field will seek to add experienced scientists' names to papers or to grant proposals to increase the perceived importance of their work. While this can lead to valuable collaborations in science, if those senior authors simply accept "honorary" authorship and do not contribute to the work, it raises ethical issues over responsibility in research publishing. A scientist's source of funding can also potentially bias their work. While scientists generally acknowledge their funding sources in their papers, there have been a number of cases in which lack of adequate disclosure has raised concern. For example, in 2006 Dr. Claudia Henschke, a radiologist at the Weill Cornell Medical College, published a paper that suggested that screening smokers and former smokers with CT chest scans could dramatically reduce the number of lung cancer deaths (Henschke *et al.*, 2006). However, Henschke failed to disclose that the foundation through which her research was funded, was itself almost wholly funded by Liggett Tobacco. The case caused an outcry in the scientific community because of the potential bias toward trivializing the impact of lung cancer. Almost two years later Dr. Henschke published a correction in the journal that provided disclosure of the funding sources of the study (Henschke, 2008). As a result of this and other cases, many journals instituted stricter requirements regarding disclosure of funding sources for published research.

Enforcing ethical standards

A number of incidents have prompted the development of clear and legally enforceable ethical standards in science. For example, in 1932, the U.S. Public Health Service located in Tuskegee, Alabama initiated a study of the effects of syphilis in men. When the study began, medical treatments available for syphilis were highly toxic and of questionable effectiveness. Thus, the study sought to determine if patients with syphilis were better off receiving those dangerous treatments or not. The researchers recruited 399 black men who had syphilis, and 201 men without syphilis (as a control). Individuals enrolled in what eventually became known as the Tuskegee Syphilis Study were not asked to give their consent and were not informed of their diagnosis; instead they were told they had "bad blood" and could receive free medical treatment (which often consisted of nothing), rides to the clinic, meals and burial insurance in case of death in return for participating.

By 1947, penicillin appeared to be an effective treatment for syphilis. However, rather than treat the infected participants with penicillin and close the study, the Tuskegee researchers withheld penicillin and information about the drug in the name of studying how syphilis spreads and kills its victims. The unconscionable study continued until 1972, when a leak to the press resulted in a public outcry and its termination. By that time, however, 28 of the original participants had died of syphilis and another 100 had died from medical complications related to syphilis. Further, 40 wives of participants had been infected with syphilis, and 19 children had contracted the disease at birth.

As a result of the Tuskegee Syphilis Study and the Nuremberg Doctors' trial, the United States Congress passed the National Research Act in 1974. The Act created the National Commission for the Protection of Human Subjects of Biomedical and Behavioral Research to oversee and regulate the use of human experimentation and it defined the requirements for Institutional Review Boards (IRBs). As a result, all institutions that receive federal research funding must establish and maintain an IRB, an independent board of trained researchers who review research plans that involve human subjects to assure that ethical standards are maintained. An institution's IRB must approve any research with human subjects before it is initiated. Regulations governing the operation of the IRB are issued by the U.S. Department of Health and Human Services.

Equally important, individual scientists enforce ethical standards in the profession by promoting open publication and presentation of methods and results that allow for other scientists to reproduce and validate their work and findings. Federal government-based organizations, like the National Academy of Sciences, publish ethical guidelines for individuals like the book *On Being a Scientist* (National Academy of Sciences, 1995). The U.S. Office of Research Integrity also promotes ethics in research by monitoring institutional investigations of research misconduct and promoting education on the issue.

Ethics in science are similar to ethics in our broader society: they promote reasonable conduct and effective cooperation between individuals. While breaches of scientific ethics do occur, as they do in society in general, they are generally dealt with swiftly when identified and help us to understand the importance of ethical behavior in our professional practices. Adhering to the scientific ethic assures that data collected during research are reliable and that interpretations are reasonable and with merit, thus allowing the work of a scientist to become part of the growing body of scientific knowledge.

Key Concepts for this chapter

▶ Ethical conduct in science assures the reliability of research results and the safety of research subjects.

▶ Ethics in science include: a) standards of methods and process that address research design, procedures, data analysis, interpretation, and reporting; and b) standards of topics and findings that address the use of human and animal subjects in research.

▶ Replication, collaboration, and peer review all help to minimize ethical breaches, and identify them when they do occur.

References

Bolton, P. A. (2002). Scientific Ethics. In *WREN, Management benchmarking study*, Washington, DC.

DOE SC (2004). Report of the Review of Low Energy Nuclear Reactions. U.S. Department of Energy, Office of Science, retrieved April 29, 2008 from http://www.science.doe.gov/Sub/Newsroom/News_Releases/DOE-SC/2004/low_energy/CF_Final_120104.pdf.

Fisher, R.A. (1936). Has Mendel's work been rediscovered? *Annals of Science*, 1:115-137.

Fleischmann, M., Pons, S., Anderson, M. W., Li, L. J., Hawkins, M. (1990) Calorimetry of the Palladium--Deuterium--Heavy Water System. *Journal of Electroanalytical Chemistry and Interfacial Electrochemistry*, 287(2):293-348.

Grant, P.M. (2002). Scientific credit and credibility. *Nature Materials*, 1:139-141.

Henschke, C.I. (2008). Clarification of funding of early cancer study. *N Engl J Med*, 358:1862.

Henschke, C.I., Yankelevitz, D.F., Libby, D.M., Pasmantier, M.W., Smith, J.P., Miettinen, O.S. (2006). Survival of patients with stage I lung cancer detected on CT screening. *N Engl J Med*, 3:1763–1771.

Louis, K.S., Jones, L.M., Campbell, E.G. (2002). Sharing in science. *American Scientist* 90(4):304

National Academy of Sciences (1992). Responsible Science, Volume I: Ensuring the Integrity of the Research Process. Panel on Scientific Responsibility and the Conduct of Research Committee on Science, Engineering, and Public Policy, National Academy Press, Washington, DC.

Nature Editorial (2007). Who is accountable? *Nature*, 450(7166):1.

Resnik, D. (2008). Philosophical Foundations of Scientific Ethics. Retrieved February 9, 2008 from the University of Wyoming

Schön, J. H., Meng, H., Bao, Z. (2001). Self-assembled monolayer organic field-effect transistors. *Nature*, 413:713-716.

Service, R.F. (2001). Breakthrough of 2001: Nanoelectronics. *ScienceNOW*

Service, R.F. (2002). Pioneering Physics Papers Under Suspicion for Data Manipulation. *Science*, 296(5572):1376-1377.

University of Konstanz (2004). "Universität Konstanz entzieht Jan Hendrik Schön den Doktortitel" (in German). Press release # 85, http://www.uni-konstanz.de/struktur/service/presse/mittshow.php?nr=85&jj=2004.

Waldrop, M.M. (1989). Cold Water from Caltech. *Science*, 244(4904):523.

National Academy of Sciences. (1995). *On Being a Scientist: Responsible Conduct in Research*: National Academy Press.

Research Methods

The Practice of Science

"If we knew what it was we were doing, it would not be called research, would it?"

~ Albert Einstein

When some people think of science, they think of formulas and facts to memorize. Many of us probably studied for a test in a science class by memorizing the names of the four nucleotides in DNA (adenine, cytosine, guanine, and thymine) or by practicing with one of Newton's laws of motion, like $f = ma$ (force equals mass times acceleration). While this knowledge is an important part of science, it is not all of science. In addition to a body of knowledge that includes formulas and facts, science is a practice by which we pursue answers to questions that can be approached scientifically. This practice is referred to collectively as scientific research and while the techniques that scientists use to conduct research may differ between disciplines, the underlying principles and objectives are similar. Whether you are talking about biology, chemistry, geology, physics, or any other scientific field, the body of knowledge that is built through these disciplines is based on the collection of data that is then analyzed and interpreted in light of other research findings. How do we know about adenine, cytosine, guanine, and thymine? These were not revealed by chance, but through the work of many scientists collecting data, evaluating the results, and putting together a comprehensive theory that explained their observations.

A brief history of scientific practice

The recorded roots of formal scientific research lie in the collective work of a number of individuals in ancient Greek, Persian, Indian, Chinese, and European cultures, rather than from a single person or event. The Greek mathematician Pythagoras is regarded as the first person to promote a scientific hypothesis when, based on his descriptive study of the movement of stars in the sky in the 5th century BCE, he proposed that the earth was round. The Indian mathematician and astronomer Aryabhata used descriptive records regarding the movement of objects in the night sky to propose in the 6th century CE that the sun was the center of the solar system. In the 9th century, Chinese alchemists invented gunpowder while performing experiments attempting to make gold from other substances. And the Persian scientist Alhazen is credited with devising the concept of the scientific experiment while researching properties related to vision and light around 1000 CE.

These and other events demonstrate that a scientific approach to addressing questions about the natural world has long been present in many cultures. The roots of modern scientific research methods, however, are considered by many historians to lie in the Scientific Revolution that occurred in Europe in the 16th and 17th centuries. Most historians cite the beginning of the Scientific Revolution as the publication of *De Revolutionibus Orbium Coelestium* (*On the Revolutions of the Heavenly Spheres*) in 1543 by the Polish astronomer Nicolaus Copernicus. Copernicus's careful observation and description of the movement of planets in relation to the earth led him to hypothesize that the sun was the center of the solar system and the planets revolved around the sun in progressively larger orbits in the following order: Mercury, Venus, Earth, Mars, Jupiter, and Saturn (Figure 1). Though Copernicus was not the first person to propose a heliocentric view of the solar system, his systematic gathering of data provided a rigorous argument that challenged the commonly held belief that the earth was the center of the universe.

The Scientific Revolution was subsequently fueled by the work of Galileo Galilei, Johannes Kepler, Isaac Newton, and others, who not only challenged the traditional geocentric view of the universe, but explicitly rejected the older philosophical approaches to natural science popularized by Aristotle. A key event marking the rejection of the philosophical method was the publication of *Novum Organum: New Directions Concerning the Interpretation of Nature* by Francis Bacon in 1620. Bacon was not a scientist, but rather an English philosopher and essayist, and *Novum* is a work on logic. In it, Bacon presented an inductive method of reasoning that he argued was superior to the philosophical approach of Aristotle. The Baconian method involved a repeating cycle of observation, hypothesis, experimentation, and the need

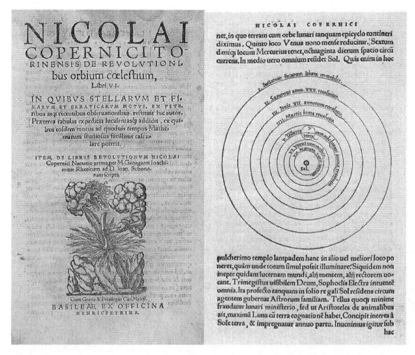

Figure 1: The front cover and an inner page from De Revolutionibus *showing Copernicus's hypothesis regarding the revolution of planets around the sun (from the 2nd edition, Basel, 1566).*

for independent verification. Bacon's work championed a method that was objective, logical and empirical, and provided a basis for the development of scientific research methodology.

Bacon's method of scientific reasoning was further refined by the publication of *Philosophiæ Naturalis Principia Mathematica* (*Mathematical Principles of Natural Philosophy*) by the English physicist and mathematician Isaac Newton in 1686 (Figure 2). *Principia* established four rules (described in more detail on page 92) that have become the basis of modern approaches to science. In brief, Newton's rules proposed that the simplest explanation of natural phenomena is often the best, countering the practice that was common in his day of assigning complicated explanations derived from belief systems, the occult, and observations of natural events. And *Principia*

Figure 2: Sir Isaac Newton

Four Rules of Scientific Reasoning
from *Principia Mathematica*
by Isaac Newton

Sir Isaac Newton was a significant contributor to the Scientific Revolution. Newton believed that scientific theory should be coupled with rigorous experimentation, and he published four rules of scientific reasoning in *Principia Mathematica* (1686) that form part of modern approaches to science:

1. admit no more causes of natural things than are both true and sufficient to explain their appearances,
2. to the same natural effect, assign the same causes,
3. qualities of bodies, which are found to belong to all bodies within experiments, are to be esteemed universal, and
4. propositions collected from observation of phenomena should be viewed as accurate or very nearly true until contradicted by other phenomena.

Newton's rules of scientific reasoning have proved remarkably enduring. His first rule is now commonly called the Principle of Parsimony, and states that the simplest explanation is generally the most likely. The second rule essentially means that special interpretations of data should not be used if a reasonable explanation already exists. The third rule suggests that explanations of phenomena determined through scientific investigation should apply to all instances of that phenomenon. Finally, the fourth rule lays the philosophical foundation of modern scientific theories, which are held to be true unless demonstrated otherwise. This is not to say that theories are accepted without evidence, nor that they can't change – theories are built upon long lines of evidence, often from multiple pieces of research, and they are subject to change as that evidence grows.

maintained that special explanations of new data should not be used when a reasonable explanation already exists, specifically criticizing the tendency of many of Newton's contemporaries to embellish the significance of their findings with exotic new explanations.

Bacon and Newton laid the foundation that has been built upon by modern scientists and researchers in developing a rigorous methodology for investigating natural phenomena. In particular, the English statisticians Karl Pearson and Ronald Fisher significantly refined scientific research in the 20th century by developing statistical techniques for data analysis and research design. And the practice of science continues to evolve today, as new tools and technologies become available and our knowledge about the natural world grows. The practice of science is commonly misrepresented as a simple, four- or five-step path to answering a scientific question, called "The

Scientific Method." In reality, scientists rarely follow such a straightforward path through their research. Instead, scientific research includes many possible paths, not all of which lead to unequivocal answers. The real scientific method, or practice of science, is much more dynamic and interesting.

More than one scientific method

The typical presentation of "The Scientific Method" (Figure 3) suggests that scientific research follows a linear path, proceeding from a question through observation, hypothesis formation, experimentation and finally producing results and a conclusion. However, scientific research does not always proceed linearly. For example, prior to the mid-1800s, a popular scientific hypothesis held that maggots and microorganisms could be spontaneously generated from the inherent life-force that existed in some foods. Louis Pasteur doubted this hypothesis and this led him to conduct a series of experiments that would eventually disprove the theory of spontaneous generation (see the chapter on Experimentation). Pasteur's work would be difficult to characterize using Figure 3 – while it did involve experimentation, he did not developed an hypothesis prior to his experiments, instead he was motivated to disprove an existing hypothesis. Or consider the work of Grove Karl Gilbert who conducted research on the Henry Mountains in Utah in the late 1800s (see the Description chapter). Gilbert was not drawn to the area by a pressing scientific question, but rather he was sent there by the U.S. government to explore the region. Further, Gilbert did not perform a single experiment in the Henry Mountains; his work was based solely on observation and description, yet no one would dispute that Gilbert was practicing science. The traditional and simplistic scientific method presented in Figure 3 does not begin to reflect the richness or diversity of scientific research, let alone the diversity of scientists themselves.

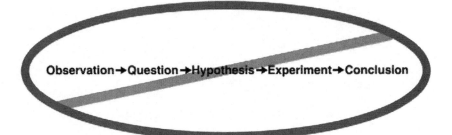

Figure 3: The classic view of the scientific method is misleading in its representation of scientific practice.

Scientific research methods

Scientific research is a robust and dynamic practice that employs multiple methods toward investigating phenomena, including experimentation, description, comparison, and modeling. Though these methods are described separately both here and in more detail in subsequent chapters, many of these methods overlap or are used in combination. For example, when NASA scientists purposefully slammed a 370 kg spacecraft named Deep Impact into a passing comet in 2005, the study had some aspects of descriptive research and some aspects of experimental research. Many scientific investigations largely employ one method, but different methods may be combined in a single study, or a single study may have characteristics of more than one method. The choice of which research method to use is personal and depends on the experiences of the scientists conducting the research and the nature of the question they are seeking to address. Despite the overlap and interconnectedness of these research methods, it is useful to discuss them separately to understand the principal characteristics of each and the ways they can be used to investigate a question.

Experimentation: Experimental methods are used to investigate the relationship(s) between two or more variables when at least one of those variables can be intentionally controlled or manipulated. The resulting effect of that manipulation (often called a treatment) can then be measured on another variable or variables. The work of the French scientist Louis Pasteur is a classic example. Pasteur put soup broth in a series of flasks, some open to the atmosphere and others sealed. He then measured the effect that the flask type had on the appearance of microorganisms in the soup broth in an effort to study the source of those microorganisms.

Description: Description is used to gather data regarding natural phenomena and natural relationships and includes observations and measurements of behaviors. A classic example of a descriptive study is Copernicus's observations and sketches of the movement of planets in the sky in an effort to determine if the earth or the sun is the orbital center of those objects.

Comparison: Comparison is used to determine and quantify relationships between two or more variables by observing different groups that either by choice or circumstance are exposed to different treatments. Examples of comparative research are the studies that were initiated in the 1950s to investigate the relationship between cigarette smoking and lung cancer in which scientists compared individuals who had chosen to smoke of their own accord with non-smokers and correlated the decision to smoke (the treatment) with various health problems including lung cancer.

Modeling: Both physical and computer-based models are built to mimic natural systems and then used to conduct experiments or make observations. Weather forecasts are an example of scientific modeling that we see every day, where data collected on temperature, wind speed, and direction are used in combination with known physics of atmospheric circulation to predict the path of storms and other weather patterns.

These methods are interconnected and are often used in combination to fully understand complex phenomenon. Modeling and experimentation are ways of simplifying systems towards understanding causality and future events. However, both rely on assumptions and knowledge of existing systems that can be provided by descriptive studies or other experiments. Description and comparison are used to understand existing systems and are used to examine the application of experimental and modeling results in real-world systems. Results from descriptive and comparative studies are often used to confirm causal relationships identified by models and experiments. While some questions lend themselves to one or another strategy due to the scope or nature of the problem under investigation, most areas of scientific research employ all of these methods as a means of complementing one another towards clarifying a specific hypothesis, theory, or idea in science. Scientific theories are clarified and strengthened through the collection of data from more than one method that generate multiple lines of evidence. Take, for example, the various research methods used to investigate what came to be known as the "ozone hole."

Research methods in practice:
The investigation of stratospheric ozone depletion

Early descriptive and comparative studies point to problem: In 1957, the British Antarctic Survey (BAS) began a descriptive study of stratospheric ozone levels in an effort to better understand the role that ozone plays in absorbing solar energy (MacDowall and Sutcliffe, 1960). For the next 20 years, the BAS recorded ozone levels and observed seasonal shifts in ozone levels, which they attributed to natural fluctuations. In the mid-1970s, however, the BAS began to note a dramatic drop in ozone levels that they correlated with the change of seasons in the Antarctic. Within a decade, they noted that a seasonal "ozone hole" (Figure 4) had begun to appear over the South Pole (Farman *et al.*, 1985).

The development of new technology opens novel research paths: Concurrent with the early BAS studies, the British scientist James Lovelock was working on developing new technology for the detection of trace concentrations of gases and vapors in the atmosphere (Lovelock, 1960). One instrument that Lovelock invented was a sensitive electron capture detector that could quantify atmospheric levels of chlorofluorocarbons (CFCs). At the time, CFCs were widely used as refrigerants and as propellants in aerosol cans and they were thought to be stable in the atmosphere and thus harmless chemicals. In 1970, Lovelock began an observational study of atmospheric CFCs and found that the chemicals were indeed very stable and

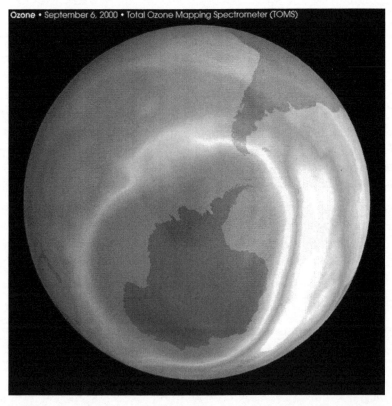

Figure 4: A picture of the Antarctic Ozone Hole in 2000, one of the largest holes on record. Ozone levels are given in Dobson Units, a measurement specific to stratospheric ozone research and named in honor of G.M.B. Dobson, one of the first scientists to investigate atmospheric ozone. For more information see http://toms.gsfc.nasa.gov/teacher/basics/dobson.html.

could be carried long distances from major urban air pollution sources by prevailing winds. Under the impression that CFCs were chemically inert, Lovelock proposed that the chemicals could be used as benign atmospheric tracers of large air mass movements (Lovelock, 1971).

Modeling and experimental research are used to draw causal connections: In 1972, F. Sherwood Rowland, a chemist at the University of California at Irvine, attended a lecture on Lovelock's work. Rowland became interested in CFCs and began studying the subject with a colleague at Irvine, Mario Molina. Molina and Rowland were familiar with modeling research by Paul Crutzen, a researcher at the National Center for Atmospheric Research in Colorado, that had previously shown that nitrogen oxides are involved in chemical reactions in the stratosphere and can influence upper atmosphere ozone levels (Crutzen, 1970). They were also familiar with modeling research by Harold Johnston, an atmospheric chemist at the University of California at Berkeley, which suggested that nitrogen oxide emissions from supersonic jets could reduce stratospheric ozone levels (Johnston, 1971). With these studies in mind, they consulted experimental research published by Michael Clyne and Ronald Walker, two British chemists, regarding the reaction rates of several chlorine containing compounds (Clyne and Walker, 1973). In 1974, Molina and Rowland published a landmark study in the journal *Nature* in which they modeled chemical kinetics to show that CFCs were not completely inert, and that they could be transported to high altitudes where they would break apart in strong sunlight and release chlorine radicals (Molina and Rowland, 1974). Molina and Rowland's model predicted that the chlorine radicals, which are reactive, would cause the destruction of significant amounts of ozone in the stratosphere.

Descriptive and comparative research provide real-world confirmation: In 1976, a group of scientists led by Allan Lazrus at the National Center for Atmospheric Research in Boulder, Colorado used balloons to carry instruments aloft that could sample air at high altitudes. In these samples, they were able to detect the presence of CFCs above the troposphere – confirming that CFCs did indeed reach the stratosphere and that once there, they could decompose in light (Lazrus *et al.*, 1976). Further research conducted using balloons and high-atmosphere aircraft in the 1980s confirmed that chlorine and chlorine oxide radicals contribute to the loss of ozone over the Antarctic (McElroy *et al.*, 1986). By the late 1980s, scientists began to examine the possible link between ozone loss and skin cancer because high levels of ultraviolet light, as would exist under an ozone hole, can cause skin cancer. In areas such as Southern Chile, where the Antarctic ozone hole overlaps with a populated land mass, a significant correlation was indeed found between the growing ozone hole and increasing rates of skin cancer (Abarca and Casiccia, 2002).

As a result of this collection of diverse yet complementary scientific evidence, the world community began to limit the use of CFCs and ratified the Montreal Protocol in 1988, which imposed strict international limits on CFC use. In 1995, Molina, Rowland, and Crutzen shared the Nobel Prize in chemistry for their research that contributed to our understanding of ozone chemistry.

The ozone story highlights an important point: scientific research is multi-dimensional, non-linear, and often leads down unexpected pathways. James Lovelock had no intention of contributing to the ozone depletion story; his work was directed at quantifying atmospheric CFC levels. Although gaining an understanding of the ozone hole may appear as a linear progression of events when viewed in hindsight, this was not the case at the time. While each researcher or research team built on previous work, it is more accurate to portray the relationships between their studies as a web of networked events, not as a linear series. Lovelock's work led Molina and Rowland to their ozone depletion models, but Lovelock's work is also widely cited by researchers developing improved electron capture detectors. Molina and Rowland not only used Lovelock's work, but they drew on the research of Crutzen, Johnston, Clyne, Walker and many others. Any single research advance was subsequently pursued in a number of different directions that complemented and reinforced one another – a common phenomenon in science. The entire ozone story required modeling, experiments, comparative research, and descriptive studies to develop a coherent theory about the role of ozone in the atmosphere, how we as humans are affecting it, and how we are also affected by it.

The real practice of science

Scientific research methods are part of the practice through which questions can be addressed scientifically. These methods all produce data that are subject to analysis and interpretation and lead to ideas in science such as hypotheses, theories, and laws. Scientific ideas are developed and disseminated through the literature where individuals and groups may debate the interpretations and significance of the results. Eventually, as multiple lines of evidence add weight to an idea it becomes an integral part of the body of knowledge that exists in science and feeds back into the research process.

The scientific community: Scientists draw on their background, experiences, and even prejudices in deciding on the types of questions they pursue and the research methods that they employ, and they are supported in their efforts by the scientific institutions and the community in which they work. Human nature makes it impossible for any scientist to be completely objective, but an important aspect of scientific research is that scientists are open to any potential result. Science emphasizes the use of multiple lines of evidence as a check on the objectivity of both individual scientists and the community at large. Research is repeated, multiple methods are used to investigate the same phenomenon, and scientists report these methods and their interpretations when publishing their work. Assuring the objectivity of data and interpretation is built into the culture of science. These common practices unite a community of science made up of individuals and institutions that are dedicated to advancing science. Rowland, Molina, Lovelock, and Crutzen each were guided by their personal interests and supported by their respective institutions. For example, in addition to his work with CFCs, James Lovelock is credited with proposing the Gaia hypothesis that all living and non-living things on the planet interact with one another much like a large, single organism. This perspective influenced his interest in looking at the movement of large air masses across the globe, work that was supported by funding from the National Aeronautics and Space Administration (NASA).

Data: Science is a way of understanding the world around us that is founded on the principal of gathering and analyzing data. In contrast, before the popularization of science, philosophical explanations of natural phenomena based on reasoning rather than data were common, and these led to a host of unsupported ideas, many of which have proven incorrect. For example, in addition to his ideas on vision, the Greek philosopher Empedocles also reasoned that because most animals are warm to the touch, they must contain fire inside of them. In contrast, the initial conclusion of the presence of a hole in the stratospheric ozone layer was based on years of data collected by scientists at the British Antarctic Survey. The amount of uncertainty and error associated with these data was critical to record as well – a small error in Dobson units would have made the hole seemingly disappear. Using statistical methods and data visualization techniques to analyze data, the scientists at the BAS drew on their own experience and knowledge to interpret that data, demonstrating that the "hole" was more than a seasonal, natural shift in ozone levels.

Ideas in science: Scientific research contributes to the body of scientific knowledge, held in record in the scientific literature so that future scientists can learn from past work. The literature does not simply hold a record of all of the data that scientists have collected: it also includes scientists' interpretations of that data. To express their ideas, scientists propose hypotheses to explain observations. For example, after observing, collecting, and interpreting data, Lovelock hypothesized that CFCs could be used by meteorologists as benign tracers of the movement of large air masses. While Lovelock was correct in his prediction that CFCs could be used to trace air movement, later research showed that they are not benign. This hypothesis was just one piece of evidence that Molina and Rowland used to form their theory of ozone depletion. Scientific theories are ideas that have held up under scrutiny and are supported by multiple lines of evidence. The ozone depletion theory is based on results from all of the studies described above, not just Lovelock's work. Unlike hypotheses, which can be tenuous in nature, theories rely on multiple lines of evidence and so are durable. Still, theories may change and be refined as new evidence and analyses come to light. For example, in 2007, a group of NASA scientists reported experimental results showing that chlorine peroxide, a compound formed when CFCs are transported to the stratosphere and which participates in the destruction of ozone, has a slower reaction rate in the presence of ultraviolet light than previously thought (Pope *et al.*, 2007). The work by Pope and his colleagues does not dispute the theory of ozone destruction; rather, it does suggest that some modifications may be necessary in terms of the reaction rates used in atmospheric chemistry models.

Despite the fact that different scientists use different methods, they can easily share results and communicate with one another because of the common language that has developed to present and interpret data and construct ideas. These shared characteristics allow studies as disparate as atmospheric chemistry, plant biology, and paleontology to be grouped together under the heading of "science" – although a practicing scientist in any one of those disciplines will require very specialized factual knowledge to conduct their research, the broad similarities in methodology allow that knowledge to be shared across many disciplines.

Key Concepts for this chapter

▶ The practice of science involves many possible pathways. The classic description of the scientific method as a linear or circular process does not adequately capture the dynamic yet rigorous nature of the practice.

▶ Scientists use multiple research methods to gather data and develop hypotheses. These methods include experimentation, description, comparison, and modeling.

▶ Scientific research methods are complementary; when multiple lines of evidence independently support one another, hypotheses are strengthened and confidence in scientific conclusions improves.

References

Abarca, F., Casiccia, C.C. (2002). Skin cancer and ultraviolet-B radiation under the Antarctic ozone hole: southern Chile, 1987-2000. *Photodermatology, Photoimmunology & Photomedicine* 18 (6), 294–302.

Agar, D. (2001). Arabic Studies in Physics and Astronomy During 800-1400 AD. University of Jyväskylä, accessed September 22, 2008

Clyne, M.A.A., Walker, R.F. (1973). Absolute rate constants for elementary reactions in the chlorination of CH4, CD4, CH3Cl, CH2Cl2, CHCl3, CDCl3 and CBrCl3. *J. Chem. Soc.*, Faraday Trans. 1, 69:1547 – 1567.

Cohn, D. (2004).*The Life and Times of Louis Pasteur.* University of Louisville.

Crutzen, P.J. (1970). The influence of nitrogen oxides on the atmospheric ozone content. *Quarterly Journal of the Royal Meteorological Society*, 96(408):320-325.

Environment Canada (2006). Protocol to the Vienna Convention on Substances that Deplete the Ozone Layer (Montreal Protocol).

Farman, J.C., Gardiner, B.G., Shanklin, J.D. (1985). Large losses of total ozone in Antarctica reveal seasonal ClOx/NOx interaction. *Nature* 315:207 - 210.

Johnston, H. (1971). Reduction of Stratospheric Ozone by Nitrogen Oxide Catalysts from Supersonic Transport Exhaust. *Science* 173(3996):517.

Kelly, J. (2004). Gunpowder. Basic Books, New York.

Lazrus, A.L., Gandrud, B.W., Woodard, R.N., Sedlacek, W.A. (1976). Direct measurements of stratospheric chlorine and bromine. *Journal of Geophysical Research*, 81(C6):1067-1070.

Lovelock, J.E. (1960). A photoionization detector for gases and vapors. *Nature,* 188:401.

Lovelock, J.E. (1971). Atmospheric fluorine compounds as indicators of air movements. *Nature,* 230(5293):379.

MacDowall, J., Sutcliffe, R.C. (1960). Some Observations at Halley Bay in Seismology, Glaciology and Meteorology [and Discussion]. *Proceedings of the Royal Society of London. Series A, Mathematical and Physical Sciences.* 256(1285):149-197.

McElroy, M.B., Salawitch, R.J., Wofsy, S.C., Logan, J.A. (1986). Reductions of Antarctic ozone due to synergistic interactions of chlorine and bromine. *Nature* 321:759 - 762.

Molina, M.J., Rowland, F.S. (1974). Stratospheric sink for chlorofluoromethanes: chlorine atom-catalysed destruction of ozone. *Nature*, 249(5460):810.

Newton, I. (1686). *Book 3: The System of the World. Philosophiae Naturalis Principia Mathematica*, translated by Andrew Motte, 1729.

Pasteur, L. (1880). De l'atténuation du virus du choléra des poules. *Comptes rendus de l'Academie des Sciences*, 91:673.

Pope, F. D., J. C. Hansen, et al. (2007). Ultraviolet Absorption Spectrum of Chlorine Peroxide, ClOOCl. *J. Phys. Chem.* A 111(20): 4322-4332.

Rowland, F.S. (2004). The Changing Atmosphere. April 5, Lecture to Bibliotheca Alexandrina, Egypt, accessed September 22, 2008

Williams, H.S. (1999). *A History of Science, The World Wide School*. Seattle, WA

Wyckoff, S. How Did Scientific Inquiry Begin? *Scientific Inquiry*, ACEPT, Arizona State University

Experimentation

"There is no such thing as a failed experiment, only experiments with unexpected outcomes."

~ R. Buckminster Fuller

Anyone who has used a cellular phone knows that certain situations require a bit of research: if you suddenly find yourself in an area with poor phone reception you might move a bit to the left or right, walk a few steps forward or back, or even hold the phone over your head to get a better signal. While the actions of a cell phone user might seem obvious, the person seeking cell phone reception is actually performing a scientific experiment: consciously manipulating one component (the location of the cell phone) and observing the effect of that action on another component (the phone's reception). Scientific experiments are obviously a bit more complicated, and generally involve more rigorous use of controls, but they draw on the same type of reasoning that we use in many everyday situations. In fact, the earliest documented scientific experiments were devised to answer a very common everyday question: how vision works.

A brief history of experimental methods

One of the first ideas regarding how human vision works came from the Greek philosopher Empedocles around 450 BCE. Empedocles reasoned that the Greek goddess Aphrodite had lit a fire in the human eye, and vision was possible because light rays from this fire emanated from the eye illuminating objects around us. While a number of people challenged this proposal, the idea that light radiated from the human eye proved surprisingly persistent until around 1000 CE, when a Persian scientist advanced our knowledge of the nature of light and, in so doing, developed a new and more rigorous approach to scientific research. Abu 'Ali al-Hasan ibn al-Hasan ibn al-Haytham, also known as Alhazen, was born in 965 CE in the Arab city of Basra in what is now present day Iraq. He began his scientific studies in physics, mathematics, and other sciences after reading the works of several Greek philosophers. One of Alhazen's most significant contributions was a seven-volume work on optics titled *Kitab al-Manazir* (later translated to Latin as *Opticae Thesaurus Alhazeni – Alhazen's Book of Optics*). Beyond the contributions this book made to the field of optics, it was a remarkable work in that it based conclusions on experimental evidence rather than abstract reasoning – the first major publication to do so. Alhazen's contributions have proved so significant that his likeness was immortalized on the 2003 10,000-dinar note issued by Iraq (Figure 1).

Figure 1: Alhazen (965–ca.1039) as pictured on an Iraqi 10,000-dinar note.

Alhazen invested significant time studying light, color, shadows, rainbows, and other optical phenomena. Among this work was a study in which he stood in a darkened room with a small hole in one wall. Outside of the room, he hung two lanterns at different heights. Alhazen observed that the light from each lantern illuminated a different spot in the room, and each lighted spot formed a direct line with the hole and one of the lanterns outside the room. He also found that covering a lantern caused the spot it illuminated to darken, and exposing the lantern caused the spot to reappear. Thus, Alhazen provided some of the first experimental evidence that light does not emanate from the human eye but rather is emitted by certain objects (like lanterns) and travels from these objects in straight lines. Alhazen's experiment may seem simplistic today, but his methodology was ground-breaking: he developed a hypothesis based on observations of physical relationships (that light comes from objects), and then designed an experiment to test that hypothesis. Despite the simplicity of the method, Alhazen's experiment was a critical step in refuting the long-standing theory that light emanated from the human eye, and it was a major event in the development of modern scientific research methodology.

Experimentation as a scientific research method

Experimentation is one scientific research method, perhaps the most recognizable, in a spectrum of methods that also includes description, comparison, and modeling (see the other chapters in the Research Methods section). While all of these methods share in common a scientific approach, experimentation is unique in that it involves the conscious manipulation of certain aspects of a real system and the observation of the effects of that manipulation. You could solve a cell phone reception problem by walking around a neighborhood until you see a cell phone tower, observing other cell phone users to see where those people who get the best reception are standing, or looking on the web for a map of cell phone signal coverage. All of these methods could also provide answers, but by moving around and testing reception yourself, you are experimenting.

In the experimental method, a condition or a parameter, generally referred to as a variable, is consciously manipulated (often referred to as a treatment) and the outcome or effect of that manipulation is observed on other variables. Variables are given different names depending on whether they are the ones manipulated or the ones observed: "independent variable" refers to a condition within an experiment that is manipulated by the scientist; "dependent variable" refers to an event or outcome of an experiment that might be affected by the manipulation of the independent variable. Scientific experimentation helps to determine the nature of the relationship between independent and dependent variables. While it is often difficult, or sometimes impossible, to manipulate a single variable in an experiment, scientists often work to minimize the number of variables being manipulated. For example, as we move from one location to another to get better cell reception, we likely change the orientation of our body, perhaps from south-facing to east-facing, or we hold the cell phone at a different angle. Which variable affected reception: location, orientation, or angle of the phone? It is critical that scientists understand which aspects of their experiment they are manipulating so that they can accurately determine the impacts of that manipulation. In order to constrain the possible outcomes of an experimental procedure, most scientific experiments use a system of controls.

In a controlled study, a scientist essentially runs two (or more) parallel and simultaneous experiments: a treatment group, in which the effect of an experimental manipulation is observed on a dependent variable, and a control group, which uses all of the same conditions as the first with the exception of the actual treatment. Controls can fall into one of two groups: negative controls and positive controls. In a negative control, the control group is exposed to all of the experimental conditions except for the actual treatment. The need to match all experimental conditions exactly is so great that, for example, in a trial for a new drug, the negative control group will be given a pill or liquid that looks exactly like the drug, except that it will not contain the drug itself, a control often referred to as a placebo. Negative controls allow scientists to measure the natural variability of the dependent variable(s), provide a means of measuring error in the experiment, and also provide a baseline to measure against the experimental treatment.

Some experimental designs also make use of positive controls. A positive control is run as a parallel experiment and generally involves the use of an alternative treatment that the researcher knows will have an effect on the dependent variable. For example, when testing the effectiveness of a new drug for pain relief, a scientist might administer a treatment placebo to one group of patients as a negative control, and a known treatment like aspirin to a separate group of individuals as a positive control since the pain-relieving aspects of aspirin are well documented. In both cases, the controls allow scientists to quantify background variability and reject alternative hypotheses that might otherwise explain the effect of the treatment on the dependent variable.

Experimentation in practice: The case of Louis Pasteur

Well-controlled experiments generally provide strong evidence of causality, demonstrating whether the manipulation of one variable causes a response in another variable. For example, as early as the 6th century BCE, Anaximander, a Greek philosopher, speculated that life could be formed from a mixture of sea water, mud and sunlight. The idea probably stemmed from the observation of worms, mosquitoes, and other insects "magically" appearing in mudflats and other shallow areas. While the suggestion was challenged on a number of occasions, the idea that living microorganisms could be spontaneously generated from air persisted until the middle of the 18th century. In the 1750s, John Needham, a Scottish clergyman and naturalist, claimed to have proved that spontaneous generation does occur when he showed that microorganisms flourished in certain foods such as soup broth, even after they had been briefly boiled and covered. Several years later, the Italian abbot and biologist Lazzaro Spallanzani, boiled soup broth for over an hour and then placed bowls of this soup in different conditions, sealing some and leaving others exposed to air. Spallanzani found that microorganisms grew in the soup exposed to air but were absent from the sealed soup. He therefore challenged Needham's conclusions and hypothesized that microorganisms suspended in air settled onto the exposed soup but not the sealed soup, and rejected the idea of spontaneous generation.

Needham countered, arguing that the growth of bacteria in the soup was not due to microbes settling onto the soup from the air, but rather because spontaneous generation required contact with an intangible "life force" in the air itself. He proposed that Spallanzani's extensive boiling destroyed the "life force" present in the soup, preventing spontaneous generation in the sealed bowls but allowing air to replenish the life force in the open bowls. For several decades, scientists continued to debate the spontaneous generation theory of life, with support for the theory coming from several notable scientists including Félix Pouchet and Henry Bastion. Pouchet, Director of the Rouen Museum of Natural History in France, and Bastion, a well-known British bacteriologist, argued that living organisms could spontaneously arise from chemical processes such as fermentation and putrefaction. The debate became so heated that in 1860, the French Academy of Sciences established the Alhumbert prize of 2,500 francs to the first person who could conclusively resolve the conflict. In 1864, Louis Pasteur achieved that result with a series of well-controlled experiments and in doing so claimed the Alhumbert prize.

Pasteur prepared for his experiments by studying the work of others that came before him. In fact, in April, 1861, Pasteur wrote to Pouchet to obtain a research description that Pouchet had published. In this letter, Pasteur writes:

Paris, 3 April 1861

Dear Colleague,

The difference of our opinions on the famous question of spontaneous generation does not prevent me from esteeming highly your labor and praiseworthy efforts... The sincerity of these sentiments... permits me to have recourse to your obligingness in full confidence. I read with great care everything that you write on the subject that occupies both of us. Now, I cannot obtain a brochure that I understand you have just published.... I would be happy to have a copy of it because I am at present editing the totality of my observations, where naturally I criticize your assertions.

L. Pasteur

(Porter, 1961)

Pasteur received the brochure from Pouchet several days later and went on to conduct his own experiments. In these, he repeated Spallanzani's method of boiling soup broth, but he divided the broth into portions and exposed these portions to different controlled conditions. Some broth was placed in flasks that had straight necks that were open to the air, some broth was placed in sealed flasks that were not open to the air, and some broth was placed into a specially designed set of swan-necked flasks, in which the broth would be open to the air but the air would have to travel a curved path before reaching the broth, thus preventing anything that might be present in the air from simply settling onto the soup (Figure 2). Pasteur then observed the response of the dependent variable (the growth of microorganisms) in response to the independent variable (the design of the flask). Pasteur's experiments contained both positive controls (samples in the straight necked flasks that he knew would become contaminated with microorganisms) and negative controls (samples in the sealed flasks that he knew would remain sterile). If spontaneous generation did indeed occur upon exposure to air, Pasteur hypothesized, microorganisms would be found in both the swan-neck flasks and the straight-necked flasks, but not in the sealed flasks. Instead, Pasteur found that microorganisms appeared in the straight necked flasks, but not in the sealed flasks or the swan-necked flasks.

By using controls and replicating his experiment (he used more than one of each type of flask), Pasteur was able to answer many of the questions that still surrounded the issue of spontaneous generation. Pasteur said of his experimental design, "I affirm with the most perfect sincerity that I have never had a single experiment, arranged as I have just explained, which gave me a doubtful result" (Porter, 1961). Pasteur's work helped refute the theory of spontaneous generation – his experiments showed that air alone was not the cause of bacterial growth in the flask, and his research supported the hypothesis that live microorganisms suspended in air could settle onto the broth in open-necked flasks via gravity.

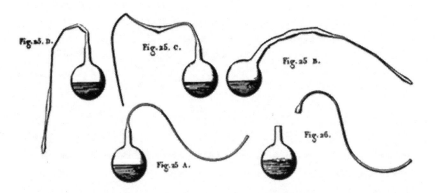

Figure 2: Pasteur's drawings of the flasks he used (Pasteur, 1861). Fig. 25 D, C, and B (top) show various sealed flasks (negative controls); Fig. 26 (bottom right) illustrates a straight-necked flask directly open to the atmosphere (positive control); and Fig. 25 A (bottom left) illustrates the specially designed swan-necked flask (treatment group).

Experimentation across disciplines

Experiments are used across all scientific disciplines to investigate a multitude of questions. In some cases, scientific experiments are used for exploratory purposes in which the scientist does not know what the dependent variable is. In this type of experiment, the scientist will manipulate an independent variable and observe what the effect of the manipulation is in order to identify a dependent variable (or variables). Exploratory experiments are sometimes used in nutritional biology when scientists probe the function and purpose of dietary nutrients. In one approach, a scientist will expose one group of animals to a normal diet, and a second group to a similar diet except that it is lacking a specific vitamin or nutrient. The researcher will then observe the two groups to see what specific physiological changes or medical problems arise in the group lacking the nutrient being studied.

Scientific experiments are also commonly used to quantify the magnitude of a relationship between two or more variables. For example, in the fields of pharmacology and toxicology, scientific experiments are used to determine the dose-response relationship of a new drug or chemical. In these approaches, researchers perform a series of experiments in which a population of organisms, such as laboratory mice, is separated into groups and each group is exposed to a different amount of the drug or chemical of interest. The analysis of the data that result from these experiments involves comparing the degree of the organism's response to the dose of the substance administered.

In this context, experiments can provide additional evidence to complement other research methods. For example, in the 1950s a great debate ensued over whether or not the chemicals in cigarette smoke cause cancer. Several researchers had conducted comparative studies (see our Comparison chapter) that indicated that patients who smoked had a higher probability for developing lung cancer when compared to non-smokers. Comparative studies differ slightly from experimental methods in that you do not consciously manipulate a variable; rather you observe differences between two or more groups depending on whether or not they fall into a treatment or control group. Cigarette companies and lobbyists criticized these studies, suggesting that the relationship between smoking and lung cancer was coincidental. Several researchers noted the need for a clear dose-response study; however, the difficulties in getting cigarette smoke into the lungs of laboratory animals prevented this research. In the mid-1950s, Ernest Wynder and colleagues had an ingenious idea: they condensed the chemicals from cigarette smoke into a liquid and applied this in various doses to the skin of groups of mice. The researchers published data from a dose-response experiment of the effect of tobacco-smoke condensate on mice (Wynder *et. al.*, 1957). As seen in Figure 3, the researchers found a positive relationship between the amount of condensate applied to the skin of mice and the number of cancers that developed. This study was one of the first pieces of experimental evidence in the cigarette smoking debate, and it helped strengthen the case for cigarette smoke as the causative agent in lung cancer in smokers.

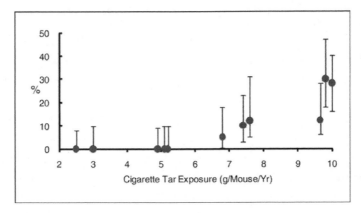

Figure 3: Percentage of mice with cancer versus the amount cigarette smoke "condensate" applied to their skin (source: Wynder et al., 1957).

Sometimes experimental approaches and other research methods are not clearly distinct, or scientists may even use multiple research approaches in combination. For example, at 1:52 a.m. EDT on July 4, 2005, scientists with the National Aeronautics and Space Administration (NASA) conducted a study in which a 370 kg spacecraft named Deep Impact was purposely slammed into passing comet Tempel 1. A nearby spacecraft observed the impact and radioed data back to earth. The research was partially descriptive in that it documented the chemical composition of the comet, but it was also partly experimental in that the effect of slamming the Deep Impact probe into the comet on the volatilization of previously undetected compounds, such as

Figure 4: An image of comet Tempel 1 67 seconds after collision with the Deep Impact impactor.

water, was assessed (A'Hearn *et al.*, 2005). It is particularly common that experimentation and description overlap: another example is Jane Goodall's research on the behavior of chimpanzees, detailed in the Description chapter.

Limitations of experimental methods

While scientific experiments provide invaluable data regarding causal relationships, they do have limitations. One criticism of experiments is that they do not necessarily represent real-world situations. In order to clearly identify the relationship between an independent variable and a dependent variable, experiments are designed so that many other contributing variables are fixed or eliminated. For example, in an experiment designed to quantify the effect of Vitamin A dose on the metabolism of beta-carotene in humans, Shawna Lemke and colleagues had to precisely control the diet of their human volunteers (Lemke, Dueker *et al.* 2003). They asked their participants to limit their intake of foods rich in Vitamin A and further asked that they maintain a precise log of all foods eaten for 1 week prior to their study. At the time of their study, they controlled their participants' diet by feeding them all the same meals, described in the methods section of their research article in this way:

> Meals were controlled for time and content on the dose administration day. Lunch was served at 5.5 h postdosing and consisted of a frozen dinner (Enchiladas, Amy's Kitchen, Petaluma, CA), a blueberry bagel with jelly, 1 apple and 1 banana, and a large chocolate chunk cookie (Pepperidge Farm). Dinner was served 10.5 h post dose and consisted of a frozen dinner (Chinese Stir Fry, Amy's Kitchen) plus the bagel and fruit taken for lunch.

While this is an important aspect of making an experiment manageable and informative, it is often not representative of the real world, in which many variables may change at once, including the foods you eat. Still, experimental research is an excellent way of determining relationships between variables that can be later validated in real world settings through descriptive or comparative studies.

Design is critical to the success or failure of an experiment. Slight variations in the experimental set-up could strongly affect the outcome being measured. During the 1950s, a number of experiments were conducted to evaluate the toxicity in mammals of the metal molybdenum, using rats as experimental subjects. Unexpectedly, these experiments seemed to indicate that the type of cage the rats were housed in affected the toxicity of molybdenum. In response, G. Brinkman and Russell Miller set up an experiment to investigate this observation (Brinkman and Miller, 1961). Brinkman and Miller fed two groups of rats a normal diet that was supplemented with 200 parts per million (ppm) of molybdenum. One group of rats was housed in galvanized steel (steel coated with zinc to reduce corrosion) cages and the second group was housed in stainless steel cages. Rats housed in the galvanized steel cages suffered more from molybdenum toxicity than the other group: they had higher concentrations of molybdenum in their livers and lower blood hemoglobin levels. It was then shown that when the rats chewed on their cages, those housed in the galvanized metal cages absorbed zinc plated onto the metal bars. Zinc is now known to affect the toxicity of molybdenum. In order to control for zinc exposure, then, stainless steel cages needed to be used for all rats.

Scientists also have an obligation to adhere to ethical limits in designing and conducting experiments. During World War II doctors working in Nazi Germany conducted many heinous experiments using human subjects. Among them was an experiment meant to identify effective treatments for hypothermia in humans, in which concentration camp prisoners were forced to sit in ice water or left naked outdoors in freezing temperatures and then re-warmed by various means. Many of the exposed victims froze to death or suffered permanent injuries. As a result of the Nazi experiments and other unethical research, strict scientific ethical standards have been adopted by the United States and other governments, and by the scientific community at large. Among other things, ethical standards require that the benefits of research outweigh the risks to human subjects, and those who participate do so voluntarily and only after they have been made fully aware of all the risks posed by the research (see the Scientific Ethics chapter for more). These guidelines have far-reaching effects: while the clearest indication of causation in the cigarette smoke and lung cancer debate would have been to design an experiment in which one group of people was asked to take up smoking and another group was asked to refrain from smoking, it would be highly unethical for a scientist to purposefully expose a group of healthy people to a suspected cancer causing agent. As an alternative, comparative studies were initiated in humans, and experimental studies focused on animal subjects. The combination of these and other studies provided even stronger evidence of the link between smoking and lung cancer than either one method alone would have.

Experimentation in modern practice

Like all scientific research, the results of experiments are shared with the scientific community, are built upon, and inspire additional experiments and research. For example, once Alhazen established that light given off by objects enters the human eye, and the natural question that was asked was "what is the nature of light that enters the human eye?" Two common theories about the nature of light were debated for many years. Sir Isaac Newton was among the principal proponents of a theory suggesting that light was made of small particles. The English naturalist Robert Hooke (who held the interesting title of Curator of Experiments at the Royal Society of London) supported a different theory stating that light was a type of wave, like sound waves. In 1801, Thomas Young conducted a now classic scientific experiment that helped resolve this controversy. Young, like Alhazen, worked in a darkened room and allowed light to enter only through a small hole in a window shade (Figure 5). Young refocused the beam of light with mirrors and split the beam with a paper-thin card. The split light beams were then projected onto a screen, and formed an alternating light and dark banding pattern – that was a sign that light was indeed a wave.

Approximately 100 years later, in 1905, new experiments led Albert Einstein to conclude that light exhibits properties of both waves and particles. Einstein's dual wave–particle theory is now generally accepted by scientists.

Figure 5: Young's split-light beam experiment helped clarify the wave nature of light.

Experiments continue to help refine our understanding of light even today. In addition to his wave–particle theory, Einstein also proposed that the speed of light was unchanging and absolute. Yet in 1998 a group of scientists led by Lene Hau showed that light could be slowed from its normal speed of 3 x 108 meters per second to a mere 17 meters per second with a special experimental apparatus (Hau *et al.*, 1999). The series of experiments that began with Alhazen's work 1000 years ago has led to a progressively deeper understanding of the nature of light. Although the tools with which scientists conduct experiments may have become more complex, the principles behind controlled experiments are remarkably similar to those used by Pasteur and Alhazen hundreds of years ago.

Key Concepts for this chapter

▶ Experimentation is a research method in which one or more variables are consciously manipulated and the outcome or effect of that manipulation on other variables is observed.

▶ Experimental designs often make use of controls that provide a measure of variability within a system and a check for sources of error.

▶ Experimental methods are commonly applied to determine causal relationships or to quantify the magnitude of response of a variable.

References

Agar, D. (2001). Arabic Studies in Physics and Astronomy During 800-1400 AD. Retrieved August 1, 2007, from the University of Jyväskylä

Alberts, B., Johnson, A., Lewis, J., Raff, M., Roberts, K., & Walter, P. (2002). *Molecular Biology of the Cell* (4th ed.), London: Taylor & Francis.

Bajcsy, M., Zibrov, A.S., & Lukin, M.D. (2003). Stationary pulses of light in an atomic medium. *Nature* 426, 638-641.

Brinkman, G.L., & Miller, R.F. (1961). Influence of Cage Type and Dietary Zinc Oxide upon Molybdenum Toxicity. *Science*, 134(3489), 1531.

Code of Federal Regulations, 45 CFR §46,

Corbie-Smith, G. (1999). The Continuing Legacy of the Tuskegee Syphilis Study. *American Journal of the Medical Sciences* 317(1), 5-8.

Fankhauser, D.B., & Stein Carter, J. (2004). Spontaneous Generation. Retrieved August 1, 2007, from the Clermont College Biology Department

Gorini, R. (2003). Al-Haytham the Man of Experience. First Steps in the Science of Vision. *Journal of the International Society for the History of Islamic Medicine*, 2(4), 53-55

Hau, L.V., Harris, S.E., Dutton, Z., & Behroozi, C.H. (1999). Light speed reduction to 17 metres per second in an ultracold atomic gas. *Nature*, 397, 594-598.

A'Hearn, M. F., Belton, M. J. S., Delamere, W. A., Kissel, J., Klaasen, K. P., McFadden, L. A., Meech, K. J., Melosh, H. J., Schultz, P. H., Sunshine, J. M., Thomas, P. C., Veverka, J., Yeomans, D. K., Baca, M. W., Busko, I., Crockett, C. J., Collins, S. M., Desnoyer, M., Eberhardy, C. A., Ernst, C. M., Farnham, T. L., Feaga, L., Groussin, O., Hampton, D., Ipatov, S. I., Li, J.-Y., Lindler, D., Lisse, C. M., Mastrodemos, N., Owen, Jr., W. M., Richardson, J. E., Wellnitz, D. D. & White, R. L. (2005). Deep Impact: Excavating Comet Tempel 1. *Science*, 310(5746), 258.

Kent, J. (2006, January). The Impact of the Scientific Revolution: A Brief History of the Experimental Method in the 17th Century. Retrieved August 1, 2007, from *Connexions*

Lemke, S. L., S. R. Dueker, et al. (2003). "Absorption and retinol equivalence of beta-carotene in humans is influenced by dietary vitamin A intake." *J Lipid Res* 44(8): 1591-600.

O'Connor, J.J., & Robertson, E.F. (1999). Abu Ali al-Hasan ibn al-Haytham. Retrieved August 1, 2007, from the MacTutor History of Mathematics Archive, School of Mathematics and Statistics, University of St. Andrews, Scotland

O'Connor, J.J., & Robertson, E.F. (2002). Light through the ages: Ancient Greece to Maxwell. Retrieved August 1, 2007, from the MacTutor History of Mathematics Archive, School of Mathematics and Statistics, University of St. Andrews, Scotland

Pasteur, L. (1861). Sur les corpuscules organizes qui existent dans l'atmosphère. Examen de la doctrine des générations spontanées. (Legon professée á la Societé chimique de Paris, le 19 mai). Mémoire sur les corpuscules organisés qui existent en suspension dans l'atmosphère. Examen de la doctrine des générations spontanées (Extrait). Compt. rend. 52(1), 1142-1143, 3 juin. Mémoire sur les corpuscules organisés qui existent dans l'atmosphère. Examen de la doctrine des générations spontanées. *Ann. sci. naturelles (partie zoologique)* (Sér. 4) 16, 5-98.

Porter, J.R. (1961). *Louis Pasteur: Achievements and Disappointments*, 1861.

Reuben, A. (2004). Au Conntraire, professeur Pasteur! *Hepatology* 40(6), 1478-1482.

Wynder, E.L., Kopf, P., & Ziegler, H. (1957). A Study of Tobacco Carcinogenesis: II. Dose-Response Studies. *Cancer* 10(6)

Description

"Darwin was a prolific describer of everything from barnacles to orchid pollination and animal emotions.... [His work] succeeded so well because it assembled and explained vast descriptive evidence."

~ Grimaldi and Engel, 2007

An eclipse is a dramatic event: the sky goes dark during the day in a solar eclipse, and the moon turns red during a lunar eclipse. As a result, many cultures have revered both solar and lunar eclipses, and their occurrences are noted frequently in prehistoric art, oral histories, and historical records. The Chinese began systematically recording the time and location of eclipses on what they called oracle bones as early as 2000 BCE. Astronomers in ancient Mesopotamia kept detailed records of lunar eclipses engraved on 70 tablets dating back to 600 BCE (such as shown in Figure 1), and these records were used to accurately predict future eclipses (Steele, 2000). By the 4th century BCE, the Mesopotamians had developed a comprehensive lunar theory from these observations – a mathematical description of the movements of the sun and moon through the sky – that was the first of its kind (Britton, 2007). These records define an early stage in the develop-

Figure 1: *Clay tablet listing eclipses between 518 and 465 BCE from the ancient city of Babylon in Mesopotamia.*

ment of the science of astronomy, which relied on quantitative description as a research method. The ancient astronomers observed and described the motion of objects in the sky, noted the time and location of events, developed mathematical models based on the phenomena they observed, and then used those models to predict future eclipses through mathematical computations.

Around 340 BCE, the Greek astronomer Eudoxus developed his own geometrical theory of the universe (Goldstein and Bowen, 1983): he proposed that the universe consisted of nested spheres with a non-moving earth at the center. This theory was based on his recorded observations of the paths that planets took through the sky, and the relationships of the planets to the earth, moon, and sun. However, Eudoxus was not able to quantify these relationships and thus was unable to use his observations predictively. In the 2nd century BCE, the Mesopotamian records reached Greece, and the mathematician Hipparchus revolutionized Greek astronomy by combining Greek and Mesopotamian observations and descriptions. Though the exact method of transmission of ideas is not clear, the presence and use of these long-term descriptive records was at the core of the development of the science of astronomy. Those early data are so significant, in fact, that they are still being revisited today: both the Chinese and Mesopotamian eclipse catalogs have been used by modern scientists to approach new scientific questions, like measuring the rate of slowing of the earth's rotation over time (Pang, Yau, Chou, and Wolff, 1988).

Description as a scientific research method

These early astronomers used descriptions of natural phenomena to make scientific inferences about broad physical principles, like the rotation of the earth or the nature of the solar system. As discussed in the chapter "The Practice of Science," all research methods involve data gathering and hypothesis development and testing, and the descriptive method is no different. This method usually involves an initial observation and detailed description of some phenomenon – e.g. the frequency of lunar eclipses, the composition and orientation of rock layers in Utah, or the behavior of chimpanzees in the wild. A scientist then develops a hypothesis or multiple working hypotheses to explain the phenomenon. Additional observations are made to test the hypothesis or to determine the most likely of the competing hypotheses. Eventually, a scientist can develop an explanatory theory that fits the observations. This is an iterative process that happens on many scales: the entire process may happen within a few days for one scientist, or over many decades or centuries and involve the contributions of many scientists, sometimes from many fields of science.

Descriptive studies can also be exploratory rather than driven by hypothesis testing. The U.S. Geological Survey, for example, maintains stream gauges on many streams and rivers in the United States, which record daily observations of the amount of water flowing at that point. These were not established to test any specific hypothesis, but simply to keep a record. The records have proven useful in addressing questions about flood recurrence intervals, daily and seasonal fluctuations in stream flow, and other watershed-related questions. Not all descriptions of streamflow are scientific, however. Part of the reason that these records are so useful is because the descriptions are systematic, and involve the same rigor and consistency that is required in designing a well-controlled experiment or in building a useful mathematical model. The location of each stream gauge was surveyed and calibrated to accurately record the flow. Streamflow is measured at the same time each day, and in the same location. The same parameters are recorded each day at each station, including stream height, water temperature, and volume of flow. Without that consistency, it would be difficult to establish the accuracy and reliability of the data that were collected.

Though it can stand alone as a research method, systematic description is often a component of other types of scientific research. Scientists who conduct experiments must first study and describe the system with which they experiment, researchers who initiate comparative studies need descriptive data regarding the population they are investigating, and scientists who build models must have an accurate representation of the system they are modeling.

Description in practice:
G.K. Gilbert and the geology of the Henry Mountains

In the United States, description was used as a scientific research method extensively during the exploration of the west. In the 1860s, the U.S. government launched a series of four surveys into the American west: the King, Wheeler, Hayden, and Powell surveys lasted from 1860 until 1879. Each of these survey teams included a geologist whose job was to observe and describe the landscape. The geological exploration of the Henry Mountains in southern Utah provides insight into the research method of description and one of its most respected practitioners, G.K. Gilbert.

On his two trips down the Colorado River in the 1870s, John Wesley Powell had noted the Henry Mountains with interest. They lay west of the river as it wound through Glen Canyon, rising abruptly from the surrounding mesas. Their dark peaks contrasted sharply with the light-colored, layered rocks that surrounded the river on all sides (see Figure 2). He did not have time to explore the mountains himself, and thus gave the task to Grove Karl Gilbert, a young geologist who had worked with him previously. Gilbert spent a week in the mountains in 1875, and returned for a month in 1876, emerging with several notebooks filled with carefully recorded notes, sketches, and hypotheses. In August of 1875, he wrote the following observations:

> The rock which rises towards Hillers from the south is the B Cliff. It is lost in the 'debris' without increasing the dip (7°) with which it approaches. But beyond are red and white sands – [deeper] rocks tilted almost to the vertical and interspersed with dikes. Moreover these sandstone hogbacks seem to trend in a curve around the mountain as far as they extend.

He made a sketch, shown in Figure 3 on the next page, in which he indicated where he had taken measurements and summarized his descriptions.

Gilbert collected samples of each of the rock types labeled in Figure 3 and described them. The layered rocks (labeled b, c, d, s, and p) were all sedimentary rocks that he had seen before in his travels, and he described them by color, grain size, and the fossils they contained. The core of Mt. Hillers was different, however: an igneous rock formed from cooling magma. He described this rock as "a pale gray paste with large white crystals of feldspar and crystals large and small of hornblende." Based on this composition he determined it was trachyte, labeled t in Figure 3. Gilbert sketched the same

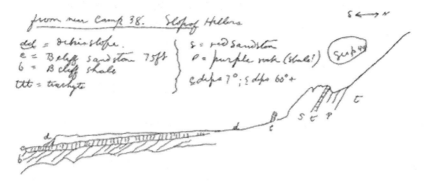

Figure 3: G. K. Gilbert's sketch of the rocks surrounding Mt. Hillers to accompany his notes; the small letter b on the left side of the diagram corresponds with the "B Cliff" in his notes. *(Hunt, 1988)*

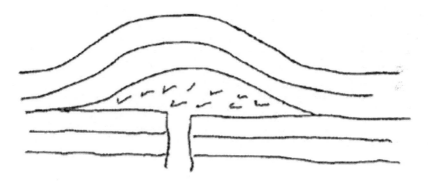

Figure 4: Gilbert's drawing representing a hypothesis for the formation of Mt. Hillers.

mountain from several different angles and collected measurements on the orientation of rock layers all the way around it, while also collecting basic survey data like elevation.

Just a few notebook pages and one day later, Gilbert takes the first leap from observation and data collection to hypothesis. He sketches a cross-section that is no longer a faithful depiction of the landscape, but is a hypothesis for the formation of Mt. Hillers (Figure 4). This initial model takes all of his observations thus far into account: the gentle slopes of the sedimentary rock units leading up to the peak, the steeply dipping rocks that continue all the way around the mountain, and the igneous rock at the center. He devotes little text to explaining his idea at this point, writing only about a "reservoir" of magma forming below the surface and deforming the rock layers above it. He knew he had more data to collect in order to test this initial hypothesis; the next day, he wrote in his notes, "I don't understand the NE side of Hillers." He could not yet explain what was going on there through his initial hypothesis.

Gilbert had only a few days left in the Henry Mountains that summer as he continued on his exploratory journey. The next year (1876) he returned, however, to the task of collecting more data to revise his initial, simple hypothesis. After a month of collecting survey data and rock unit orientations, Gilbert and his team were stuck in camp because of rain and snow. Gilbert took the opportunity to summarize his findings and display the development of his thinking over the course of his explorations. He re-drew the sketch from the previous year and wrote an explanation for his new model:

> The simplest type of Henry Mt. structure is a lenticular mass of trap [an early word for igneous rock] above which the strata were arched... The form of the trap mass is never fully shown but it can be described in a general way in several cases... Injections are combined and grouped variously. A trap mass with sheets above and below may be regarded as a system of exudations from one chimney.

He includes a more realistic representation of the process as it applies to the Henry Mountains specifically (Figure 5). Gilbert then poses a question about these intrusions: Why didn't the magma reach the surface?

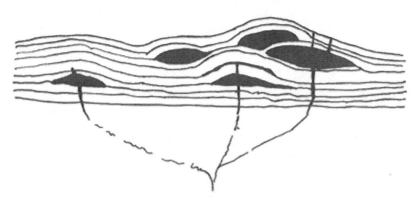

Figure 5: Gilbert's 1876 drawing representing a revised hypothesis for the formation of the Henry Mountains.

Gilbert published his "Report on the Geology of the Henry Mountains" in 1877 (Gilbert, 1877). In the publication, he named this newly discovered type of intrusion a laccolite (later changed to laccolith). He formalized his field sketches, measurements, and research questions into a coherent theory about the formation of the Henry Mountains and noted that many other mountains in the region were likely formed through the same process. He proposed two different answers for his question about the underlying causes of the intrusion relating to relative densities and the "penetrability" of the sedimentary rocks, but his question has still not been resolved today. Gilbert's report is considered a key milestone in geology, not only for the new type of intrusion he proposed, but for the highly systematic way in which he used the descriptive method of science; as a result, Gilbert went on to become a highly valued and respected leader of the new U.S. Geological Survey and two-time president of the Geological Society of America.

Gilbert's work also laid the foundation for further research on the Henry Mountains. More detailed measurements of the folding and faulting in the rock layers gave strong support to Gilbert's laccolith hypothesis (Jackson and Pollard, 1988). More recently, researchers have experimented with physical analogue models to try to understand why the magma did not make it to the surface by building sedimentary layers out of sand and injecting the layers from below with silica gel to simulate magma (Roman-Berdiel, Gapais, and Brun, 1995).

Description across disciplines

Description as a research method is not a thing of the past, nor does it consist solely of sketches. Ongoing measurements of CO_2 concentrations in the atmosphere, such as those begun by Charles Keeling on the Hawaiian volcano Mauna Loa in 1958, are a quantitative description of the composition of the atmosphere over time (see our online module the Carbon Cycle). These daily, worldwide measurements have allowed climate scientists to develop hypotheses about the atmospheric response to volcanic eruptions, pollutants, and the steadily increasing emissions of greenhouse gases. The atmospheric record has been extended back 650,000 years through the sampling and description of CO_2 concentrations in air bubbles trapped in ice cores drilled in Greenland and Antarctica (Figure 6). These data reveal a cyclical pattern in CO_2 concentrations that has helped climate scientists develop an understanding of long-term climate. Based on these findings, climatologists can develop models to assess the possible impacts of a continued increase in CO_2 concentration in the atmosphere.

In contrast with experimentation, sometimes the main goal of the descriptive method is explicitly to avoid manipulating any variables, such as in some ecological studies that seek to describe the natural interactions

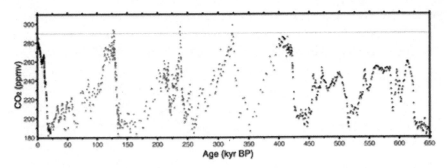

Figure 6: Data from the European Project for Ice-Coring in Antarctica (EPICA), showing CO_2 concentrations over time (graph is from Siegenthaler et al., 2005). The three different shades represent data collected from three separate ice cores.

between organisms in the environment. Jane Goodall's goal in the Gombe National Park in Tanzania when she began working there in the 1960s was the non-invasive observation of chimpanzees in the wild. One of her first papers, "Tool-using and aimed throwing in a community of free-living chimpanzees," published in 1964, opened with the fact that tool-use had been observed in chimpanzees in captivity, but many people wanted to know if the behavior existed in wild populations.

In order to answer this question, Goodall observed chimpanzees in their natural habitat and took detailed notes. Goodall's work involved long days, weeks, and months in the field. In the beginning of her study, she simply sat near the chimps to assure that the animals would become comfortable with her presence and would act normally, as she did not want her presence to be a variable affecting their behavior. Goodall then placed boxes full of bananas in areas where she knew the chimpanzees would find them. The kinds of data she presented in her paper included descriptions like the following, "After pulling and pushing at the boxes for up to 5 min., each one broke off a stick and stripped it of its leaves. Two individuals then tried to push their sticks under the box lids…. None of the three had seen either of the others trying to solve the problem in this way." It is important to recognize that Goodall did manipulate the environment (she gave the chimpanzees something new to look at – boxes of bananas) but she did not attempt to manipulate their behavior – that was the object of her observations and descriptions. She used these and other observations to develop new ideas about chimpanzees as tool-users who think independently and can learn from one another (Goodall, 1964), revolutionizing our understanding of non-human primates and human origins.

In fact, Goodall was performing an experiment, in a sense, with the chimpanzees: what will they do with a sealed box of bananas? That particular research question falls somewhere on a continuum between experimentation and description, and highlights how different research methods complement each other. It is particularly common that experimentation and description overlap: another example is NASA's Deep Impact mission, which is described in our Experimentation chapter.

Limitations of the descriptive method

Description is very widely used throughout scientific research, and there are few limitations on its use. It is a very useful research method for questions where experimentation is impossible, such as determining events in earth history. Despite the wide applicability of the method in science, it is challenging to establish cause and effect relationships through description alone. Instead, descriptive studies lead most often to information about the function or form of phenomena, like Gilbert's work, and the establishment of physical, spatial, and temporal relationships.

Systematic description can also easily lead to unscientific explanations, as is evident in the mythologies and legends of many cultures. The early Greeks were excellent observers of their environment, and they developed mythological explanations for natural processes that we now understand in a scientific sense. For example, like most agricultural peoples, the Greeks observed and monitored the change of the seasons, the regular cycle of budding and growth in the spring, followed by a season of abundance in the summer, the fall harvest, and barren fields in the winter. These observations are encapsulated in the myth of Demeter, the goddess of agriculture, and her daughter Persephone, who was kidnapped by Hades and taken to the Underworld. In the myth, Demeter strikes a deal with Hades to share Persephone – for six months of the year, Persephone lives with her mother on the surface, and Demeter's happiness is reflected in the seasons of spring and summer, while the six months when Persephone returns to the Underworld are marked by Demeter's grief and the crops wither and die. Clearly, the observations of seasonal changes are valid, but the mythological explanation is not scientific.

In some cases, even descriptions that weren't meant to be scientific at the time can be utilized by scientists later. For example, many historical figures have been diagnosed with diseases or afflictions long after their deaths by historians and scientists who peruse diaries, letters, and other primary sources for descriptions of symptoms. In 1979, Peter Spargo, a chemist at the University of Cape Town teamed with a forensic scientist, C.A. Pounds, to determine the cause of a period of "madness" experienced by Isaac Newton in 1692–93. Many historians had noted oddities in Newton's behavior during this time as reflected in his letters and records. Based on the descriptions of his actions contained in these letters and records, Spargo and Pounds summarized the symptoms of Newton's illness as "severe insomnia, extreme sensitivity in personal relations, loss of appetite, delusions of persecution, and amnesia". They noted that during this same time period, Newton was engaged in intense alchemical experimentation and hypothesized he was experiencing heavy metal poisoning (Spargo and Pounds, 1979). In other words, though the descriptions of Newton's behavior were not meant to thoroughly document his ailment, they were still useful in developing a scientific hypothesis. Spargo and Pounds were able to test their hypothesis by obtaining a sample of Newton's hair, which indeed revealed significantly elevated levels of mercury, arsenic, gold, chlorine, antimony, and lead – all metals capable of producing temporary neurological disorders such as those he experienced.

Description in modern practice

Although many scientists still sketch their descriptions with pencil and paper, the tools available for descriptive studies have proliferated and grown more powerful. For example, the use of X-ray diffraction allows geologists to go beyond a field description of a rock to a detailed description of the chemical make-up of individual minerals. This same technique allowed Crick, Franklin, Watson, and Wilson to describe the structure of the DNA molecule as a double helix (see our online module DNA II). Other instruments, like mass spectrometers, make it possible to determine the absolute ages of things like lavas from volcanic eruptions and bones from archaeological sites, whereas scientists like Gilbert, who worked before such technology was invented, could only assign relative ages to the rocks he studied. Many of our most advanced and costly technologies are based on making highly accurate descriptions: for example, global positioning satellite (GPS) technology allows ecologists, oceanographers, and many others to accurately pinpoint their sample locations and make more detailed analyses of spatial data; magnetic resonance imaging (or MRI) allows us to see the organs inside our bodies for more accurate medical diagnoses. These techniques are in use today in a variety of scientific disciplines, bringing new understanding to large-scale, complex, interacting systems.

Key Concepts for this chapter

▶ Description involves the systematic observation and cataloging of components of a natural system in a manner that can be
utilized and replicated by other scientists.

▶ Description is commonly used as a research method to explain
unique natural systems (such as in ecology or chemistry),
large-scale phenomena (such as in astronomy), or past events
(such as in geology or forensic science).

References

Britton, J. P. (2007). Studies in Babylonian Lunar Theory: Part I. Empirical Elements for Modeling Lunar and Solar Anomalies. *Archive for the History of Exact Sciences*, 61(2), 83-145.

Gilbert, G. K. (1877). Report on the geology of the Henry Mountains.

Goldstein, B. R., & Bowen, A. C. (1983). A New View of Early Greek Astronomy. *Isis*, 74(3),
330-340.

Goodall, J. (1964). Tool-Using and Aimed Throwing in a Community of Free-Living Chimpanzees. *Nature*, 201(4926), 1264-1266.

Grimaldi, D., and Engel, M., 2007, Why descriptive science still matters: *BioScience*, v. 57, p.
646-647

Hunt, C. B. (Ed.). (1988). *Geology of the Henry Mountains, Utah, as recorded in the notebooks of
G.K. Gilbert, 1875-76 (Vol. 167)*. Boulder, CO: Geological Society of America.

Jackson, M. D., & Pollard, D. D. (1988). The laccolith-stock controversy: New results from the
southern Henry Mountains, Utah. *Geological Society of America Bulletin*, 100(1), 117-139.

Pang, K. D., Yau, K., Chou, H.-h., & Wolff, R. (1988). Computer analysis of some ancient Chinese sunrise eclipse records to determine the Earth's rotation rate. *Vistas in Astronomy*,
31, 833-847.

Roman-Berdiel, T., Gapais, D., & Brun, J. P. (1995). Analogue models of laccolith formation.
Journal of Structural Geology, 17(9), 1337-1346.

Siegenthaler, U., Stocker, T. F., Monnin, E., Luthi, D., Schwander, J., Stauffer, B., et al. (2005).
Stable Carbon Cycle-Climate Relationship During the Late Pleistocene. *Science*,
310(5752), 1313-1317.

Spargo, P. E., & Pounds, C. A. (1979). Newton's 'Derangement of the Intellect'. New Light on
an Old Problem. *Notes and Records of the Royal Society of London*, 34(1), 11-32.

Steele, J. M. (2000). Eclipse Prediction in Mesopotamia. *Archive for History of Exact Sciences*,
54(5), 421.

Comparison

*"[T]he amount of evidence accumulated to indict cigarette
smoke as a health hazard is overwhelming. The evidence
challenging such an indictment is scant."*

~ R.J. Reynolds Tobacco Company memo, 1962

Anyone who has stared at a chimpanzee in a zoo (Figure 1) has probably wondered about the animal's similarity to humans. Chimps
make facial expressions that resemble humans, use their hands in
much the same way we do, are adept at using different objects as tools, and
even laugh when they are tickled. It may not be surprising to learn then, that
when the first captured chimpanzees were brought to Europe in the 17th century, people were confused, labeling the animals "pygmies" and speculat-
ing that they were stunted versions of
"full-grown" humans. A London physician named Edward Tyson obtained
a "pygmie" that had died of an infection shortly after arriving in London,
and began a systematic study of the
animal that cataloged the differences
between chimpanzees and humans,
thus helping to establish comparative
research as a scientific method.

Figure 1: Chimpanzee

A brief history of comparative methods

In 1698, Tyson, a member of the Royal Society of London, began a detailed dissection of the "pygmie" he had obtained and published his findings in the 1699 work: *Orang-Outang, sive Homo Sylvestris: or, the Anatomy of
a Pygmie Compared with that of a Monkey, an Ape, and a Man.* The title of the
work further reflects the misconception that existed at the time – Tyson did

not use the term Orang-Outang in its modern sense to refer to the orangutan, he used it in its literal translation from the Malay language as "man of the woods," as that is how the chimps were viewed.

Tyson took great care in his dissection. He precisely measured and compared a number of anatomical variables such as brain size of the "pygmie," ape, and human. He recorded his measurements of the "pygmie," even down to the direction in which the animal's hair grew: "The tendency of the Hair of all of the Body was downwards; but only from the Wrists to the Elbows 'twas upwards" (Russell, 1967). Aided by William Cowper, Tyson made drawings of various anatomical structures, taking great care to accurately depict the dimensions of these structures so that they could be compared to those in humans (Figures 2 and 3). His systematic comparative study of the dimensions of anatomical structures in the chimp, ape, and human led him to state, "...in the Organization of abundance of its Parts, it more approached to the Structure of the same in Men: But where it differs from a Man, there it resembles plainly the Common Ape, more than any other Animal" (Russell, 1967). Tyson's comparative studies proved exceptionally accurate and his research was used by others, including Thomas Henry Huxley in *Evidence as to Man's Place in Nature* (1863) and Charles Darwin in *The Descent of Man* (1871).

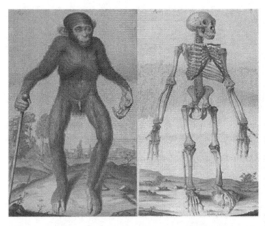

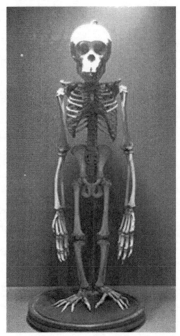

Figure 2, above: Edward Tyson's drawing of the external appearance of a "pygmie" (left) and the animal's skeleton (right) from The Anatomy of a Pygmie Compared with that of a Monkey, an Ape, and a Man *from the second edition, London, printed for T. Osborne, 1751.*

Figure 3, right: Skeleton of the juvenile chimpanzee dissected by Edward Tyson, currently displayed at the Natural History Museum, London.

Tyson's methodical and scientific approach to anatomical dissection contributed to the development of evolutionary theory and helped establish the field of comparative anatomy. Further, Tyson's work helps to highlight the importance of comparison as a scientific research method.

Comparison as a scientific research method

Comparative research represents one approach in the spectrum of scientific research methods and in some ways is a hybrid of other methods, drawing on aspects of both experimental science and descriptive research. Similar to experimentation, comparison seeks to decipher the relationship between two or more variables by documenting observed differences and similarities between two or more subjects or groups. In contrast to experimentation, the comparative researcher does not subject one of those groups to a treatment, but rather observes a group that either by choice or circumstance has been subject to a treatment. Thus comparison involves observation in a more "natural" setting, not subject to experimental confines, and in this way evokes similarities with description. Importantly, the simple comparison of two variables or objects is not comparative research. Tyson's work would not have been considered scientific research if he had simply noted that "pygmies" looked like humans without measuring bone lengths and hair growth patterns. Instead, comparative research involves the systematic cataloging of the nature and/or behavior of two or more variables, and the quantification of the relationship between them.

While the choice of which research method to use is a personal decision based in part on the training of the researchers conducting the study, there are a number of scenarios in which comparative research would likely be the primary choice. The first scenario is one in which the scientist is not trying to measure a response to change, but rather he or she may be trying to understand the similarities and differences between two subjects. For example, Tyson was not observing a change in his "pygmie" in response to an experimental treatment. Instead, his research was a comparison of the unknown "pygmie" to humans and apes in order to determine the relationship between them.

A second scenario in which comparative studies are common is when the physical scale or timeline of a question may prevent experimentation. For example, in the field of paleoclimatology, researchers have compared cores taken from sediments deposited millions of years ago in the world's oceans to see if the sedimentary composition is similar across all oceans or differs according to geographic location. Because the sediments in these cores were deposited millions of years ago, it would be impossible to obtain these results through the experimental method. Research designed to look at past events such as sediment cores deposited millions of years ago is referred to as retrospective research. A third common comparative scenario is when the ethical implications of an experimental treatment preclude an experimental design. Researchers who study the toxicity of environmental pollutants or the spread of disease in humans are precluded from purposefully exposing a group of individuals to the toxin or disease for ethical reasons. In these situations, researchers would set up a comparative study by identifying individuals who have been accidentally exposed to the pollutant or disease and comparing their symptoms to those of a control group of people who were not exposed. Research designed to look at events from the present into the future, such as a study looking at the development of symptoms in individuals exposed to a pollutant, is referred to as prospective research.

The utility of comparative science was significantly strengthened in the late 19th and early 20th centuries with the invention and popularization of modern statistical methods for quantifying the association between variables (see the Statistics chapter). Today, these statistical methods are critical for quantifying the nature of relationships examined in many comparative research studies. The outcome of comparative research is often presented as a probability, statement of statistical significance, or declaration of risk. For example, Kristensen and Bjerkedal recently showed that there is a statistically significant relationship (at the 95% confidence level) between birth order and IQ by comparing test scores of first-born children to those of their younger siblings (Kristensen and Bjerkedal, 2007). And numerous studies have now contributed to the determination that the risk of developing lung cancer is 30 times greater in smokers than in nonsmokers (NCI, 1997).

Comparison in practice: The case of cigarettes

In 1919, Dr. George Dock, chairman of the Department of Medicine at Barnes Hospital in St. Louis asked all of the third- and fourth-year medical students at the teaching hospital to observe an autopsy of a man with a disease so rare, he claimed, that most of the students would likely never see another case of it in their careers. With the medical students gathered around, the physicians conducting the autopsy observed that the patient's lungs were speckled with large dark masses of cells that had caused extensive damage to the lung tissue and had forced the airways to close and collapse. Dr. Alton Ochsner, one of the students who observed the autopsy, would write years later: "I did not see another case until 1936, seventeen years later, when in a period of six months, I saw nine patients with cancer of the lung.... All the afflicted patients were men who smoked heavily and had smoked since World War I" (Meyer, 1992).

The American physician Dr. Isaac Adler was the first scientist to propose a link between cigarette smoking and lung cancer in 1912, based on his observation that lung cancer patients often reported that they were smokers. Adler's observations, however, were anecdotal, and provided no scientific evidence toward demonstrating a relationship. The German epidemiologist Franz Müller is credited with the first case-control study of smoking and lung cancer in the 1930s. Müller sent a survey to the relatives of individuals who had died of cancer, and asked them about the smoking habits of the deceased. Based on the responses he received, Müller reported a higher incidence of lung cancer among heavy smokers compared to light smokers; however, the study had a number of problems. First, it relied on the memory of relatives of deceased individuals rather than first-hand observations, and second, no statistical association was made. Soon after this, the tobacco industry began to sponsor research with the biased goal of repudiating negative health claims against cigarettes (see our Scientific Institutions and Societies chapter for more information on sponsored research).

Figure 4: *Image from a stereoptic card showing a woman smoking a cigarette, circa 1900.*

Beginning in the 1950s, several well-controlled comparative studies were initiated. In 1950, Ernest Wynder and Evarts Graham published a retrospective study comparing the smoking habits of 605 hospital patients with lung cancer to 780 hospital patients with other diseases (Wynder and Graham, 1950). Their study showed that 1.3% of lung cancer patients were nonsmokers while 14.6% of patients with other diseases were nonsmokers. In addition, 51.2% of lung cancer patients were "excessive" smokers while only 19.1% of other patients were excessive smokers. Both of these comparisons proved to be statistically significant differences. The statisticians who analyzed the data concluded, "when the nonsmokers and the total of the high smoking classes of patients with lung cancer are compared with patients who have other diseases, we can reject the null hypothesis that smoking has no effect on the induction of cancer of the lungs." Wynder and Graham also suggested that there might be a lag of ten years or more between the period of smoking in an individual and the onset of clinical symptoms of cancer; this would present a major challenge to researchers as any study that investigated the relationship between smoking and lung cancer in a prospective fashion would have to last many years.

Richard Doll and Austin Hill published a similar comparative study in 1950 in which they showed that there was a statistically higher incidence of smoking among lung cancer patients compared to patients with other diseases (Doll and Hill, 1950). In their discussion, Doll and Hill raise an interesting point regarding comparative research methods by saying, "This is not necessarily to state that smoking causes carcinoma of the lung. The association would occur if carcinoma of the lung caused people to smoke or if both attributes were end-effects of a common cause." They go on to assert that because the habit of smoking was seen to develop before the onset of lung cancer, the argument that lung cancer leads to smoking can be rejected. They therefore conclude, "that smoking is a factor, and an important factor, in the production of carcinoma of the lung."

Despite this substantial evidence, both the tobacco industry and unbiased scientists raised objections, claiming that the retrospective research on smoking was "limited, inconclusive, and controversial." The industry stated that the studies published did not demonstrate cause and effect, but rather a spurious association between two variables. Dr. Wilhelm Hueper of the National Cancer Institute, a scientist with a long history of research into occupational causes of cancers, argued that the emphasis on cigarettes as the only cause of lung cancer would compromise research support for other causes of lung cancer. Ronald Fisher, a renowned statistician, also was opposed to the conclusions of Doll and others, purportedly because they promoted a "puritanical" view of smoking. The tobacco industry mounted an extensive campaign of misinformation, sponsoring and then citing research that showed that smoking did not cause "cardiac pain" as a distraction from the studies that were being published regarding cigarettes and lung cancer. The industry also highlighted studies that showed that individuals who quit smoking suffered from mild depression, and they pointed to the fact that even some doctors themselves smoked cigarettes as evidence that cigarettes were not harmful (Figure 5).

While the scientific research began to impact health officials and some legislators, the industry's ad campaign was effective. The U.S. Federal Trade Commission banned tobacco companies from making health claims about their products in 1955; however, more significant regulation was averted. An editorial that appeared in the *New York Times* in 1963 summed up the national sentiment when it stated that the tobacco industry made a "valid point," and the public should refrain from making a decision regarding cigarettes until further reports were issued by the U.S. Surgeon General.

Figure 5: Cigarette advertisement, circa 1946.

In 1951, Doll and Hill enrolled 40,000 British physicians in a prospective comparative study to examine the association between smoking and the development of lung cancer. In contrast to the retrospective studies that followed patients with lung cancer back in time, the prospective study was designed to follow the group forward in time. In 1952, Drs. E. Cuyler Hammond and Daniel Horn enrolled 187,783 white males in the United States in a similar prospective study. And in 1959, the American Cancer Society (ACS) began the first of two large-scale prospective studies of the association between smoking and the development of lung cancer. The first ACS study, named Cancer Prevention Study I, enrolled more than 1 million individuals and tracked their health, smoking and other lifestyle habits, development of diseases, cause of death, and life expectancy for almost 13 years (Garfinkel, 1985). All of the studies demonstrated that smokers are at a higher risk of developing and dying from lung cancer than non-smokers. The ACS study further showed that smokers have elevated rates of other pulmonary diseases, coronary artery disease, stroke, and cardiovascular problems. The two ACS Cancer Prevention Studies would eventually show that 52% of deaths among smokers enrolled in the studies were attributed to cigarettes.

In the second half of the 20th century, evidence from other scientific research methods would contribute multiple lines of evidence to the conclusion that cigarette smoke is a major cause of lung cancer. Descriptive studies of the pathology of lungs of deceased smokers would demonstrate that smoking causes significant physiological damage to the lungs. Experiments that exposed mice, rats, and other laboratory animals to cigarette smoke showed that it caused cancer in these animals (see the chapter on Experimentation for more information). And physiological models would help demonstrate the mechanism by which cigarette smoke causes cancer.

As evidence linking cigarette smoke, lung cancer and other diseases accumulated, the public, the legal community and regulators slowly responded. In 1957, the U.S. Surgeon General first acknowledged an association between smoking and lung cancer when a report was issued stating, "It is clear that there is an increasing and consistent body of evidence that excessive cigarette smoking is one of the causative factors in lung cancer." In 1965, over objections by the tobacco industry and the American Medical Association which had just accepted a $10 million grant from the tobacco companies, the U.S. Congress passed the Federal Cigarette Labeling and Advertising Act which required that cigarette packs carry the warning: "Caution: Cigarette Smoking May Be Hazardous to Your Health." In 1967, the U.S. Surgeon General issued a second report stating that cigarette smoking is the principal cause of lung cancer in the United States. While the tobacco companies found legal means to protect themselves for decades following this, in 1996, Brown and Williamson Tobacco Company was ordered to pay $750,000 in a tobacco liability lawsuit; it became the first liability award paid to an individual by a tobacco company.

Comparison across disciplines

Comparative studies are used in a host of scientific disciplines, from anthropology to archaeology, comparative biology, epidemiology, psychology, and even forensic science. DNA fingerprinting, a technique used to incriminate or exonerate a suspect using biological evidence, is based on comparative science. In DNA fingerprinting, segments of DNA are isolated from a suspect and from biological evidence such as blood, semen, or other tissue left at a crime scene. Up to 20 different segments of DNA are compared between that of the suspect and the DNA found at the crime scene. If all of the segments match, the investigator can calculate the statistical probability that the DNA came from the suspect as opposed to someone else. Thus DNA matches are described in terms of a "1 in 1 million" or "1 in 1 billion" chance of error.

Comparative methods are also commonly used in studies involving humans due to the ethical limits of experimental treatment. For example, in 2007, Petter Kristensen and Tor Bjerkedal published a study in which they compared the IQ of over 250,000 male Norwegians in the military (Kristensen and Bjerkedal, 2007). The researchers found a significant relationship between birth order and IQ, where the average IQ of first-born male children was approximately three points higher than the average IQ of the second-born male in the same family. The researchers further showed that this relationship was correlated with social, rather than biological factors, as second born males who grew up in families in which the first-born child died had average IQs similar to other first-born children. One might imagine a scenario in which this type of study could be carried out experimentally, for example, purposefully removing first-born male children from certain families, but the ethics of such an experiment preclude it from ever being conducted.

Limitations of comparative methods

One of the primary limitations of comparative methods is the control of other variables that might influence a study. For example, as pointed out by Doll and Hill in 1950, the association between smoking and cancer deaths could have meant that: a) smoking caused lung cancer, b) lung cancer caused individuals to take up smoking, or c) a third unknown variable caused lung cancer AND caused individuals to smoke (Doll and Hill, 1950). As a result, comparative researchers often go to great lengths to choose two different study groups that are similar in almost all respects except for the treatment in question. In fact, many comparative studies in humans are carried out on identical twins for this exact reason. For example, in the field of tobacco research, dozens of comparative twin studies have been used to examine everything from the health effects of cigarette smoke to the genetic basis of addiction.

Comparison in modern practice

Despite the lessons learned during the debate that ensued over the possible effects of cigarette smoke, misconceptions still surround comparative science. For example, in the late 1950s, Charles Keeling, an oceanographer at the Scripps Institute of Oceanography, began to publish data he had gathered from a long-term descriptive study of atmospheric carbon dioxide (CO_2) levels at the Mauna Loa observatory in Hawaii (Keeling, 1958). Keeling observed that atmospheric CO_2 levels were increasing at a rapid rate (Figure 6). He and other researchers began to suspect that rising CO_2 levels were associated with increasing global mean temperatures, and several comparative studies have since correlated rising CO_2 levels with rising global temperature (Keeling, 1970). Together with research from modeling studies, this research has provided evidence for an association between global climate change and the burning of fossil fuels (which emits CO_2). Yet in a move reminiscent of the fight launched by the tobacco companies, the oil and fossil fuel industry launched a major public relations campaign against climate change research. As late as 1989, scientists funded by the oil industry were producing reports that called the research on climate change "noisy junk science" (Roberts, 1989). As with the tobacco issue, challenges to early comparative studies tried to paint the method as less reliable than experimental methods. But the challenges actually strengthened the science by prompting more researchers to launch investigations, thus providing multiple lines of evidence supporting an association between atmospheric CO_2 concentrations and climate change. As a result, the culmination of multiple lines of scientific evidence prompted the Intergovernmental Panel on Climate Change organized by the United Nations to issue a report stating that "Warming of the climate system is unequivocal" and "Carbon dioxide is the most important anthropogenic greenhouse gas" (IPCC, 2007).

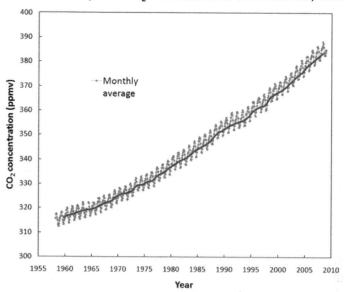

Atmospheric CO$_2$ Concentrations at Mauna Loa, Hawaii

Figure 6: *The "Keeling curve," a long-term record of atmospheric CO$_2$ concentration measured at the Mauna Loa Observatory (Keeling et al.). Although the annual oscillations represent natural, seasonal variations, the long-term increase means that concentrations are higher than they have been in 400,000 years.*

Comparative studies are a critical part of the spectrum of research methods currently used in science. They allow scientists to apply a treatment-control design in settings that preclude experimentation, and they can provide invaluable information about the relationships between variables. The intense scrutiny that comparison has undergone in the public arena due to cases involving cigarettes and climate change have actually strengthened the method by clarifying its role in science and emphasizing the reliability of data obtained from these studies.

Key Concepts for this chapter

▶ Comparison is used to determine and quantify relationships between two or more variables by observing different groups that either by choice or circumstance are exposed to different treatments.

▶ Comparison includes both retrospective studies that look at events that have already occurred, and prospective studies, that examine variables from the present forward.

▶ Comparative research is similar to experimentation in that it involves comparing a treatment group to a control, but it differs in that the treatment is observed rather than being consciously imposed due to ethical concerns, or because it is not possible, such as in a retrospective study.

References

Borio, G. (2003). *The Twentieth Century 1950 – 1999: The Battle is Joined*. Retrieved August 1, 2007, from the Tobacco Timeline, tobacco.org.

Dremann, S. (2007). Got a light? *Palo Alto Weekly*, March 14, 2007

Doll, R. (1999). Tobacco: A Medical History. *Journal of Urban Health: Bulletin of the New York Academy of Medicine* 76(3), 289-313.

Doll, R., & Hill, A.B. (1950). Smoking and Carcinoma of the lung. *British Medical Journal* 2(4682), 739-748.

Enersen, O.D. (2007). Edward Tyson. Retrieved August 1, 2007, from *Who Named It*

Forest, C., Webster, M., & Reilly, J. (2004). Narrowing uncertainty in global climate change. *The Industrial Physicist* issue 7/23

Garfinkel, L. (1985). Selection, Follow-up, and Analysis in the American Cancer Society Prospective Studies. *NCI Monograph No. 67*, 49–52. Bethesda, MD: U.S. Department of Health and Human Services, National Cancer Institute.

IPCC – Intergovernmental Panel on Climate Change (2007). Working Group I Report: The Physical Science Basis. United Nations Environment Program, Geneva, http://www.ipcc.ch/.

Keeling, C. (1958) The concentration and isotopic abundances of atmospheric carbon dioxide in rural areas. *Geochimica et Cosmochimica Acta*, 13(4), 322-334

Keeling, C. (1970). Is Carbon Dioxide from Fossil Fuel Changing Man's Environment? *Proceedings of the American Philosophical Society* 114(1), 10-17.

Kristensen, P., & Bjerkedal, T. (2007). Explaining the Relation between Birth Order and Intelligence. *Science* 316(5832), 1717.

Kundi, M. (2006). Causality and the interpretation of epidemiologic evidence. *Environ. Health Perspect.* 114(7), 969–974.

Maisel, A.Q. (1950). Don't Smoke - Unless You Like It. *Collier's*, November 4, 1950, 18.

Meyer, J.A. (1992). Cigarette Century. *American Heritage Magazine* 43(8)

NCI - National Cancer Institute (1997). Changes in Cigarette-Related Disease Risks and Their Implications for Prevention and Control. *Smoking and Tobacco Control Monographs*, National Institutes of Health

Newman, C. (1975). Edward Tyson. *British Medical Journal* 4, 96-97.

Roberts, L. (1989). Global Warming: Blaming the Sun. *Science* 246(4933), 992-93.

Russell, K.F. (1967). Edward Tyson's Orang-Outang. *Medical History* 11(4), 417-423.

Salsburg, D. (2001). *The Lady Tasting Tea: How Statistics Revolutionized Science in the Twentieth Century*, W.H. Freeman & Company, New York.

Witschi, H. (2001). A Short History of Lung Cancer. *Toxicological Sciences* 4(1), 4-6.

Wynder, E.L., & Graham, E.A. (1950). Tobacco smoking as a possible etiological factor in bronchiogenic carcinoma. *Journal of the American Medical Association* 143(4), 329-338.

Modeling

"Dr. Richardson said that the atmosphere resembled
London for in both there were always far more things
going on than anyone could properly attend to."

~ George C. Simpson

LEGO® bricks have been a staple of the toy world since they were first manufactured in Denmark in 1953. The interlocking plastic bricks can be assembled into an endless variety of objects (see Figure 1). Some kids (and even many adults) are interested in building the perfect model – finding the bricks of the right color, shape, and size, and assembling them into a replica of a familiar object in the real world, like a castle, the space shuttle, or London Bridge. Others focus on using the object they build – moving LEGO knights in and out of the castle shown in Figure 1, for example, or enacting a space shuttle mission to Mars. Still others may have no particular end product in mind when they start snapping bricks together and just want to see what they can do with the pieces they have.

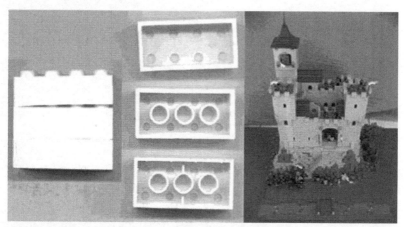

Figure 1: On the left, individual LEGO® bricks, showing how they interlock. On the right, a model of a castle, complete with moat and castle guards, built with LEGO bricks.

On the most basic level, scientists use models in much the same way that people play with LEGO bricks. Scientific models may or may not be physical entities, but scientists build them for the same variety of reasons: to replicate systems in the real world through simplification, to perform an experiment that cannot be done in the real world, or to assemble several known ideas into a coherent whole to build and test hypotheses. At the St. Anthony Falls Laboratory at the University of Minnesota, for example, a group of engineers and geologists have built a room-sized physical replica of a river delta similar to a real one like the Mississippi River delta in the Gulf of Mexico (Paola *et al.*, 2001). These researchers have successfully incorporated into their model the key processes that control river deltas (like the variability of water flow, the deposition of sediments transported by the river, and the compaction and subsidence of the coastline under the pressure of constant sediment additions) in order to better understand how those processes interact. With their physical model, they can mimic the general setting of the Mississippi River delta and then do things they can't do in the real world, like take a slice through the resulting sedimentary deposits to analyze the layers within the sediments. Or they can experiment with changing parameters like sea level and sedimentary input to see how those changes affect deposition of sediments within the delta, the same way you might "experiment" with the placement of the knights in your LEGO castle.

Figure 2: A photograph of the St. Anthony Falls lab river delta model, showing the experimental set-up with water flowing over sediments.

Not all models used in scientific research are physical models. Some are conceptual, and involve assembling all of the known components of a system into a coherent whole. This is a little like building an abstract sculpture out of LEGO bricks rather than building a castle. For example, over the past several hundred years, scientists have developed a series of models for the structure of an atom. The earliest known model of the atom compared it to a billiard ball, reflecting what scientists knew at the time – they were the smallest piece of an element that maintained the properties of that element. Despite the fact that this was a purely conceptual model, it could be used to predict some of the behavior that atoms exhibit. However, it did not explain all of the properties of atoms accurately. With the discovery of subatomic particles like the proton and electron, the physicist Ernest Rutherford proposed a "solar system" model of the atom, in which electrons orbited around a nucleus that included protons. While the Rutherford model is useful for understanding basic properties of atoms, it eventually proved insufficient to explain all of the behavior of atoms. The current quantum model of the atom depicts electrons not as pure particles, but as having the properties of both particles and waves, and these electrons are located in specific probability density clouds around the atom's nucleus.

Both physical and conceptual models continue to be important components of scientific research. In addition, many scientists now build models mathematically through computer programming. These computer-based models serve many of the same purposes as physical models, but are determined entirely by mathematical relationships between variables that are defined numerically. The mathematical relationships are kind of like individual LEGO bricks: they are basic building blocks that can be assembled in many different ways. In this case, the building blocks are fundamental concepts and theories like the mathematical description of turbulent flow in a liquid, the law of conservation of energy, or the laws of thermodynamics, which can be assembled into a wide variety of models for, say, the flow of contaminants released into a groundwater reservoir or for global climate change.

Modeling as a scientific research method

Whether developing a conceptual model like the atomic model, a physical model like a miniature river delta, or a computer model like a global climate model, the first step is to define the system that is to be modeled and the goals for the model. "System" is a generic term that can apply to something very small (like a single atom), something very large (the earth's atmosphere), or something in between, like the distribution of nutrients in a local stream. So defining the system generally involves drawing the boundaries (literally or figuratively) around what you want to model, and then determining the key variables and the relationships between those variables.

Though this initial step may seem straightforward, it can be quite complicated. Inevitably, there are many more variables within a system than can be realistically included in a model, so scientists need to simplify. To do this, they make assumptions about which variables are most important. In building a physical model of a river delta, for example, the scientists made the assumption that biological processes like burrowing clams were not important to the large-scale structure of the delta, even though they are clearly a component of the real system. Determining where simplification is appropriate takes a detailed understanding of the real system – and in fact, sometimes models are used to help determine exactly which aspects of the system can be simplified. For example, the scientists who built the model of the river delta did not incorporate burrowing clams into their model because they knew from experience that the clams would not affect the overall layering of sediments within the delta. On the other hand, they were aware that vegetation strongly affects the shape of the river channel (and thus the distribution of sediments), and therefore conducted an experiment to determine the nature of the relationship between vegetation density and river channel shape (Gran and Paola, 2001).

Once a model is built (either in concept, physical space or in a computer), it can be tested using a given set of conditions. The results of these tests can then be compared against reality in order to validate the model; in other words, how well does the model match what we see in the real world? In the physical model of delta sediments, the scientists who built the model looked for features like the layering of sand that they have seen in the real world. If the model shows something really different than what the scientists expect, the relationships between variables may need to be redefined or the scientists may have oversimplified the system. Then the model is revised, improved, tested again, and compared to observations again in an ongoing, iterative process. For example, the conceptual "billiard ball" model of the atom used in the early 1800s worked for some aspects of the behavior of gases, but when that hypothesis was tested for chemical reactions, it didn't do a good job of explaining how they occur – billiard balls do not normally interact with one another. John Dalton envisioned a revision of the model in which he added "hooks" to the billiard ball model to account for the fact that atoms could join together in reactions, as conceptualized in Figure 3.

While conceptual and physical models have long been a component of all scientific disciplines, computer-based modeling is a more recent development, and one that is frequently misunderstood. Computer models are based on exactly the same principles as conceptual and physical models, however, and they take advantage of relatively recent advances in computing power to mimic real systems.

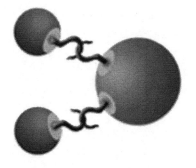

Figure 3. Dalton's ball and hook model for the atom.

The beginning of computer modeling: Numerical weather prediction

In the late 19th century, Vilhelm Bjerknes, a Norwegian mathematician and physicist, became interested in deriving equations that govern the large-scale motion of air in the atmosphere. Importantly, he recognized that circulation was the result not just of thermodynamic properties (like the tendency of hot air to rise), but of hydrodynamic properties as well, which describe the behavior of fluid flow. Through his work, he developed an equation that described the physical processes involved in atmospheric circulation, which he published in 1897. The complexity of the equation reflected the complexity of the atmosphere, and Bjerknes was able to use it to describe why weather fronts develop and move.

Bjerknes had another vision for his mathematical work, however: he wanted to predict the weather. The goal of weather prediction, he realized, is not to know the paths of individual air molecules over time, but to provide the public with "average values over large areas and long periods of time." Because his equation was based on physical principles, he saw that by entering the present values of atmospheric variables like air pressure and temperature, he could solve it to predict the air pressure and temperature at some time in the future. In 1904, Bjerknes published a short paper describing what he called "the principle of predictive meteorology" (Bjerknes, 1904). In it, he says:

> Based upon the observations that have been made, the initial state of the atmosphere is represented by a number of charts which give the distribution of seven variables from level to level in the atmosphere. With these charts as the starting point, new charts of a similar kind are to be drawn, which represent the new state from hour to hour.

In other words, Bjerknes envisioned drawing a series of weather charts for the future based on using known quantities and physical principles. He proposed that solving the complex equation could be made more manageable by breaking it down into a series of smaller, sequential calculations, where the results of one calculation are used as input for the next. As a simple example, imagine predicting traffic patterns in your neighborhood. You start by drawing a map of your neighborhood showing the location, speed, and direction of every car within a square mile. Using these parameters, you then calculate where all of those cars are one minute later. Then again after a second minute. Your calculations will likely look pretty good after the first minute. After the second, third, and fourth minutes, however, they begin to become less accurate. Other factors you had not included in your calculations begin to exert an influence, like where the person driving the car wants to go, the right- or left-hand turns that they make, delays at traffic lights and stop signs, and how many new drivers have entered the roads. Trying to include all of this information simultaneously would be mathematically difficult, so, as proposed by Bjerknes, the problem can be solved with sequential calculations. To do this, you would take the first step as described above: use location, speed, and direction to calculate where all the cars are after one minute. Then you would use information on right- and left-hand turn frequency to calculate changes in direction, then you would use information on traffic light delays and new traffic to calculate changes in speed. After these three steps are done, you would then solve your first equation again for the second minute time sequence, using location, speed, and direction to calculate where the cars are after the second minute. Though it would certainly be rather tiresome to do by hand, this series of sequential calculations would provide a manageable way to estimate traffic patterns over time.

Although this method made calculations tedious, Bjerknes imagined "no intractable mathematical difficulties" with predicting the weather. The method he proposed (but never used himself) became known as numerical weather prediction, and it represents one of the first approaches towards numerical modeling of a complex, dynamic system.

Bjerknes' challenge for numerical weather prediction was taken up sixteen years later in 1922 by the English scientist Lewis Fry Richardson. Richardson related seven differential equations that built on Bjerknes' atmospheric circulation equation to include additional atmospheric processes. One of Richardson's great contributions to mathematical modeling was to solve the equations for boxes within a grid; he divided the atmosphere over Germany into 25 squares that corresponded with available weather station data (see Figure 4), then divided the atmosphere into five layers, creating a three-dimensional grid of 125 boxes. This was the first use of a technique that is now standard in many types of modeling. For each box, he calculated each of nine variables in seven equations for a single time step of three hours. This was not a simple sequential calculation, however, since the values in each box depended on the values in the adjacent boxes, in part because the air in each box does not simply stay there – it moves from box to box.

Richardson's attempt to make a six-hour forecast took him nearly six weeks of work with pencil and paper and was considered an utter failure, as it resulted in calculated barometric pressures that exceeded any historically measured value (Dalmedico, 2001). Probably influenced by Bjerknes, Richardson attributed the failure to inaccurate input data, whose errors were magnified through successive calculations (see more about error propagation in the Uncertainty, Error, and Confidence chapter).

In addition to his concerns about inaccurate input parameters, Richardson realized that weather prediction was limited in large part by the speed at which individuals could calculate by hand. He thus envisioned a "forecast factory," in which thousands of people would each complete one small part of the necessary calculations for rapid weather forecasting. His vision became reality in a sense with the birth of the computer, which was able to do calculations far faster and with fewer errors than humans. The computer used for the first one-day weather prediction in 1950, nicknamed ENIAC (Electronic Numerical Integrator and Computer), was 8 feet tall, 3 feet wide,

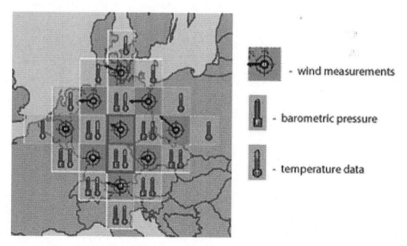

Figure 4: Data for Richardson's forecast included measurements of winds, barometric pressure and temperature. Initial data were recorded in 25 squares, each 200 kilometers on a side, but conditions were forecast only for the two central squares outlined in dark gray.

and 100 feet long – a behemoth by modern standards, but it was so much faster than Richardson's hand calculations that by 1955, meteorologists were using it to make forecasts twice a day (Weart, 2003). Over time, the accuracy of the forecasts increased as better data became available over the entire globe through radar technology and eventually, satellites.

The process of numerical weather prediction developed by Bjerknes and Richardson laid the foundation not only for modern meteorology, but for computer-based, mathematical modeling as we know it today. In fact, after Bjerknes died in 1951, the Norwegian government recognized the importance of his contributions to the science of meteorology by issuing a stamp bearing his portrait in 1962 (Figure 5).

Figure 5: Norwegian stamp bearing an image of Vilhelm Bjerknes.

Modeling in practice:
The development of global climate models

The desire to model earth's climate on a long-term, global scale grew naturally out of numerical weather prediction. The goal was to use equations to describe atmospheric circulation in order to understand not just tomorrow's weather, but large-scale patterns in global climate, including dynamic features like the jet stream and major climatic shifts over time like ice ages. Initially, scientists were hindered in the development of valid models by three things: a lack of data from the more inaccessible components of the system like the upper atmosphere, the sheer complexity of a system that involved so many interacting components, and limited computing powers. Unexpectedly, World War II helped solve one problem as the newly-developed technology of high altitude aircraft offered a window into the upper atmosphere. The jet stream, now a familiar feature of the weather broadcast on the news, was in fact first documented by American bombers flying westward to Japan.

As a result, global atmospheric models began to feel more within reach. In the early 1950s, Norman Phillips, a meteorologist at Princeton University, built a mathematical model of the atmosphere based on fundamental thermodynamic equations (Phillips, 1956). He defined 26 variables related through 47 equations, which described things like evaporation from the earth's surface, the rotation of the earth, and the change in air pressure with temperature. In the model, each of the 26 variables was calculated in each square of a 16 x 17 grid that represented a piece of the northern hemisphere. The grid represented an extremely simple landscape – it had no continents or oceans, no mountain ranges or topography at all. This was not because Phillips thought it was an accurate representation of reality, but because it simplified the calculations. He started his model with the atmosphere "at rest," with no predetermined air movement, and with yearly averages of input parameters, like air temperature.

Phillips ran the model through 26 simulated day-night cycles by using the same kind of sequential calculations Bjerknes proposed. Within only one "day," a pattern in atmospheric pressure developed that strongly resembled the typical weather systems of the portion of the northern hemisphere he was modeling (see Figure 6). In other words, despite the simplicity of the model, Phillips was able to reproduce key features of atmospheric circulation, showing that the topography of the earth was not of primary importance in atmospheric circulation. His work laid the foundation for an entire subdiscipline within climate science: development and refinement of General Circulation Models (GCMs).

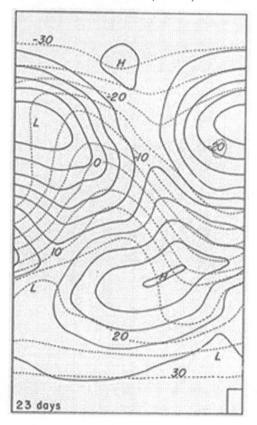

Figure 6: A model result from Phillips' 1956 paper. The box in the lower right shows the size of a grid cell. The solid lines represent the elevation of the 1000 millibar pressure, so the H and L represent areas of high and low pressure, respectively. The dashed lines represent lines of constant temperature, indicating a decreasing temperature at higher latitudes. This is the 23rd simulated day.

By the 1980s, computing power had increased to the point where modelers could incorporate the distribution of oceans and continents into their models. In 1991, the eruption of Mt. Pinatubo in the Philippines provided a natural experiment: how would the addition of a significant volume of sulfuric acid, carbon dioxide, and volcanic ash affect global climate? In the aftermath of the eruption, descriptive methods were used to document its effect on global climate: worldwide measurements of sulfuric acid and other components were taken, along with the usual air temperature measurements. Scientists could see that the large eruption had affected climate, and they quantified the extent to which it had done so. This provided a perfect test for the GCMs: given the inputs from the eruption, could they accurately reproduce the effects that descriptive research had shown? Within a few years, scientists had demonstrated that GCMs could indeed reproduce the climatic effects induced by the eruption, and confidence in the abilities of GCMs to provide reasonable scenarios for future climate change grew. The validity of these models has been further substantiated by their ability to simulate past events, like ice ages, and the agreement of many different models on the range of possibilities for warming in the future, one of which is shown in Figure 7.

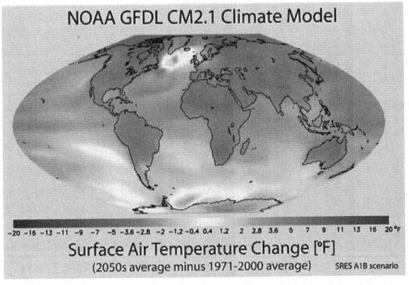

Figure 7: Projected change in annual mean surface air temperature from the late 20th century (1971-2000 average) to the middle 21st century (2051-2060 average).

Limitations and misconceptions of models

The widespread use of modeling has also led to widespread misconceptions about models, particularly with respect to their ability to predict. Some models are widely used for prediction, such as weather and streamflow forecasts, yet we know that weather forecasts are often wrong. Modeling still cannot predict exactly what will happen to the earth's climate, but it can help us see the range of possibilities with a given set of changes. For example, many scientists have modeled what might happen to average global temperatures if the concentration of carbon dioxide (CO_2) in the atmosphere is doubled from pre-industrial levels (pre 1950); though individual models differ in exact output, they all fall in the range of an increase of 2 to 6° C (IPCC, 2007).

All models are also limited by the availability of data from the real system. As the amount of data from a system increases, so will the accuracy of the model. For climate modeling, that is why scientists continue to gather data about climate in the geologic past and monitor things like ocean temperatures with satellites – all that data helps define parameters within the model. The same is true of physical and conceptual models, too, well-illustrated by the evolution of our model of the atom as our knowledge about subatomic particles increased.

Modeling in modern practice

The various types of modeling play important roles in virtually every scientific discipline, from ecology to analytical chemistry and from population dynamics to geology. Physical models such as the river delta take advantage of cutting edge technology to integrate multiple large-scale processes. As computer processing speed and power have increased, so has the ability to run models on them. From the room-sized ENIAC in the 1950s to the closet-sized Cray supercomputer in the 1980s to today's laptop, processing speed has increased over a million-fold, allowing scientists to run models on their own computers rather than booking time on one of only a few supercomputers in the world. Our conceptual models continue to evolve, and one of the more recent theories in theoretical physics digs even deeper into the structure of the atom to propose that what we once thought were the most fundamental particles – quarks – are in fact composed of vibrating filaments, or strings. String theory is a complex conceptual model that may help explain gravitational force in a way that has not been done before. Modeling has also moved out of the realm of science into recreation, and many computer games like SimCity® involve both conceptual modeling (answering the question, "What would it be like to run a city?") and computer modeling, using the same kinds of equations that are used model traffic flow patterns in real cities. The accessibility of modeling as a research method allows it to be easily combined with other scientific research methods, and scientists often incorporate modeling into experimental, descriptive, and comparative studies.

Key Concepts for this chapter

▶ Modeling involves developing physical, conceptual, or computer-based representations of systems.

▶ Scientists build models to replicate systems in the real world through simplification, to perform an experiment that cannot be done in the real world, or to assemble several known ideas into a coherent whole to build and test hypotheses.

▶ Computer modeling is a relatively new scientific research method, but it is based on the same principles as physical and conceptual modeling.

References

Bjerknes, V. (1904). Das Problem der Wettervorhersage, betrachtet vom Standpunkte der Mechanik und der Physik. *Meteorologische Zeitschrift*, 21, 1-7.

Dalmedico, A. D. (2001). History and Epistemology of Models: Meteorology (1946-1963) as a Case Study. *Archive for History of Exact Sciences*, 55(5), 395.

Gran, K., & Paola, C. (2001). Riparian vegetation controls on braided stream dynamics. *Water Resources Research*, 37(12), 3275-3283.

IPCC. (2007). *Climate Change 2007: The Physical Science Basis. Contribution of Working Group I to the Fourth Assessment Report of the Intergovernmental Panel on Climate Change.* New York, NY: Cambridge University Press.

Paola, C., Mullin, J., Ellis, C., Mohrig, D. C., Swenson, J. B., Parker, G., et al. (2001). Experimental Stratigraphy. *GSA Today*, 11(7), 4-9.

Phillips, N. A. (1956). The general circulation of the atmosphere: a numerical experiment. *Quarterly Journal of the Royal Meteorological Society*, 82(352), 123-164.

Scientific Data

Analysis and Interpretation

"The goal is to transform data into information, and information into insight."

~ Carly Fiorina

Before you decide what to wear in the morning, you collect a variety of data: the season of the year, what the forecast says the weather is going to be like, which clothes are clean and which are dirty, and what you will be doing during the day. You then analyze that data. Perhaps you think, "It's summer, so it's usually warm." That analysis helps you determine the best course of action, and you base your apparel decision on your interpretation of the information. You might choose a t-shirt and shorts on a summer day when you know you'll be outside, but bring a sweater with you if you know you'll be in an air-conditioned building.

Though this example may seem simplistic, it reflects the way scientists pursue data collection, analysis, and interpretation. Data (the plural form of the word datum) are scientific observations and measurements that, once analyzed and interpreted, can be developed into evidence to address a question. Data lie at the heart of all scientific investigations, and all scientists collect data in one form or another. The weather forecast that helped you decide what to wear, for example, was an interpretation made by a meteorologist who analyzed data collected by satellites. Data may take the form of the number of bacteria colonies growing in soup broth, a series of drawings or photographs of the different layers of rock that form a mountain range, a tally of lung cancer victims in populations of cigarette smokers and non-smokers, or the changes in average annual temperature predicted by a model of global climate (see the Research Methods section). Scientific data collection involves more care than you might use in a casual glance at the thermometer to see what you should wear. Because scientists build on their own work and the work of others, it is important that they are systematic and consistent in their data collection methods and make detailed records so that others can see and use the data they collect.

But collecting data is only one step in a scientific investigation, and scientific knowledge is much more than a simple compilation of data points. The world is full of observations that can be made, but not every observation constitutes a useful piece of data. For example, your meteorologist could record the outside air temperature every second of the day, but would that make the forecast any more accurate than recording it once an hour? Probably not. All scientists make choices about which data are most relevant to their research and what to do with that data: how to turn a collection of measurements into a useful dataset through processing and analysis, and how to interpret those analyzed data in the context of what they already know. The thoughtful and systematic collection, analysis, and interpretation of data allow it to be developed into evidence that supports scientific ideas, arguments, and hypotheses.

Data collection, analysis, and interpretation: Weather and climate

The weather has long been a subject of widespread data collection, analysis, and interpretation. Accurate measurements of air temperature became possible in the early 1700s when Daniel Gabriel Fahrenheit invented the first standardized mercury thermometer. Air temperature, wind speed, and wind direction are all critical navigational information for sailors on the ocean, but in the late 1700s and early 1800s, as sailing expeditions became common, this information was not easy to come by. The lack of reliable data was of great concern to Matthew Fontaine Maury, the superintendent of the Depot of Charts and Instruments of the U.S. Navy. As a result, Maury organized the first international Maritime Conference, held in Brussels, Belgium, in 1853. At this meeting, international standards for taking weather measurements on ships were established and a system for sharing this information between countries was founded. Defining uniform data collection standards was an important step in producing a truly global dataset of meteorological information, allowing data collected by many different people in different parts of the world to be gathered together into a single database. Maury's compilation of sailors' standardized data on wind and currents is shown in Figure 1. The early international cooperation and investment in weather-related data collection has produced a valuable long-term record of air temperature that goes back to the 1850s.

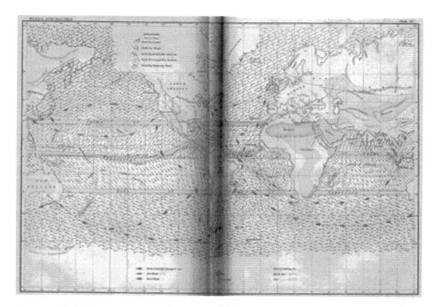

Figure 1: *Plate XV from Maury, Matthew F. 1858. The Winds. Chapter in:* Explanations and Sailing Directions. *Washington: Hon. Issaac Toucey.*

This vast store of information is considered "raw" data: tables of numbers (dates and temperatures), descriptions (cloud cover), location, etc. Raw data can be useful in and of itself – for example, if you wanted to know the air temperature in London on June 5th, 1801. But the data alone cannot tell you anything about how temperature has changed in London over the past two hundred years, or how that information is related to global-scale climate change. In order to see patterns and trends in the data, they must be analyzed and interpreted first. The analyzed and interpreted data may then be used as evidence in scientific arguments, to support an hypothesis or a theory.

error

Good data is a potential treasure trove – it can be mined by scientists at any time – and thus an important part of any scientific investigation is accurate and consistent recording of data and the methods used to collect that data. The weather data collected since the 1850s has been just such a treasure trove, based in part upon the standards established by Matthew Maury. These standards provided guidelines for data collections and recording that assured consistency within the dataset. At the time, ship captains were able to utilize the data to determine the most reliable routes to sail across the oceans. Many modern scientists studying climate change have taken advantage of this same dataset to understand how global air temperatures have changed over the recent past. In neither case can one simply look at the table of numbers and observations and answer the questions of which route to take or how global climate has changed. Instead, both questions require analysis and interpretation of the data.

Though it may sound simple to take 150 years of air temperature data and describe how global climate has changed, the process of analyzing and interpreting that data is actually quite complex. Consider the range of temperatures around the world on any given day in January (see Figure 2): in Johannesburg, South Africa, where it is summer, the air temperature can reach 35° C (95° F), and in Fairbanks, Alaska at that same time of year, it is the middle of winter and air temperatures might be -35° C (-31° F). Now consider the huge expanses of ocean, where no consistent measurements are available. One could simply take an average of all of the available measurements for a single day to get a global air temperature average for that day, but that number would not take into account the natural variability and uneven distribution of those measurements.

Defining a single global average temperature requires scientists to make several decisions about how to process all of that data into a meaningful set of numbers. In 1986, climatologists Phil Jones, Tom Wigley, and Peter Wright published one of the first attempts to assess changes in global mean surface air temperature from 1861 to 1984 (Jones, Wigley, and Wright, 1986). The majority of their paper – three out of five pages – describes the processing techniques they used to correct for the problems and inconsistencies in the historical data that would not be related to climate. For example, the authors note that::

> early SSTs [sea surface temperatures] were measured using water collected in uninsulated, canvas buckets, while more recent data come either from insulated bucket or cooling water intake measurements, with the latter considered to be 0.3-0.7° C warmer that uninsulated bucket measurements.

Correcting for this bias may seem simple, just adding ~0.5° C to early canvas bucket measurements, but it becomes more complicated than that because, the authors continue, the majority of SST data does not include a description of what kind of bucket or system was used.

Similar problems were encountered with marine air temperature data. Historical air temperature measurements over the ocean were taken aboard ships, but the type and size of ship could affect the measurement because size "determines the height at which observations were taken." Air tem-

Figure 2: Satellite image composite of average air temperatures (in degrees Celsius) across the globe on January 2, 2008.

perature can change rapidly with height above the ocean. The authors therefore applied a correction for ship size in their data. Once Jones, Wigley, and Wright had made several of these kinds of corrections, they analyzed their data using a spatial averaging technique that placed measurements within grid cells on the earth's surface in order to account for the fact that there were many more measurements taken on land than over the oceans. Developing this grid required many decisions based on their experience and judgment, such as how large each grid cell needed to be and how to distribute the cells over the earth. They then calculated the mean temperature within each grid cell, and combined all of these means to calculate a global average air temperature for each year. Statistical techniques such as averaging are commonly used in the research process and can help identify trends and relationships within and between data sets (see the Statistics chapter later in this section).

Once these spatially averaged global mean temperatures were calculated, the authors compared the means over time, from 1861 to 1984. A common method for analyzing data that occurs in a series, such as temperature measurements over time, is to look at anomalies, or differences from a pre-defined reference value. In this case, the authors compared their temperature values to the mean of the years 1970–1979 (see Figure 3). This reference mean is subtracted from each annual mean to produce the jagged lines, which display positive or negative anomalies (values greater or less than zero). Though this may seem to be a circular or complex way to display this data, it is useful because the goal is to show change in mean temperatures rather than absolute values.

Putting data into a visual format can facilitate additional analysis (see the chapter on Using Graphs and Visual Data). Figure 3 shows a lot of variability in the data: there are a number of spikes and dips in global temperature throughout the period examined. It can be challenging to see trends in data that have so much variability; our eyes are drawn to the extreme values in the jagged lines like the large spike in temperature around 1876 or the significant dip around 1918. However, these extremes do not necessarily reflect long-term trends in the data. In order to more clearly see long-term patterns and trends, Jones and his co-authors used another processing technique and applied a filter to the data by calculating a 10-year running average to smooth the data. The smooth lines in the graph represent the filtered data. The smooth line follows the data closely, but it does not reach the extreme values.

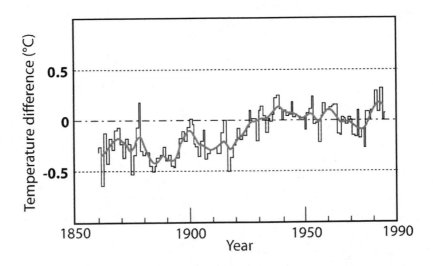

Figure 3: *The black line shows global temperature anomalies, or differences between averaged yearly temperature measurements and the reference value for the entire globe. The smooth, gray line is a filtered 10-year average. (Based on Figure 5 in Jones et al., 1986).*

Data processing and analysis are sometimes misinterpreted as manipulating data to achieve the desired results, but in reality, the goal of these methods is to make the data clearer, not to change it fundamentally. As described above, scientists report the data processing and analysis methods they use in addition to the data itself when they publish their work, allowing their peers the opportunity to assess both the raw data and the techniques used to analyze them.

The analyzed data can then be interpreted and explained. In general, when scientists interpret data, they attempt to explain the patterns and trends uncovered through analysis, bringing all of their background knowledge, experience, and skills to bear on the question and relating their data to existing scientific ideas. Given the personal nature of the knowledge they draw upon, this step can be subjective, but that subjectivity is scrutinized through the peer review process (see the Peer Review chapter). Based on the smoothed curves, Jones, Wigley, and Wright interpreted their data to show a long-term warming trend. They note that the three warmest years in the entire data set are 1980, 1981, and 1983. They do not go further in their interpretation to suggest possible causes for the temperature increase, however, but merely state that the results are "extremely interesting when viewed in the light of recent ideas of the causes of climate change."

The data presented in this study were widely accepted throughout the scientific community, in large part due to their careful description of the data and their process of analysis. Through the 1980s, however, a few scientists remained skeptical about their interpretation of a warming trend. In 1990, Richard Lindzen, a meteorologist at the Massachusetts Institute of Technology, published a paper expressing his concerns with the warming interpretation (Lindzen, 1990). Lindzen highlighted several issues that he believed weakened the arguments for global temperature increases. First, he argued that the data collection was inadequate, suggesting that the current network of data collection stations was not sufficient to correct for the uncertainty inherent in data with so much natural variability (consider how different the weather is in Antarctica and the Sahara Desert on any given day). Secondly, he argued that the data analysis was faulty, and that the substantial gaps in coverage, particularly over the ocean, raised questions regarding the ability of such a data set to adequately represent the global system. Finally, Lindzen suggested that the interpretation of the global mean temperature data is inappropriate, and that there is no trend in the data. He noted a decrease in the mean temperature from 1940 to 1970 at a time when atmospheric CO_2 levels, a proposed cause for the temperature increases, were increasing rapidly. In other words, Lindzen brought a differ-ent background and set of experiences and ideas to bear on the same dataset, and came to very different conclusions.

This type of disagreement is common in science, and generally leads to more data collection and research. In fact, the differences in interpreta-tion over the presence or absence of a trend motivated climate scientists to extend the temperature record in both directions – going back further into the past and continuing forward with the establishment of dedicated weath-er stations around the world. In 1998, Michael Mann, Raymond Bradley, and Malcolm Hughes published a paper that greatly expanded the record originally cited by Jones, Wigley, and Wright (Mann, Bradley, and Hughes, 1998). Of course, they were not able to use air temperature readings from thermometers to extend the record back to 1000 CE; instead, the authors used data from other sources that could provide information about air tempera-ture to reconstruct past climate, like tree ring width, ice core data, and coral growth records (Figure 4).

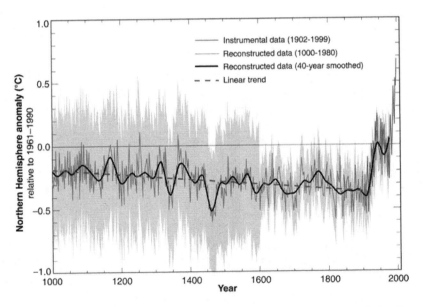

Figure 4: Differences between annual mean temperature and mean temperature during the reference period. Medium gray line represents data from tree ring, ice core and coral growth records, light dotted line represents data measured with modern instruments. Graph adapted from Mann et al. published in IPCC Third Assessment Report.

Mann, Bradley, and Hughes used many of the same analysis techniques as Jones and co-authors, such as applying a ten-year running average, and in addition, they included measurement uncertainty on their graph: the gray region shown on the graph in Figure 3. Reporting error and uncertainty for data does not imply that the measurements are wrong or faulty – in fact, just the opposite is true. The magnitude of the error describes how confident the scientists are in the accuracy of the data, so bigger reported errors indicate less confidence (see the Uncertainty, Error, and Confidence chapter). They note that the magnitude of the uncertainty increases going further back in time, but becomes more tightly constrained around 1900. In their interpretation, the authors describe several trends they see in the data: several warmer and colder periods throughout the record (for example, compare the data around year 1360 to 1460 in Figure 3), and a pronounced warming trend in the 20th century. In fact, they note that "almost all years before the twentieth century [are] well below the twentieth-century... mean," and these show a linear trend of decreasing temperature (Figure 3, light dashed line). Interestingly, where Jones *et al.* reported that the three warmest years were all within the last decade of their record, the same is true for the much more extensive dataset: Mann *et al.* report that the warmest years in their dataset, which runs through 1998, were 1990, 1995, and 1997.

The debate over the interpretation of data related to climate change as well as the interest in the consequences of these changes have led to an enormous increase in the number of scientific research studies addressing climate change, and multiple lines of scientific evidence now support the conclusions initially made by Jones, Wigley, and Wright in the mid-1980s. All of these results are summarized in the Fourth Assessment Report (AR4) of the Intergovernmental Panel on Climate Change (IPCC), released to the public in 2007 (IPCC, 2007). Based on the agreement between these multiple datasets, the team of contributing scientists wrote that, "Warming of the climate system is unequivocal, as is now evident from observations of increases in global average air and ocean temperatures, widespread melting of snow and ice, and rising global average sea level." The short phrase "now evident" reflects the accumulation of data over time, including the most recent data up to 2007.

A higher level of data interpretation involves determining the reason for the temperature increases. The AR4 goes on to say that "Most of the observed increase in global average temperatures since the mid-20th century is very likely due to the observed increase in anthropogenic greenhouse gas concentrations." This statement relies on many data sources in addition to the temperature data, including data as diverse as the timing of the first appearance of tree buds in spring, greenhouse gas concentrations in the atmosphere, and measurements of isotopes of oxygen and hydrogen from ice cores. Analyzing and interpreting such a diverse array of datasets requires the combined expertise of the many scientists that contributed to the IPCC report. This type of broad synthesis of data and interpretation is critical to the process of science, highlighting how individual scientists build on the work of others and potentially inspiring collaboration for further research between scientists in different disciplines.

Data interpretation is not a free-for-all, nor are all interpretations equally valid. Interpretation involves constructing a logical scientific argument that explains the data. Scientific interpretations are neither absolute truth nor personal opinion: they are inferences, suggestions, or hypotheses about what the data mean, based on a foundation of scientific knowledge and individual expertise. When scientists begin to interpret their data, they draw on their personal and collective knowledge, often talking over results with a colleague across the hall or on another continent. They use experience, logic, and parsimony to construct one or more plausible explanations for the data. As within any human endeavor, scientists can make mistakes or even intentionally deceive their peers (see the Scientific Ethics chapter), but the vast majority of scientists present interpretations that they feel are most reasonable and supported by the data.

Making data available

The process of data collection, analysis, and interpretation happens on multiple scales. It occurs over the course of a day, a year, or many years, and may involve one or many scientists whose priorities change over time. One of the fundamentally important components of the practice of science is therefore the publication of data in the scientific literature. Properly collected and archived data continues to be useful as new research questions emerge. In fact, some research involves re-analysis of data with new techniques, different ways of looking at the data, or combining the results of several studies. For example, in 1997, the Collaborative Group on Hormonal Factors in Breast Cancer published a widely-publicized study in the prestigious medical journal *The Lancet* entitled, "Breast cancer and hormone replacement therapy: collaborative reanalysis of data from 51 epidemiological studies of 52,705 women with breast cancer and 108,411 women without breast cancer" (Collaborative Group on Hormonal Factors in Breast Cancer, 1997). The possible link between breast cancer and hormone replacement therapy (HRT) had been studied for years, with mixed results: some scientists suggested a small increase of cancer risk associated with HRT as early as 1981 (Brinton *et al.*, 1981), but later research suggested no increased risk (Kaufman *et al.*, 1984). By bringing together results from numerous studies and reanalyzing the data together, the researchers concluded that women who were treated with hormone replacement therapy were more likely to develop breast cancer. In describing why the re-analysis was used, the authors write, "The increase in the relative risk of breast cancer associated with each year of [HRT] use in current and recent users is small, so inevitably some studies would, by chance alone, show significant associations and others would not. Combination of the results across many studies has the obvious advantage of reducing such random fluctuations."

In many cases, data collected for other purposes can be used to address new questions. The initial reason for collecting weather data, for example, was to better predict winds and storms to help assure safe travel for trading ships. It is only more recently that interest shifted to long-term changes in the weather, but the same data easily contributes to answering both of those questions.

For that reason, one of the most exciting advances in science today is the development of public databases of scientific information that can be accessed and used by anyone. For example, climatic and oceanographic data, which are generally very expensive to obtain because they require large-scale operations like drilling ice cores or establishing a network of buoys across the Pacific Ocean, are shared online through several web sites run by agencies responsible for maintaining and distributing that data, such as the Carbon Dioxide Information Analysis Center run by the U.S. Department of Energy. Anyone can download that data to conduct their own analyses and make interpretations. Likewise, the Human Genome Project has a searchable database of the human genome, where researchers can both upload and download their data. The number of these widely available datasets has grown to the point where the National Institute of Standards and Technology actually maintains a database of databases. Some organizations require their participants to make their data publicly available, such as the Incorporated Research Institutions for Seismology (IRIS): the instrumentation branch of IRIS provides support for researchers by offering seismic instrumentation, equipment maintenance and training, and logistical field support for experiments. Anyone can apply to use the instruments as long as they provide IRIS with the data they collect during their seismic experiments. IRIS then makes these data available to the public.

Making data available to other scientists is not a new idea, but having that data available on the Internet in a searchable format has revolutionized the way that scientists can interact with it, allowing for research efforts that would have been impossible before. This collective pooling of data also allows for new kinds of analysis and interpretation on global scales and over long periods of time. In addition, making data easily accessible helps promote interdisciplinary research by opening the doors to exploration by diverse scientists in many fields.

Key Concepts for this chapter

▶ Data collection is the systematic recording of information; data analysis involves working to uncover patterns and trends in data sets; data interpretation involves explaining those patterns and trends.

▶ Scientists interpret data based on their background knowledge and experience, thus different scientists can interpret the same data in different ways.

▶ By publishing their data and the techniques they used to analyze and interpret that data, scientists give the community the opportunity to both review the data and use it in future research.

References

Brinton, L. A., Hoover, R. N., Szklo, M., & Fraumeni, J. F. J. (1981). Menopausal estrogen use and risk of breast cancer. *Cancer*, 47(10), 2517-2522.

Collaborative Group on Hormonal Factors in Breast Cancer. (1997). Breast cancer and hormone replacement therapy: collaborative reanalysis of data from 51 epidemiological studies of 52,705 women with breast cancer and 108,411 women without breast cancer. *The Lancet*, 350(9084), 1047-1059.

IPCC. (2007). *Climate Change 2007: The Physical Science Basis. Contribution of Working Group I to the Fourth Assessment Report of the Intergovernmental Panel on Climate Change*. New York, NY: Cambridge University Press.

Jones, P. D., Wigley, T. M. L., & Wright, P. B. (1986). Global temperature variations between 1861 and 1984. *Nature*, 322(6078), 430-434.

Kaufman, D. W., Miller, D. R., Rosenberg, L., Helmrich, S. P., Stolley, P., Schottenfeld, D., et al. (1984). Noncontraceptive estrogen use and the risk of breast cancer. *JAMA*, 252(1), 63-67.

Lindzen, R. S. (1990). Some Coolness Concerning Global Warming. *Bulletin of the American Meteorological Society*, 71(3), 288-299.

Mann, M. E., Bradley, R. S., & Hughes, M. K. (1998). Global-scale temperature patterns and climate forcing over the past six centuries. *Nature*, 392(6678), 779-787.

Uncertainty, Error, and Confidence

"It is in the admission of ignorance and the admission of uncertainty that there is a hope for the continuous motion of human beings..."

~ Richard Feynman

The Olympic sport of biathlon (Figure 1) is a cross-country ski race of 20 km in which the athletes stop on four occasions to shoot 0.57 cm diameter bullets from a .22 caliber rifle at targets. The sport not only requires great endurance, but exceptional accuracy as the athletes shoot on two occasions from the prone position (lying down) and on two occasions while standing. The targets the athletes aim for are all 50 m away, but the size varies to match the precision expected of them; those targeted while shooting in the prone position are 4.5 cm in diameter while those targeted from the more difficult standing position are 11.5 cm in diameter. In both cases, however, the diameter of the target is many times larger than the diameter of the bullet itself – why?

While the legend of Robin Hood splitting one arrow with another is well-known, it is also unrealistic. Biathlon targets are purposely sized many times larger than the bullets the athletes shoot to account for the inherent error and uncertainty involved in long distance riflery. Even the most skilled marksman cannot account for every variable affecting the path of the bullet, like sudden gusts of wind or variations in air pressure. Shooting from the standing position involves even greater uncertainty, as indi-

Figure 1: *Biathletes in the shooting area of the competition.*

cated by the larger targets used, because even the simple rise and fall of an athlete's chest as they breathe can affect the aim of their rifle.

Scientific measurements also incorporate variability, and scientists report this as uncertainty in an effort to share with others the level of error that they found acceptable in their measurements. But uncertainty in science does not imply doubt as it does in everyday use. Scientific uncertainty is a quantitative measurement of variability in the data. In other words, uncertainty in science refers to the idea that all data have a range of expected values as opposed to a precise point value. This uncertainty can be categorized in two ways: accuracy and precision. Accuracy is a term that describes how well a measurement approximates the theoretically correct value of that measurement, for example, how close the arrow is to the bullseye (Figure 2). The term precision, by comparison, describes the degree to which individual measurements vary around a central value. Measurements with high precision are highly reproducible because repeated measurement will reliably give a similar result; however, they may or may not be accurate.

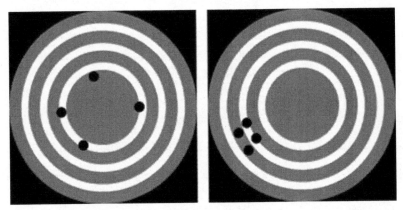

Figure 2: A representation of accuracy and precision as hits on a target. The target at left depicts good accuracy as the marks are close to the bullseye, but poor precision; while the target at right depicts good precision as the marks are grouped closely, but poor accuracy.

Uncertainty in nature

Karl Pearson, the English statistician and geneticist, is commonly credited with first describing the concept of uncertainty as a measure of data variability in the late 1800s (Salsburg, 2001). Before Pearson, scientists realized that their measurements incorporated variability, but they assumed that this variability was simply due to error. For example, measurement of the orbits of planets around the sun taken by different scientists at different times varied, and this variability was thought to be due to errors caused by inadequate instrumentation. The French mathematician Pierre-Simon Laplace discussed a method for quantifying error distributions of astronomical measurements caused by small errors associated with instrument shortcomings as early as 1820. As technology improved through the 1800s, astronomers realized that they could reduce, but not eliminate this error in their measurements. Pearson put forward a revolutionary idea: uncertainty, he proposed, was not simply due to the limits of technology in measuring certain events – it was inherent in nature. Even the most careful and rigorous scientific investigation (or any type of investigation for that matter) could not yield an exact measurement. Rather, repeating an investigation would yield a scatter of measurements that are distributed around some central value. This scatter would be caused not only by error, but also by natural variability. In other words, measurements themselves, independent of any human or instrument inaccuracies, exhibit scatter. Whether it is the flight path of an arrow, the resting heart rate of an adult male, or the age of a historical artifact, measurements do not have exact values, but instead always exhibit a range of values, and that range can be quantified as uncertainty. This uncertainty can be expressed as a plot of the probability of obtaining a certain value, and the probabilities are distributed about some central, or mean, value.

Uncertainty and error in practice – Carbon-14 dating

Archaeologists, paleontologists, and other researchers have long been interested in dating objects and artifacts in an effort to understand their history and use. Unfortunately, written records are a relatively recent human invention, and few historical artifacts are accompanied by precise written histories. In the first half of the 20th century, an American nuclear chemist by the name of Willard F. Libby became interested in using the radioactive isotope ^{14}C to date certain objects. The theory of radiocarbon dating is relatively simple. Most carbon in the earth's atmosphere is in the form of ^{12}C, but a small amount of the isotope ^{14}C is produced naturally through the bombardment of ^{14}N with cosmic rays (W. F. Libby, 1946). As plants take up carbon from the atmosphere through respiration, they incorporate both ^{14}C as well as the more abundant ^{12}C into their tissues. Animals also take up both carbon isotopes through the foods that they eat. Thus, all living organisms have the same ratio of ^{14}C and ^{12}C isotopes in their body as the atmosphere. Unlike ^{12}C, ^{14}C is a radioactive isotope that is constantly undergoing decay to its daughter product ^{14}N at a known rate. While an organism is alive, it is taking up new ^{14}C from the environment and thus remains in equilibrium with it. When that organism dies, however, the carbon in its tissues is no longer replaced, and the amount of ^{14}C slowly decreases in time as it decays to ^{14}N. Thus, the amount of radioactive ^{14}C remaining in a piece of wood or an animal bone can be used to determine when that organism died. In essence, the longer the organism has been dead, the lower the ^{14}C levels.

The amount of radioactive material (such as ^{14}C) in a sample can be quantified by counting the number of decays that the material undergoes in a specific amount of time, usually reported in counts per minute (cpm). When Libby began his radiocarbon work in the 1940s, the technology available was still quite new. A simple Geiger counter was only first invented in 1908 by the German scientist Hans Wilhelm Geiger, a student of Ernest Rutherford's, and it was not perfected until 1928 when Walther Müller, a student of Geiger's, improved on the design allowing it to detect all types of radiation. Libby himself is credited with building the first Geiger counter in the United States in the 1930s. But he faced a major hurdle with using the instrument to measure ^{14}C – naturally occurring background radiation from cosmic rays and the earth and the variability associated with that background signal would overwhelm the small ^{14}C signal he expected to see. In 1949, he reported on a method for reducing the background signal and variability, he placed the entire sample and the detector inside of a tube shielded by 2 inches of lead and 4 inches of iron (W. F. Libby, Anderson, and Arnold, 1949). In this way, Libby and his colleagues reduced the background signal from 150 cpm to 10 cpm and minimized the variability associated with the signal to "about 5–10% error" or less than 1 cpm. Libby and colleagues do not use the word error as we do in common language, where it refers to a mistake such as a typographical error or a baseball error. The Latin origin of the word error (errorem) means wandering or straying, and the scientific use of the word is closer to this original meaning. Libby calculated the error associated with his measurements by counting the number of decay events in the sample in a known amount of time, repeating the measurement over multiple periods, and then using statistical techniques to quantify the error.

In 1949, Libby, working with his post-doctoral student James Arnold, reported the first use of radiocarbon dating for determining the age of wood fragments from archaeological sites around the world (Arnold and Libby, 1949). Because the method was new, Arnold and Libby were careful to replicate their measurements to provide a detailed estimate of different types of error, and they compared the results of their method with samples of a known age as a control (Table 1).

Table 1: Age determinations on samples of known age, reproduced from Arnold and Libby (1949).

Sample	Specific Activity (cpm/g of carbon)	Age (years)	
Tree Ring	Found	Found	Expected
	11.10 ± 0.31	1100 ± 150	1372 ± 50
	11.52 ± 0.35		
	11.34 ± 0.25		
	10.15 ± 0.44		
	11.08 ± 0.31		
	Average: 10.99 ± 0.15		

The specific activities for five different replicates of a sample of wood from a Douglas fir excavated from the Red Rock Valley are shown in the second column of Table 1. Each individual measurement has an error shown to the right of it, indicated by the ± sign. Arnold and Libby describe these measurements in their paper, stating "The errors quoted for the specific activity measurements are standard deviations as computed from the Poisson statistics of counting random events." In other words, the individual error is calculated from the expected uncertainties associated with radioactive decay for each sample. As seen in Table 1, an average specific activity value (10.99) is provided at the bottom with an overall error. The overall error (0.15) is smaller than the individual error reported with each measurement. This is an important feature of the statistical calculation of error associated with scientific data – as you increase the number of measurements of a value, you decrease the uncertainty and increase the confidence associated with the approximation of the value. The error reported alongside the specific activity provides a measure of the precision of the value, and is commonly referred to as statistical error. Statistical error is what Pearson described as the inherent uncertainty of a measurement. It is caused by random fluctuations within a system, such as the random fluctuation of radioactive decay, and is sometimes referred to as random error as the researcher has little control over it. Statistical error cannot be eliminated, as Pearson described, but it can be measured and reduced by conducting repeated observations of a specific event.

In column 3 of Table 1, Arnold and Libby estimate the age of the Douglas fir sample based on the ^{14}C activity as 1,100 years old (placing its first season of growth in the year 849 CE). In column 4 of Table 1, they report the actual age of the Douglas fir as calculated by counting tree rings in the sample as 1,372 years old (placing its first season in the year 577 CE). By comparing the ^{14}C age to a theoretically correct value as determined by the tree ring count, Arnold and Libby allow the reader to gauge the accuracy of their method, and this provides a measure of a second type of error encountered in science: systematic error. Based on their data, Arnold and Libby state that the "agreement between prediction and observation is seen to be satisfactory." However, as he continued to do research to establish the method of ^{14}C dating, Libby began to recognize that the discrepancy between radiocarbon dating and other methods was even larger for older objects, especially those greater than 4,000 years old (W.F. Libby, 1963). Where theoretically correct dates on very old objects could be established by other means, such as in samples from the temples of Egypt where a calendar system was well-established, the ages obtained through the radiocarbon dating method were consistently older than the recorded dates, often by as much as 500 years. Libby knew that there was bound to be statistical error in these measurements and had anticipated using ^{14}C dating to calculate a range of dates for objects. But the problem he encountered was different: ^{14}C-dating systematically calculated ages that differed by as much as 500 years from the actual ages of older objects. Systematic error, like Libby encountered, is due to an unknown but non-random fluctuation, like instrumental bias or a faulty assumption. The radiocarbon dating method had achieved good precision, replicate analyses gave dates within 150 years of one another as seen in Table 1; but initially it showed poor precision – the ^{14}C age of the Douglas fir was almost 300 years different than the actual age, and other objects were off by some 500 years.

Unlike statistical error, systematic error can be compensated for, or sometimes even eliminated if its source can be identified. In the case of ^{14}C-dating, it was later discovered that the reason for the systematic error was a faulty assumption: Libby and many other scientists had assumed that the production rate for ^{14}C in the atmosphere was constant over time, but it is not. Instead, it fluctuates with changes in the earth's

Figure 3: Tree-ring dates have been used to recalibrate the radiocarbon dating method.

magnetic field, the uptake of carbon by plants, and other factors. In addition, levels of radioactive ^{14}C increased through the 20th century because nuclear weapons testing released high levels of radiation to the atmosphere.

In the decades since Libby first published his method, researchers have recalibrated the radiocarbon dating method with tree-ring dates from bristlecone pine trees (Damon *et al.*, 1974) and corals (Fairbanks *et al.*, 2005) to correct for the fluctuations in the production of ^{14}C in the atmosphere. As a result, both the precision and accuracy of radiocarbon dates have increased dramatically. For example, in 2000, Xiaohong Wu and colleagues at Peking University in Beijing used radiocarbon dating on bones of the Marquises (lords) of Jin recovered from a cemetery in Shanxi Province in China (Wu *et al.*, 2000). As seen in Table 2, not only is the precision of the estimates (ranging from 18 to 44 years) much tighter than Libby's reported 150 year error range for the Douglas fir samples, but the radiocarbon dates are highly accurate, with the reported deaths dates of the Jin (the theoretically correct values) falling within the statistical error ranges reported in all three cases.

Table 2: Radiocarbon estimates and documented death dates of three of the Marquises of Jin, reproduced from Wu et al. (2000).

Name of Jin Marquis	Radiocarbon Date (BCE)	Documented Death Rate (BCE)
Jing	860 - 816	841
Li	834 - 804	823
Xian	814 - 796	812

Confidence: Reporting uncertainty and error

As a result of error, scientific measurements are not reported as single values, but rather as ranges or averages with error bars in a graph or ± sign in a table. Karl Pearson first described mathematical methods for determining the probability distributions of scientific measurements, and these methods form the basis of statistical applications in scientific research (see our Statistics chapter). Statistical techniques allow us to estimate and report the error surrounding a value after repeated measurement of that value. For example, both Libby and Wu reported their estimates as ranges of one standard deviation around the mean, or average, measurement. The standard deviation provides a measure of the range of variability of individual measurements, and specifically, defines a range that encompasses 34.1% of individual measurements above the mean value and 34.1% of those below the mean. The standard deviation of a range of measurements can be used to compute a confidence interval around the value. Confidence statements do not, as some people believe, provide a measure of how "correct" a measurement is. Instead, a confidence statement describes the probability that a measurement range will overlap the mean value of a measurement when a study is repeated. This may sound a bit confusing, but consider a study by Yoshikata Morimoto and colleagues who examined the average pitch speed of eight college baseball players (Morimoto *et al.*, 2003). Each of the pitchers was required to throw six pitches and the average pitch speed was found to be 34.6 m/s (77.4 mph) with a 95% confidence interval of 34.6 ± 0.2 m/s (34.4 m/s to 34.8 m/s). When he later repeated this study requiring that each of the eight pitchers throw 18 pitches, the average speed was found to be 34.7 m/s, exactly within the confidence interval obtained during the first study. In this case, there is no "theoretically correct" value, but the confidence interval provides an estimate of the probability that a similar result will be found if the study is repeated. Given that Morimoto determined a 95% confidence interval, if he repeated his study 100 times (without exhausting his baseball pitchers), his confidence interval would overlap the mean pitch speed 95 times, and the other five studies would likely yield pitch speeds that fall outside of his confidence interval.

In science, an important indication of confidence within a measurement is the number of significant figures reported. Morimoto reported his measurement to one decimal place (34.6 m/s) because his instrumentation supported this level of precision. He was able to distinguish differences in pitches that were 34.6 m/s and 34.7 m/s. Had he just rounded his measurements to 35 m/s, he would have lost a significant amount of detail contained within his data. Further, his instrumentation did not support the precision needed to report additional significant figures (for example, 34.62 m/s). Incorrectly reporting significant figures can introduce substantial error into a data set.

Error propagation

As Pearson recognized, uncertainty is inherent in scientific research, and for that reason it is critically important for scientists to recognize and account for the errors within a dataset. Disregarding the source of an error can result in the propagation and magnification of that error. For example, in 1960 the American mathematician and meteorologist Edward Norton Lorenz was working on a mathematical model for predicting the weather (see the Modeling chapter for more on this) (Gleick, 1987; Lorenz, 1993). Lorenz was using a Royal McBee computer to iteratively solve 12 equations that expressed relationships such as that between atmospheric pressure and wind speed.

Lorenz would input starting values for several variables into his computer, such as temperature, wind speed, and barometric pressure on a given day at series of locations. The model would then calculate weather changes over a defined period of time. The model recalculated a single day's worth of weather changes in single minute increments and printed out the new parameters. On one occasion, Lorenz decided to rerun a particular model scenario. Instead of starting from the beginning, which would have taken many hours, he decided to pick up in the middle of the run, consulting the print out of parameters and re-entering these into his computer. He then left his computer for the hour it would take to recalculate the model, expecting to return and find a weather pattern similar to the one predicted previously.

Unexpectedly, Lorenz found that the resulting weather prediction was completely different from the original pattern he observed. What Lorenz did not realize at the time was that while his computer stored the numerical values of the model parameters to six significant figures (for example 0.639172), his printout, and thus the numbers he inputted when restarting the model, were rounded to three significant figures (0.639). The difference between the two numbers is minute, representing a margin of systematic error less than 0.1% – less than one thousandth of the value of each parameter. However, with each iteration of his model (and there were thousands of iterations), this error was compounded, multiplying many times over so that his end result was completely different from the first run of the model. As can be seen in Figure 4, the error appears to remain small, but after a few hundred iterations it grows exponentially until reaching a magnitude equivalent to the value of the measurement itself (~0.6).

Lorenz published his observations in the now classic work "Deterministic Nonperiodic Flow" (Lorenz, 1963). His observations led him to conclude that accurate weather prediction over a period of more than a few weeks was extremely difficult – perhaps impossible – because even infinitesimally small errors in the measurement of natural conditions were compounded and quickly reached levels equal to the measurements themselves. The work motivated other researchers to begin looking at other dynamic systems that are similarly sensitive to initial starting conditions, such as the flow of water in a stream or the dynamics of population change. In 1975, the American mathematician and physicist James Yorke and his collaborator, the Chinese-born mathematician Tien-Yien Li, coined the term "chaos" to describe these systems (Li and Yorke, 1975). Again, unlike the common use of the term chaos, which implies randomness or a state of disarray, the science of chaos is not about randomness. Rather, as Lorenz was the first to do, chaos researchers work to understand underlying patterns of behavior in complex systems toward understanding and quantifying this uncertainty.

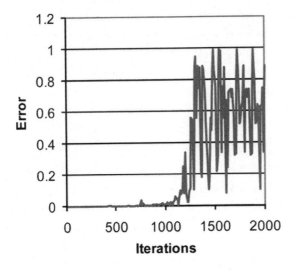

Figure 4: Representation of error propagation in an iterative, dynamic system. After ~1,000 iterations, the error is equivalent to the value of the measurement itself (~0.6) making the calculation fluctuate wildly. Adapted from IMO (2007).

Recognizing and reducing error

Error propagation is not limited to mathematical modeling. It is always a concern in scientific research, especially in studies that proceed stepwise in multiple increments because error in one step can easily be compounded in the next step. As a result, scientists have developed a number of techniques to help quantify error. The use of controls in scientific experiments helps quantify statistical error within an experiment and identify systematic error in order to either measure or eliminate it (see the Experimentation chapter). In research that involves human judgment, such as studies that try to quantify the perception of pain relief following administration of a pain-relieving drug, scientists often work to minimize error by using "blinds." In blind trials, the treatment (i.e. the drug) will be compared to a control (i.e. another drug or a placebo); neither the patient nor the researcher will know if the patient is receiving the treatment or the control. In this way, systematic error due to preconceptions about the utility of a treatment is avoided.

Error reduction and measurement efforts in scientific research are sometimes referred to as quality assurance and quality control. Quality assurance generally refers to the plans that a researcher has for minimizing and measuring error in his or her research; quality control refers to the actual procedures implemented in the research. The terms are most commonly used interchangeably and in unison, as in "quality assurance/quality control" (QA/QC). QA/QC includes steps such as calibrating instruments or measurements against known standards, reporting all instrument detection limits, implementing standardized procedures to minimize human error, thoroughly documenting research methods, replicating measurements to determine precision, and a host of other techniques, often specific to the type of research being conducted, and reported in the Materials and Methods section of a scientific paper.

Reduction of statistical error is often as simple as repeating a research measurement or observation many times to reduce the uncertainty in the range of values obtained. Systematic error can be more difficult to pin down, creeping up in research due to instrumental bias, human mistakes, poor research design, or incorrect assumptions about the behavior of variables in a system. From this standpoint, identifying and quantifying the source of systematic error in research can help scientists better understand the behavior of the system itself.

Uncertainty as a state of nature

While Karl Pearson proposed that individual measurements could not yield exact values, he felt that careful and repeated scientific investigation coupled with statistical analysis could allow one to determine the true value of a measurement. A younger contemporary of Pearson's, the English statistician Ronald Aylmer Fisher, extended and, at the same time, contradicted this concept. Fisher felt that because all measurements contained inherent error, one could never identify the exact or "correct" value of a measurement. According to Fisher, the true distribution of a measurement is unattainable; statistical techniques therefore do not estimate the "true" value of a measurement, rather they are used to minimize error and develop range estimates that approximate the theoretically correct value of the measurement. A natural consequence of his idea is that occasionally the approximation may be incorrect.

In the first half of the 20th century, the concept of uncertainty reached new heights with the discovery of quantum mechanics. In the quantum world, uncertainty is not an inconvenience; it is a state of being. For example, the decay of a radioactive element is inherently an uncertain event. We can predict the probability of the decay profile of a mass of radioactive atoms, but we can never predict the exact time that an individual radioactive atom will undergo decay. Or consider the Heisenberg Uncertainty Principle in quantum physics, which states that measuring the position of a particle makes the momentum of the particle inherently uncertain, and, conversely, measuring the particle's momentum makes its position inherently uncertain. Once we understand the concept of uncertainty as it applies to science, we can begin to see that the purpose of scientific data analysis is to identify and quantify error and variability toward uncovering the relationships, patterns, and behaviors that occur in nature. Scientific knowledge itself continues to evolve as new data and new studies help us understand and quantify uncertainty in the natural world.

Key Concepts for this chapter

▶ Uncertainty is the quantitative estimation of error present in data; all measurements contain some uncertainty generated through systematic error and/or random error.

▶ Acknowledging the uncertainty of data is an important component of reporting the results of scientific investigation.

▶ Uncertainty is commonly misunderstood to mean that scientists are not certain of their results, but the term specifies the degree to which scientists are confident in their data.

▶ Careful methodology can reduce uncertainty by correcting for systematic error and minimizing random error. However, uncertainty can never be reduced to zero.

References

Arnold, J. R., & Libby, W. F. (1949). Age Determinations by Radiocarbon Content: Checks with Samples of Known Age. *Science*, 110, 678-680.

Damon, P. E., Ferguson, C. W., Long, A., & Wallick, E. I. (1974). Dendrochronologic Calibration of the Radiocarbon Time Scale. *American Antiquity*, 39(2), 350-366.

Fairbanks, R. G., Mortlock, R. A., Chiu, T.-C., Cao, L., Kaplan, A., Guilderson, T. P., et al. (2005). Radiocarbon calibration curve spanning 0 to 50,000 years BP based on paired 230Th/ 234U/ 238U and 14C dates on pristine corals. *Quaternary Science Reviews*, 24, 1781-1796.

Gleick, J. (1987) *Chaos: Making a new science.* Penguin books, New York, USA.

IMO (2007) Long Range Weather Prediction. The Icelandic Meteorological Office, Retrieved December 18. 2007 from http://andvari.vedur.is/~halldor/HB/Met210old/pred.html.

Li, T.Y., Yorke, J.A. (1975). Period Three Implies Chaos. *Amer. Math. Monthly*, 82:985.

Libby, W. F. (1946). Atmospheric Helium Three and Radiocarbon from Cosmic Radiation. *Physical Review*, 69(11-12), 671-672.

Libby, W. F. (1963). Accuracy of Radiocarbon Dates. *Science*, 140, 278-280.

Libby, W. F., Anderson, E. C., & Arnold, J. R. (1949). Age Determination by Radiocarbon Content: World-Wide Assay of Natural Radiocarbon. *Science*, 109(2827), 227-228.

Lorenz, E. (1963) Deterministic Nonperiodic Flow. *Journal of the Atmospheric Sciences*, 20:130-141.

Lorenz, E. (1993) *The essence of chaos.* The University of Washington Press.

Morimoto, Y., Ito, K., Kawamura, T., Muraki, Y. (2003). Immediate effect of assisted and resisted training using different weight balls on ball speed and accuracy in baseball pitching. *International Journal of Sport and Health Science*, 1(2):238-246

Peat, F.D. (2002). *From Certainty to Uncertainty: The Story of Science and Ideas in the Twentieth Century.* Joseph Henry Press, National Academies Press

Salsburg, D. (2001). *The Lady Tasting Tea: How Statistics Revolutionized Science in the Twentieth Century,* W.H. Freeman & Company, New York.

Wagner, C.H. (1983). Uncertainty in Science and Statistics. *The Two-Year College Mathematics Journal,* 14(4):360-363.

Wu, X., Yuan, S., Wang, J., Guo, Z., Liu, K., Lu, X., et al. (2000). AMS radiocarbon dating of cemetery of Jin Marquises in China. *Nuclear Inst. and Methods in Physics Research,* B, 172(1-4), 732-735.

Statistics

"Statistics may be defined as a body of methods for making wise decisions in the face of uncertainty."

~ W. A. Wallis

M odern science is often based on statements of statistical significance and probability. For example: 1) studies have shown that the probability of developing lung cancer is almost 20-times greater in cigarette smokers compared to non-smokers (ACS, 2004); 2) there is a significant likelihood of a catastrophic meteorite impact on earth sometime in the next 200,000 years (Bland, 2005); and 3) first-born male children exhibit IQ test scores that are 2.82 points higher than second-born males, a difference that is significant at the 95% confidence level (Kristensen and Bjerkedal, 2007). But why do scientists speak in terms that seem obscure? If cigarette smoking causes lung cancer, why not simply say so? If we should immediately establish a colony on the moon to escape extraterrestrial disaster, why not inform people? And if older children are smarter than their younger siblings, why not let them know?

The reason is that none of these latter statements accurately reflect the data. Scientific data rarely lead to absolute conclusions. Not all smokers die from lung cancer – some smokers decide to quit, thus reducing their risk, some smokers may die prematurely from cardiovascular or diseases other than lung cancer, and some smokers may simply never contract the disease. All data exhibit variability, and it is the role of statistics to quantify this variability and allow scientists to make more accurate statements about their data.

A common misconception is that statistics provide a measure of proof that something is true, but they actually do no such thing. Instead, statistics provide a measure of the probability of observing a certain result. This is a critical distinction. For example, the American Cancer Society has conducted several massive studies of cancer in an effort to make statements about the risks of the disease in U.S. citizens. Cancer Prevention Study I enrolled approximately 1 million people between 1959 and 1960, and Cancer Prevention Study II was even larger, enrolling 1.2 million people in 1982. Both of these studies found much higher rates of lung cancer among cigarette smokers compared to non-smokers, however, not all individuals who smoked contracted lung cancer (and, in fact, some non-smokers did contract lung cancer). Thus, the development of lung cancer is a probability-based event, not a simple cause-and-effect relationship. Statistical techniques allow scientists to put numbers to this probability, moving from a statement like "if you smoke cigarettes, you are more likely to develop lung cancer" to the one that started this module: "the probability of developing lung cancer is almost 20-times greater in cigarette smokers compared to non-smokers." The quantification of probability offered by statistics is a powerful tool used widely throughout science, but it is frequently misunderstood.

What is statistics?

The field of statistics dates to 1654 when a French gambler, Antoine Gombaud, asked the noted mathematician and philosopher Blaise Pascal about how one should divide the stakes among players when a game of chance is interrupted prematurely. Pascal posed the question to the lawyer and mathematician Pierre de Fermat, and over a series of letters, Pascal and Fermat devised a mathematical system that not only answered Gombaud's original question, but laid the foundations of modern probability theory and statistics.

Figure 1: The field of statistics has its roots in calculations of the probable outcomes of games of chance.

From its roots in gambling, statistics has grown into a field of study that involves the development of methods and tests that are used to quantitatively define the variability inherent in data, the probability of certain outcomes, and the error and uncertainty associated with those outcomes (see the chapter Uncertainty, Error, and Confidence). As such, statistical methods are used extensively throughout the scientific process, from the design of research questions through data analysis and to the final interpretation of data. The specific statistical methods used vary widely between different scientific disciplines; however, the reasons that these tests and techniques are used are similar across disciplines. This chapter does not attempt to introduce the many different statistical concepts and tests that have been developed, but rather provides an overview of how various statistical methods are used in science. More information about specific statistical tests and methods can be found in the links section of this chapter on our website.

Statistics in research design

Many people misinterpret statements of likelihood and probability as a sign of weakness or uncertainty in scientific results. However, the use of statistical methods and probability tests in research is an important aspect of science that adds strength and certainty to scientific conclusions. For example, in 1843, an English entrepreneur named John Bennet Lawes founded the Rothamsted Agriculture Experimental Station in Hertfordshire, England to investigate the impact of fertilizer application on crop yield. Lawes was motivated to do so because he had established one of the first artificial fertilizer factories a year earlier. For the next 80 years, researchers at the Station conducted experiments in which they applied fertilizers, planted different crops, kept track of the amount of rain that fell, and measured the size of the harvest at the end of each growing season. By the turn of the century, the Station had a vast collection of data but few useful conclusions: one fertilizer would outperform another one year but underperform the next, certain fertilizers appeared to affect only certain crops, and the differing amounts of rainfall that fell each year continually confounded the experiments (Salsburg, 2001). The data were essentially useless because there were a large number of uncontrolled variables.

In 1919, the Rothamsted Station hired a young statistician by the name of Ronald Aylmer Fisher to try to make some sense of the data. Fisher's statistical analyses suggested that the relationship between rainfall and plant growth was far more statistically significant than the relationship between fertilizer type and plant growth. But the agricultural scientists at the station weren't out to test for weather – they wanted to know which fertilizers were most effective for which crops. No one could remove weather as a variable in the experiments, but Fisher realized that its effects could essentially be separated out if the experiments were designed appropriately. In order to share his insights with the scientific community, he published two books: *Statistical Methods for Research Workers* in 1925 and *The Design of Experiments*

Figure 2: *A building at the Rothamsted Research Station.*

A				B			
$(u_2 p)$ 480	$(m_2 p)$ 542	(c_2) 373	(I) 186	(I) 268	(p) 297	$(s_2 p)$ 536	$(s_1 p)$ 471
$(m_1 p)$ 431	(c_1) 365	(s_2) 293	(s_1) 281	(u_1) 343	$(c_2 p)$ 443	(u_2) 498	(m_2) 522
(p) 284	(p) 313	$(u_1 p)$ 336	(I) 260	(m_1) 366	$(c_1 p)$ 412	(p) 250	(I) 239
(u_2) 475	(I) 275	(I) 242	$(c_2 p)$ 395	(p) 244	(c_2) 396	(s_2) 400	(p) 228
(p) 344	(p) 277	$(s_1 p)$ 359	(m_1) 368	(s_1) 413	$(u_2 p)$ 512	(I) 259	$(m_1 p)$ 453
(u_1) 401	$(c_1 p)$ 429	$(s_2 p)$ 464	(m_2) 542	$(m_2 p)$ 504	(c_1) 409	$(u_1 p)$ 389	(I) 267
C				D			

Figure 3: *An original figure from Fisher's* The Design of Experiments *showing the arrangement of treatment groups and yields of barley in an experiment at the Rothamsted Station in 1927 (Fisher, 1935). Letters in parentheses denote control plots not treated with fertilizer (I) or those treated with different fertilizers (s = sulfate of ammonia, m = chloride of ammonia, c = cyanamide, and u = urea) with or without the addition of superphosphate (p). Subscripted numbers in parentheses indicate relative quantities of fertilizer used. Numbers at the bottom of each block indicate the relative yield of barley from the plot.*

in 1935. By highlighting the need to consider statistical analysis during the planning stages of research, Fisher revolutionized the practice of science and transformed the Rothamsted Station into a major center for research on statistics and agriculture, which it still is today.

In *The Design of Experiments*, Fisher introduced several concepts that have become hallmarks of good scientific research, including the use of controls, randomization, and replication (Figure 3).

Controls: The use of controls is based on the concept of variability. Since any phenomenon has some measure of variability, controls allow the researcher to measure natural, random, or systematic variability in a similar system and use that estimate as a baseline for comparison to the observed variable or phenomenon. At Rothamsted, a control would be a crop that did not receive the application of fertilizer (see plots labeled I in Figure 3). The variability inherent in plant growth would still produce plants of varying heights and sizes. The control then could provide a measure of the impact that weather or other variables could have on crop growth independent of fertilizer application, thus allowing the researchers to statistically remove this as a factor.

Randomization: Statistical randomization helps to manage bias in scientific research. Unlike the common use of the word random, which implies haphazard or disorganized, statistical randomization is a precise procedure in which units being observed are assigned to a treatment or control group in a manner that takes into account the potential influence of confounding variables. This allows the researcher to quantify the influence of these confounding variables by observing them in both the control and treatment groups. For example, before Fisher, fertilizers were applied along different crop rows at Rothamsted, some of which fell entirely along the edge of fields. Yet edges are known to affect agricultural yield, and so it was difficult in many cases to distinguish edge effects from fertilizer effects. Fisher introduced a process of randomly assigning different fertilizers to different plots within a field in a single year while assuring that not all of the treatment (or control) plots for any particular fertilizer fell along the edge of the field (see Figure 3).

Replication: Fisher also advocated for replicating experimental trials and measurements such that the range of variability inherently associated with the experiment or measurement could be quantified and the robustness of the results could be evaluated. At Rothamsted this meant planting multiple plots with the same crop and applying the same fertilizer to each of those plots (see Figure 3). Further, this meant repeating similar applications in different years so that the variability of different fertilizer applications as a function of different weather conditions could be quantified.

In general, scientists design research studies based on the nature of the question they are seeking to investigate, but they refine their research plan in line with many of Fisher's statistical concepts to increase the likelihood that their findings will be useful. The incorporation of these techniques facilitates the analysis and interpretation of data, another place where statistics are used.

Statistics in data analysis

A multitude of statistical techniques have been developed for data analysis, but they generally fall into two groups: descriptive and inferential.

Descriptive Statistics: Descriptive statistics allow a scientist to quickly sum up major attributes of a dataset using measures such as the mean, median, and standard deviation. These measures provide a general sense of the group being studied, allowing scientists to place the study within a larger context. For example, Cancer Prevention Study I (CPS-I) was a prospective mortality study initiated in 1959 as mentioned earlier. Researchers conducting the study reported the age and demographics of participants, among other variables, to allow a comparison between the study group and the broader population of the United States at the time. Adults participating in the study ranged from 30 to 108 years of age, with the median age reported as 52 years. The study subjects were 57% female, 97% white and 2% black. By comparison, median age in the United States in 1959 was 29.4 years of age, obviously much younger than the study group since CPS-I did not enroll anyone under 30 years of age. Further, 51% of U.S. residents were female in 1960, 89% white, and about 11% black. One recognized shortcoming of CPS I, easily identifiable from the descriptive statistics, was that with 97% participants categorized as white, the study did not adequately assess disease profiles in minority groups of the U.S.

Inferential Statistics: Inferential statistics are used to model patterns in data, make judgments about data, identify relationships between variables in datasets, and make inferences about larger populations based on smaller samples of data. It is important to keep in mind that from a statistical perspective the word "population" does not have to mean a group of people, as it does in common language. A statistical population is the larger group that a data set is used to make inferences about – this can be a group of people, corn plants, meteor impacts, oil field locations, or any other group of measurements as the case may be.

Transferring results from small sample sizes to large populations is especially important with respect to scientific studies. For example, while Cancer Prevention Studies I and II enrolled approximately 1 million and 1.2 million people, respectively, they represented a small fraction of the 179 and 226 million people who were living in the United States in 1960 and 1980. Common inferential techniques include regression, correlation, and point estimation/testing. For example, Petter Kristensen and Tor Bjerkedal (2007) examined IQ test scores in a group of 250,000 male Norwegian military personnel. Their analyses suggested that first-born male children had an average IQ test score 2.82 ± 0.07 points higher than second-born male children, a statistically significant difference at the 95% confidence level (Kristensen and Bjerkedal, 2007).

The phrase "statistically significant" is a key concept in data analysis, and it is commonly misunderstood. Many people assume that, like the common use of the word significant, calling a result statistically significant means that the result is important or momentous, but this is not the case. Instead, statistical significance is an estimate of the probability that the observed association or difference is due to chance rather than any real association. In other words, tests of statistical significance describe the likelihood that an observed association or difference would be seen even if there were no real association or difference actually present. The measure of significance is often expressed in terms of confidence, which has the same meaning in statistics as it does in common language, but can be quantified. In Kristensen's and Bjerkedal's work, for example, the IQ difference between first- and second-born men was found to be significant at a 95% confidence level, meaning that there is only a 5% probability that the IQ difference is due purely to chance. This does not mean that the difference is large or even important: 2.82 IQ points is a tiny blip on the IQ scale and hardly enough to declare first-borns geniuses in relation to their younger siblings. Nor do the findings imply that the outcome is 95% "correct." Instead, they indicate that the observed difference is not due simply to random sampling bias and that there is a 95% probability the same results would be seen again if another researcher conducted a similar study in different population of Norwegian men. A second-born Norwegian who has a higher IQ than his older brother does not disprove the research – it is just a statistically less likely outcome.

Just as revealing as a statistically significant difference or relationship, is the lack of a statistical significance difference. For example, researchers have found that the risks of dying from heart disease in men who have quit smoking for at least two years is not significantly different from the risk of the disease in male non-smokers (Rosenberg *et al.*, 1985). So, the statistics show that while smokers have a significantly higher rate of heart disease than non-smokers, this risk falls back to baseline within just two years after having quit smoking.

Limitations, misconceptions, and the misuse of statistics

Given the wide variety of possible statistical tests, it is easy to misuse statistics in data analysis, often to the point of deception. One reason for this is that statistics do not address systematic error that can be introduced into a study either intentionally or accidentally. For example, in one of the first studies that reported on the effects of quitting smoking, E. Cuyler Hammond and Daniel Horn found that individuals who smoked more than one pack of cigarettes a day but had quit smoking within the past year had a death rate of 198.0, significantly higher than the rate of 157.1 for individuals who were still smoking more than one pack a day at the time of their study (Hammond and Horn, 1958). Without a proper understanding of the study, one might conclude from the statistics that quitting smoking is actually dangerous for heavy smokers. However, Hammond later offers an explanation for this finding when he says, "This is not surprising in light of the fact that recent ex-smokers, as a group, are heavily weighted with men in ill health" (Hammond, 1965). Thus, heavy smokers who had stopped smoking included many individuals who had quit because they were already diagnosed with an illness, thus adding systematic error to the sample set. Without a complete understanding of these facts, the statistics alone could be misinterpreted. The most effective use of statistics, then, is to identifying trends and features within a dataset. These trends can then be interpreted by the researcher in light of his or her understanding of their scientific basis, possibly opening up opportunities for further study. Andrew Lang, a Scottish poet and novelist, famously summed up this aspect of statistical testing when he stated: "An unsophisticated forecaster uses statistics as a drunken man uses lamp-posts – for support rather than for illumination."

Another misconception of statistical testing is that statistical relationships and associations prove causation. In reality, identification of a correlation or association between variables does not mean that a change in one variable actually caused the change in another variable. In 1950 Richard Doll and Austin Hill, British researchers who became known for conducting one of the first scientifically valid comparative studies of smoking and the development of lung cancer, famously wrote about the correlation they uncovered: "This is not necessarily to state that smoking causes carcinoma of the lung. The association would occur if carcinoma of the lung caused people to smoke or if both attributes were end-effects of a common cause" (Doll and Hill, 1950). Doll and Hill went on to discuss the scientific basis of the correlation and the fact that the habit of smoking preceded the development of lung cancer in all of their study subjects, leading them to conclude "that smoking is a factor, and an important factor, in the production of carcinoma of the lung." As multiple lines of scientific evidence have accumulated regarding the association between smoking and lung cancer, scientists are now able to make very accurate statements about the statistical probability of risk associated with smoking cigarettes.

While statistics help uncover patterns, relationships, and variability in data, they can unfortunately be used to misrepresent data, relationships, and interpretations. For example, in the late 1950s, in light of the mounting comparative studies that demonstrated a causative relationship between cigarette smoking and lung cancer, the major tobacco companies began to investigate the viability of marketing alternative products that they could promote as "healthier" than regular cigarettes. As a result, filtered and light cigarettes were developed. The tobacco industry then sponsored and widely advertised research that suggested that the common cellulose acetate filter reduced tar in regular cigarettes by 42–46% and nicotine by 19–35%. Marlboro® filtered cigarettes claimed to have "22 percent less tar, 34 percent less nicotine" than other brands. The Tobacco industry launched a similar advertising campaign promoting low tar cigarettes (6 to 12 mg tar compared to 12 to 16 mg in "regular" cigarettes) and ultra low tar cigarettes (under 6 mg) (Glantz *et al.*, 1996). While the industry flooded the public with statistics on tar content, the tobacco companies did not advertise the

Figure 4: *Filtered and low tar cigarettes were advertised as less dangerous based on hollow statistics.*

fact that there was no research to indicate that tar or nicotine were the causative agents in the development of smoking-induced lung cancer. In fact, several research studies showed that the risks associated with low tar products were no different than regular products, and worse still, some studies showed that "low tar" cigarettes led to increased consumption of cigarettes among smokers (Stepney, 1980; NCI, 2001). Thus hollow statistics were used to mislead the public and detract from the real issue.

Statistics and scientific research

All measurements contain some uncertainty and error, and statistical methods help us quantify and characterize this uncertainty. This helps explain why scientists often speak in qualified statements. For example, no seismologist who studies earthquakes would be willing to tell you exactly when an earthquake is going to occur; instead, the U.S. Geological Survey issues statements like this: "There is…a 62% probability of at least one magnitude 6.7 or greater earthquake in the 3-decade interval 2003–2032 within the San Francisco Bay Region" (USGS, 2007). This may sound ambiguous, but it is in fact a very precise, mathematically-derived description of how confident seismologists are that a major earthquake will occur, and open reporting of error and uncertainty is a hallmark of quality scientific research.

Today, science and statistical analyses have become so intertwined that many scientific disciplines have developed their own subsets of statistical techniques and terminology. For example, the field of biostatistics (sometimes referred to as biometry) involves the application of specific statistical techniques to disciplines in biology such as population genetics, epidemiology, and public health. The field of geostatistics has evolved to develop specialized spatial analysis techniques that help geologists map the location of petroleum and mineral deposits; these spatial analysis techniques have also helped Starbuck's® determine the ideal distribution of coffee shops based on maximizing the number of customers visiting each store. Used correctly, statistical analysis goes well beyond finding the next oil field or cup of coffee to illuminating scientific data in a way that helps validate scientific knowledge.

Key Concepts for this chapter

▶ Statistics are used to describe the variability inherent in data in a quantitative fashion, and to quantify relationships between variables

▶ Statistical analysis is used in designing scientific studies to increase consistency, measure uncertainty, and produce robust datasets.

▶ There are a number of misconceptions that surround statistics, including confusion between statistical terms and the common language use of similar terms, and the role that statistics employ in data analysis.

References

ACS (2004). *Cancer Facts & Figures - 2004*. American Cancer Society, Atlanta, GA.

ACS (2007) *Cancer prevention studies overview*. American Cancer Society, Atlanta, GA

ACS (2008). *Characteristics of American Cancer Society Cohorts*, American Cancer Society, Atlanta, GA, retrieved July 18, 2008

Bland, P.A. (2005). The impact rate on Earth. *Phil. Trans. R. Soc. A*, 363:2793-2810.

Cohen, J. (1988). *Statistical power analysis for the behavioral sciences* (2nd ed.) Hillsdale, NJ: Lawrence Erlbaum Associates.

Doll, R., & Hill, A.B. (1950). Smoking and Carcinoma of the lung. *British Medical Journal* 2(4682), 739-748.

Fisher, R. A. (1935). *Design of Experiments*: Hafner Press, New York.

Glantz, S.A., Slade, J., Bero, L.A., Hanauer, P., Barnes, D.E. (1996) *The Cigarette Papers*. University of California Press, Berkeley, CA.

Hamilton, W.L., Norton, G.d., Ouellette, T.K., Rhodes, W.M., Kling, R., Connolly, G.N. (2004). Smokers' responses to advertisements for regular and light cigarettes and potential reduced-exposure tobacco products. *Nicotine & Tobacco Research*, 6(Supp. 3):S353-S362.

Hammond, E.C. (1965). Evidence of the Effects of Giving Up Cigarette Smoking. *American Journal of Public Health* 55:682-691.

Hammond, E.C., Horn, D. (1958). Smoking and death rates: report on forty-four months of follow-up of 187,783 men. 2. Death rates by cause. *J Am Med Assoc.* 166(11):1294-308.

Kristensen, P., & Bjerkedal, T. (2007). Explaining the Relation between Birth Order and Intelligence. *Science* 316(5832), 1717.

National Center for Health Statistics (2006). *Health, United States*, 2006. NCHS, Centers for Disease Control and Prevention, U.S. Department of Health and Human Services, Hyattsville, MD.

NCI – National Cancer Institute (2001). *Monograph 13: Risks Associated with Smoking Cigarettes with Low Tar Machine-Measured Yields of Tar and Nicotine.* NCI, Tobacco Control Research, Document M914.

Rosenberg, L., Kaufman, D.W., Helmrich, S.P., Shapiro, S. (1985). The risk of myocardial infarction after quitting smoking in men under 55 years of age. *N Engl J Med*, 313:1511-1514.

Salsburg, D. (2001). ,*The Lady Tasting Tea: How Statistics Revolutionized Science in the Twentieth Century*, W.H. Freeman & Company, New York.

Silverstein, B., Feld, S., Kozlowski, L.T. (1980). The Availability of Low-Nicotine Cigarettes as a Cause of Cigarette Smoking among Teenage Females (in Research Notes) *Journal of Health and Social Behavior*, 21(4):383-388.

Stepney, R. (1980). Consumption of Cigarettes of Reduced Tar and Nicotine Delivery. *Addiction*, 75(1):81–88.

Using Graphs and Visual Data

Flip through any scientific journal or textbook and you'll notice quickly that the text is interspersed with graphs and figures. In some journals, as much as 30% of the space is taken up by graphs (Cleveland, 1984), perhaps surpassing the adage that "a picture is worth a thousand words." Although many magazines and newspapers also include graphs, the visual depiction of data is fundamental to science and represents something very different from the photographs and illustrations published in magazines and newspapers. Although numerical data are initially compiled in tables or databases, they are often displayed in a graphic form to help scientists visualize and interpret the variation, patterns, and trends within the data.

Data lie at the heart of any scientific endeavor. Scientists in different fields collect data in many different forms, from the magnitude and location of earthquakes, to the length of finch beaks, to the concentration of carbon dioxide in the atmosphere and so on. Visual representations of scientific data have been used for centuries – Copernicus drew schematic sketches of planetary orbits around the sun, for example – but the visual representation of numerical data in the form of graphs is a more recent development. In 1786, William Playfair, a Scottish economist, published *The Commercial and Political Atlas*, which contained a variety of economic statistics presented in graphs. Among these was the image shown in Figure 1, a graph comparing exports from England with imports into England from Denmark and Norway from 1708 to 1780 (Playfair, 1786). (Incidentally, William Playfair was the brother of John Playfair, the geologist who elucidated James Hutton's fundamental work on geological processes to the broader public. See our online module The Rock Cycle: Uniformitarianism and Recycling.)

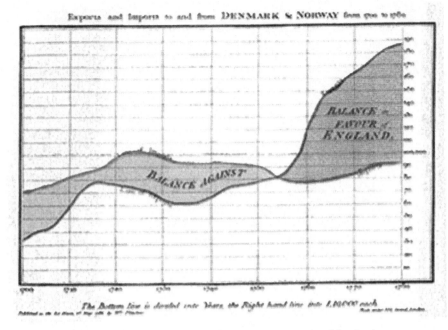

Figure 1: *William Playfair's graph was one of the first examples of the visual representation of numerical data.*

Playfair's graph displayed a powerful message very succinctly. The graph shows time on the horizontal (x) axis and money in English pounds on the vertical (y) axis. The lighter line shows the monetary value of imports to England from Denmark and Norway; the darker line shows the monetary value of exports to Denmark and Norway from England. Although a table of numerical data would show the same information, it would not be immediately apparent that something important happened in about 1753: England began exporting more than it imported, placing the "balance in favour of England." This simple visualization of a large numerical dataset made it easy to comprehend quickly.

Graphs and figures quickly became standard components of science and scientific communication, and the use of graphs has increased dramatically in scientific journals in recent years, almost doubling from an average of 35 graphs per journal issue to more than 60 between 1985 and 1994 (Zacks *et al.*, 2002). This increase has been attributed to a number of causes, including the use of computer software programs that make producing graphs easy, as well as the production of increasingly large and complex datasets that require visualization to be interpreted. Graphs are not the only form of visualized data, however – maps, satellite imagery, animations, and more specialized images like atomic orbital depictions are also composed of data, and have become more common. Creating, using, and reading visual forms of data is just one type of data analysis and interpretation, but it is ubiqui-. tous throughout all fields and methods of scientific investigation (see the chapter Analysis and Interpretation).

Interpreting graphs

The majority of graphs published in scientific journals relate two variables. As many as 85% of graphs published in the journal *Science*, in fact, show the relationship between two variables, one on the x-axis and another on the y-axis (Cleveland, 1984). Although many other kinds of graphs exist, knowing how to fully interpret a two-variable graph can help anyone decipher not only the vast majority of graphs in the scientific literature, but also offers a starting point for examining more complex graphs. As an example, imagine trying to identify any long-term trends in the data table that follows of atmospheric carbon dioxide concentrations taken over several years at Mauna Loa (Table 1).

Table 1: This is a small portion of a data table containing atmospheric carbon dioxide concentrations measured at Mauna Loa – access to the full table is available through the module on our website.

	Jan	Feb	Mar	Apr
1958			315.7	317
1959	315.62	316.38	316.71	317
1960	316.43	316.97	317.58	319
1961	316.93	317.7	318.54	319
1962	317.94	318.56	319.68	320
1963	318.74	319.08	319.86	321
1964	319.57			
1965	319.44	320.44	320.89	322
1966	320.62	321.59	322.39	323

The variables are straightforward – time in months in the top row of the table, years in the far left column of the table, and carbon dioxide (CO_2) concentrations within the individual table cells. Yet, it is challenging for most people to make sense of that much numerical information. You would have to look carefully at the entire table to see any trends. But if we take the exact same data and plot it on a graph, we get the graph in Figure 2 on the next page.

The x-axis shows the variable of time in units of years, and the y-axis shows the range of the variable of CO_2 concentration in units of parts per million (ppm). The dots are individual measurements of concentrations – the numbers

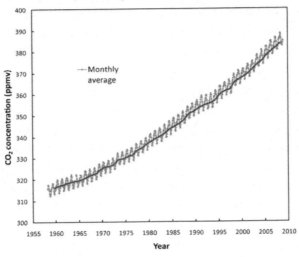

Figure 2: Data plotted from Table 1, atmospheric CO$_2$ measured at Mauna Loa (Keeling and Whorf, 2005).

shown in Table 1. Thus, the graph is showing us the change in atmospheric CO$_2$ concentrations over time. The line connects consecutive measurements, making it easier to see both the short- and long-term trends within the data. On the graph, it is easy to see that the concentration of atmospheric CO$_2$ steadily rose over time, from a low of about 315 ppm in 1958 to a current level of about 375 ppm. Within that long-term trend, it's also easy to see that there are short-term, annual cycles of about 5 ppm. On the graph, scientists can derive additional information from the numerical data, such as how fast CO$_2$ concentration is rising. This rate can be determined by calculating the slope of the long-term trend in the numerical data, and seeing this rate on a graph makes it easily apparent. While a keen observer may have been able to pick out of the table the increase in CO$_2$ concentrations over the five decades provided, it would be difficult for even a highly trained scientist to note the yearly cycling in atmospheric CO$_2$ in the numerical data – a feature elegantly demonstrated in the sawtooth pattern of the line.

Putting data into a visual format is one step in data analysis and interpretation, and well-designed graphs can help scientists interpret their data. Interpretation involves explaining why there is a long-term rise in atmospheric CO$_2$ concentrations on top of an annual fluctuation, thus moving beyond the graph itself to put the data into context. Seeing the regular and repeating cycle of about 5 ppm, scientists realized that this fluctuation must be related to natural changes on the planet due to seasonal plant activity.

Visual representation of this data also helped scientists to realize that the increase in CO_2 concentrations over the five decades shown occurs in parallel with the industrial revolution and thus are almost certainly related to the growing number of human activities that release CO_2 (IPCC, 2007).

It is important to note that neither one of these trends (the long-term rise or the annual cycling) nor the interpretation can be seen in a single measurement or data point. That's one reason why you almost never hear scientists use the singular of the word data – datum. Imagine just one point on a graph. You could draw a trend line going through it in any direction. Rigorous scientific practice requires multiple data points to make a clear interpretation, and a graph can be critical not only in showing the data itself, but demonstrating on how much data a scientist is basing his or her interpretation.

We just followed a short, logical process to extract a lot of information from this graph. Although an infinite variety of data can appear in graphical form, this same procedure can apply when reading any kind of graph:

1. **Describe the graph:** What does the title say? What variable is represented on the x-axis? What is on the y-axis? What are the units of measurement? What do the symbols and colors mean?

2. **Describe the data:** What is the numerical range of the data? What kinds of patterns can you see in the distribution of the data as they are plotted?

3. **Interpret the data:** How do the patterns you see in the graph relate to other things you know?

The same questions apply whether you are looking at a graph of two variables or something more complex. Because creating graphs is a form of data analysis and interpretation, it is important to scrutinize a scientist's graphs as much as his or her written interpretation.

Error and uncertainty estimation in visual data

Graphs and other visual representations of scientific information also commonly contain another key element of scientific data analysis – a measure of the uncertainty or error within measurements (see the chapter Uncertainty, Error, and Confidence). For example, the graph in Figure 3 presents mean measurements of mercury emissions from soil at various times over the course of a single day. The error bars on each vertical bar provide the standard deviation of each measurement and are included to demonstrate that the change in emissions with time are greater than the inherent variability within each measurement (see the Statistics chapter for more information).

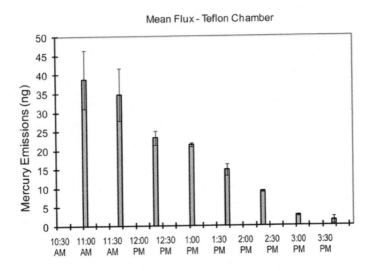

Mean Flux - Teflon Chamber

Figure 3: Error bars within this graphical display of data are used to demonstrate that the change in measurement value (thick bars) with time is greater than the inherent variability within the data (shown as thin error bars). Adapted from Carpi et al. (2007).

Graphical displays of data can also be used not just to display error, but to quantify error and uncertainty in a system. For example, Figure 4 shows a gas chromatograph of a fuel oil spill. Peaks in the chromatograph (the undulating line) provide information about the chemicals identified in the spill, and the peak size can provide an estimate of the relative concentration of that specific chemical in the spill. However, before this information can be extracted from the graph, instrument error and uncertainty must be calculated (the smooth, black line) and subtracted from the peak area. As you can see in Figure 4, instrument variability decreases as you move from left to right in the graph, and in this case, the graphical display of the error is therefore critical to accurate analysis of the data.

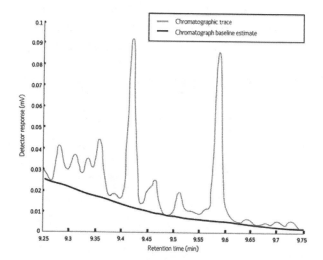

Figure 4: Graphical displays of data can be used to estimate system error and uncertainty (smooth, black line) as well as present this uncertainty.

Misuse of scientific images

Poor use of graphics can highlight trends that don't really exist, or can make real trends disappear. In 2006, Christopher Monckton, a British journalist and former government advisor, published an article in the *Daily Telegraph*, a British national daily newspaper, that disputed the concept of climate change and suggested that the United Nation's report on the topic was flawed. Monckton included Figure 5 in his article, suggesting that the bottom graph, which shows relatively little change in temperature over the past 1,000 years, disputed the top graph used by the Intergovernmental Panel on Climate Change that showed a recent, rapid temperature increase.

At first glance the bottom graph does seem to contradict the top graph. However, looking more closely you realize that the two graphs actually represent completely different data sets. The top graph is a representation of change in annual mean global temperature normalized to a 30-year period, 1960–1990, whereas the bottom graph represents average temperatures in Europe compared to an average over the 20th-century. In addition, the y-axes of the two graphs are displayed on differing scales – the bottom graph has more space between the 0.5° lines. Both of these techniques tend to exaggerate the variability in the lower graph. However, the primary reason for the difference in the graphs is not actually shown in the graphs – the author of the article, Christopher Monckton, created the graph on the bottom using different calculations that did not take into account all of the variables that climate scientists used to create the top graph. In other words, the graphs simply do not show the same data. These are common techniques used to distort visual forms of data – manipulating axes, changing one of the variables in a comparison, changing calculations without full explanation – that can obscure a true comparison.

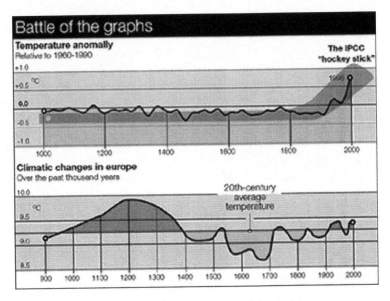

Figure 5: Poor use of graphical displays can confuse and obscure data.

Visualizing spatial and three-dimensional data

There are other kinds of visual data aside from graphs. You might think of a topographic map or a satellite image as a picture or a sketch of the surface of the earth, but both of these images are ways of visualizing spatial data. A topographic map shows data collected on elevation and the location of geographic features like lakes or mountain peaks (see Figure. 6). These data may have been collected in the field by surveyors or by looking at aerial photographs, but nonetheless, the map is not a picture of a region – it is a visual representation of data. The topographic map in Figure 6 is actually accomplishing a second goal beyond simply visualizing data: it is taking three-dimensional data (variations in land elevation) and displaying it in two dimensions on a flat piece of paper.

Likewise, satellite images are commonly misunderstood to be photographs of the earth from space, but in reality they are much more complex than that. A satellite records numerical data for each pixel, and it does so at certain predefined wavelengths in the electromagnetic spectrum. In other words, the image itself is a visualization of data that has been processed

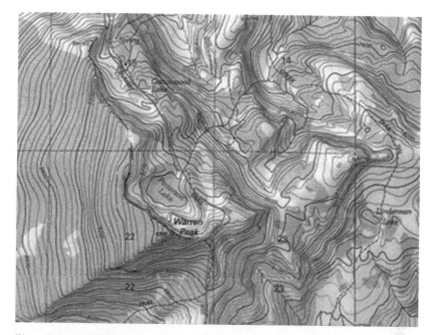

Figure 6: Portion of the Warren Peak USGS 7.5′ topographic map. Solid black lines are elevation contours. This image takes 3-dimensional data on elevation and depicts it in 2-dimensions.

Figure 7: July 2002 Landsat satellite image of the Hayman Fire, central Colorado.

from the raw data received from the satellite. For example, the Landsat satellites record data in seven different wavelengths, three in the visible spectrum, and four in the infrared wavelengths. The composite image of four of those wavelengths is displayed in the image of a portion of the Colorado Rocky Mountains shown in Figure 7. The large light region in the lower left portion of the image is not vegetation in the mountains; instead, it is a region with high values for emission of infrared (or thermal) wavelengths. In fact, this region was the site of a large forest fire, known as the Hayman Fire, a month prior to the acquisition of the satellite image in July, 2002.

Working with image-based data

The advent of satellite imagery vastly expanded one data collection method: extracting data from an image. For example, from a series of satellite images of the Hayman Fire acquired while it was burning, scientists and forest managers were able to extract data about the extent of the fire (which burned deep into National Forest land where it could not be monitored by people on the ground), the rate of spread, and the temperature at which it was burning. By comparing two satellite images, they could find the area that had burned over the course of a day, a week, or a month. Thus, although the images themselves consist of numerical data, additional information can be extracted from these images as a form of data collection.

Another example can be taken from the realm of atomic physics. In 1666 Sir Isaac Newton discovered that when light from the sun is passed through a prism it separates into a characteristic rainbow of light. Almost 200 years after Newton, John Herschel and W.H. Fox Talbot demonstrated that when substances are heated and the light they give off is passed through a prism, each element gives off a characteristic pattern of bright lines of color, but they did not understand why (see Figure 8). In 1913, the Danish physicist Neils Bohr used these images to make a startling proposal: he suggested that the line spectra of elements were due to the movement of electrons be-

Figure 8: Line spectra for helium (top) and neon (bottom). The location and color of the lines represents a unique wavelength that defines the electron configuration of the atoms.

tween different orbitals, and thus these spectra could provide information regarding the electron configuration of the elements (see our Atomic Theory II module online for more information). You can actually calculate the potential energy difference between electron orbitals in atoms by analyzing the color (and thus wavelength) of light emitted.

Photographs and videos are also visual data. In 2005, a group of scientists based in part at the Cornell Ornithology lab published their findings that a bird believed to be extinct in North America, the Ivory-billed Woodpecker, had been spotted in Arkansas (Fitzpatrick *et al.*, 2005). Their primary evidence consisted of video footage and photographs of a bird in flight, which they included in their paper along with a detailed analysis of the features of the images and video that suggested that the bird was an Ivory-billed Woodpecker.

Graphs in publications

Many areas of study within science have more specialized graphs used for specific kinds of data. Evolutionary biologists, for example, use evolutionary trees or cladograms to show how species are related to each other, what characteristics they share, and how they evolve over time. Geologists use a type of graph called a stereonet that represents the inside of a hemisphere in order to depict the orientation of rock layers in three-dimensional space. Many fields now use three-dimensional graphs to represent three variables, though they may not actually represent three-dimensional space.

Regardless of the exact type of graph, the creation of clear, understandable visualizations of data is of fundamental importance in all branches of science. In recognition of the critical contribution of visuals to science, the National Science Foundation and the American Association for the Advancement of Science sponsor an annual Science and Engineering Visualization Challenge, in which submissions are judged based on their visual impact, effective communication, and originality (NSF, 2007). Likewise, reading and interpreting graphs is a key skill at all levels, from the introductory student to the research scientist. Graphs are a key component of scientific research papers where new data are routinely presented. Presenting the data from which conclusions are drawn allows other scientists the opportunity to analyze the data for themselves, a process whose purpose is to keep scientific experiments and analysis as objective as possible. Although tables are necessary to record the data, graphs allow readers to visualize complex datasets in a simple, concise manner.

Key Concepts for this chapter

▶ Visual representations of data are essential for both data analysis and interpretation.

▶ Visualization highlights trends and patterns in numeric datasets that might not otherwise be apparent.

▶ Understanding and interpreting graphs and other visual forms of data is a critical skill for scientists and students of science.

References

Carpi, A., Frei, A., Cocris, D., McCloskey, R., Contreras, E., Ferguson, K. (2007). Analytical artifacts produced by a polycarbonate chamber compared to a Teflon chamber for measuring surface mercury fluxes. *Analytical & Bioanalytical Chemistry*, 388(2):361-365.

Cleveland, W. S. (1984). Graphs in Scientific Publications. *The American Statistician*, 38(4), 261-269.

Fitzpatrick, J. W., Lammertink, M., Luneau, M. D., Jr., Gallagher, T. W., Harrison, B. R., Sparling, G. M., et al. (2005). Ivory-billed Woodpecker (*Campephilus principalis*) Persists in Continental North America. *Science*, 308(5727), 1460-1462.

IPCC. (2007). *Climate Change 2007: The Physical Science Basis. Contribution of Working Group I to the Fourth Assessment Report of the Intergovernmental Panel on Climate Change.* New York, NY: Cambridge University Press.

Playfair, W. (1786). *The commercial and political atlas and statistical breviary* London: J.Wallis.

Keeling, R.F., S.C. Piper, A.F. Bollenbacher and J.S. Walker. 2008. Atmospheric CO2 records from sites in the SIO air sampling network. In Trends: A Compendium of Data on Global Change. Carbon Dioxide Information Analysis Center, Oak Ridge National Laboratory, U.S. Department of Energy, Oak Ridge, Tenn., U.S.A.NSF. (2007, Sept. 27, 2007).

Science & Engineering Visualization Challenge. Retrieved January 8, 2008

Zacks, J., Levy, E., Tversky, B., & Schiano, D. (2002). Graphs in Print. In M. Anderson, B. Meyer & P. Olivier (Eds.), *Diagrammatic Representation and Reasoning* (pp. 187-206): Springer.

Scientific
Communication

Understanding Scientific Journals and Articles

"In science the credit goes to the man who convinces the world, not to the man to whom the idea first occurs."

~ Sir Francis Darwin

W e've all read the headlines at the supermarket checkout line: "Aliens Abduct New Jersey School Teacher" or "Quadruplets Born to 99-Year-Old Woman: Exclusive Photos Inside." Newspapers like the *National Enquirer* sell copies by publishing sensational headlines, and most readers believe only a fraction of what is printed. A person more interested in news than gossip could buy a publication like *Time, Newsweek* or *Discover*. These magazines publish information on current news and events, including recent scientific advances. These are not original reports of scientific research, however. In fact, most of these stories include phrases like, "A group of scientists recently published their findings on ..." So where do scientists publish their findings?

Scientists publish their original research in scientific journals, which are fundamentally different from news magazines. The articles in scientific journals are not written by journalists – they are written by scientists. Scientific articles are not sensational stories intended to entertain the reader with an amazing discovery, nor are they news stories intended to summarize recent scientific events, nor even records of every successful and unsuccessful research venture. Instead, scientists write articles to describe their findings to the community in a transparent manner. Within a scientific article, scientists present their research questions, the methods by which the question was approached, and the results they achieved using those methods. In addition, they present their analysis of the data and describe some of the interpretations and implications of their work. Because these articles report new work for the first time, they are called primary literature. In contrast, articles or news stories that review or report on scientific research already published elsewhere are referred to as secondary.

The articles in scientific journals are different from news articles in another way – they must undergo a process called peer review in which other scientists (the professional peers of the authors) evaluate the quality and merit of research before recommending whether or not it should be published (see the chapter on Peer Review). This is a much lengthier and more rigorous process than the editing and fact-checking that goes on at news organizations. The reason for this thorough evaluation by peers is that a scientific article is more than a snapshot of what is going on at a certain time in a scientist's research. Instead, it is a part of what is collectively called the scientific literature, a global archive of scientific knowledge. When published, each article expands the library of scientific literature available to all scientists and contributes to the overall knowledge base of the discipline of science.

Scientific journals

There are thousands of scientific journals that publish research articles. These journals are diverse and can be distinguished according to their field of specialization. Among the most broadly targeted and competitive are journals like *Cell*, the *New England Journal of Medicine* (*NEJM*), *Nature*, and *Science* that all publish a wide variety of research articles (see Figure 1 for an example). *Cell* focuses on all areas of biology, *NEJM* on medicine, and both *Science* and *Nature* publish articles in all areas of science. Scientists submit manuscripts for publication in these journals when they feel their work deserves the broadest possible audience.

Just below these journals in terms of their reach are the top-tier disciplinary journals like *Analytical Chemistry, Applied Geochemistry, Neuron, Journal of Geophysical Research*, and many others. These journals tend to publish broad-based research focused on specific disciplines, such as chemistry, geology, neurology, nuclear physics, etc. Next in line are highly specialized journals, such as the *American Journal of Potato Research, Grass and Forage Science*, the *Journal of Shellfish Research, Neuropeptides, Paleolimnology*, and many more. While the research published in various journals does not differ in terms of the quality or the rigor of the science described,

Figure 1: Nature, *an example of a scientific journal.*

it does differ in its degree of specialization: these journals tend to be more specialized, and thus appeal to a more limited audience.

All of these journals play a critical role in the advancement of science and dissemination of information. However, to understand how science is disseminated through these journals, you must first understand how the articles themselves are formatted and what information they contain. While some details about format vary between journals and even between articles in the same journal, there are broad characteristics that all scientific journal articles share.

The format of journal articles

In June of 2005, the journal *Science* published a research report on a sighting of the ivory-billed woodpecker, a bird long considered extinct in North America (Fitzpatrick *et al.*, 2005). The work was of such significance and broad interest that it was displayed prominently on the cover (Figure 2) and highlighted by an editorial at the front of the journal (Kennedy, 2005). The authors were aware that their findings were likely to be controversial, and they worked especially hard to make their writing clear. Although the article has no headings within the text, it can easily be divided into sections:

Figure 2: *A picture of the cover of* Science *from June 3, 2005.*

Title and authors: The title of a scientific article should concisely and accurately summarize the research. Here, the title used is "Ivory-billed Woodpecker (*Campephilus principalis*) Persists in North America." While it is meant to capture attention, journals avoid using misleading or overly sensational titles (you can imagine that a tabloid might use the headline "Long-dead Giant Bird Attacks Canoeists!"). The names of all scientific contributors are listed as authors immediately after the title. You may be used to seeing one or maybe two authors for a book or newspaper article, but this article has seventeen authors! It's unlikely that all seventeen of those authors sat down in a room and wrote the manuscript together. Instead, the authorship reflects the distribution of the workload and responsibility for the research, in addition to the writing. By convention, the scientist who performed most of the work described in the article is listed first, and it is likely that the first author did most of the writing. Other authors had different contributions; for example, Gene Sparling is the person who originally spotted the bird in Arkansas and was subsequently contacted by the scientists at the Cornell Laboratory of Ornithology. In some cases, but not in the woodpecker article, the last author listed is the senior researcher on the project, or the scientist from whose lab the project originated. Increasingly, journals are requesting that authors detail their exact contributions to the research and writing associated with a particular study.

Abstract: The abstract is the first part of the article that appears right after the listing of authors in an article. In it, the authors briefly describe the research question, the general methods, and the major findings and implications of the work. Providing a summary like this at the beginning of an article serves two purposes: first, it gives readers a way to decide whether the article in question discusses research that interests them, and second, it is entered into literature databases as a means of providing more information to people doing scientific literature searches. For both purposes, it is important to have a short version of the full story. In this case, all of the critical information about the timing of the study, the type of data collected, and the potential interpretations of the findings is captured in four straightforward sentences as seen below:

> The ivory-billed woodpecker (*Campephilus principalis*), long suspected to be extinct, has been rediscovered in the Big Woods region of eastern Arkansas. Visual encounters during 2004 and 2005, and analysis of a video clip from April 2004, confirm the existence of at least one male. Acoustic signatures consistent with *Campephilus* display drums also have been heard from the region. Extensive efforts to find birds away from the primary encounter site remain unsuccessful, but potential habitat for a thinly distributed source population is vast (over 220,000 hectares).

Introduction: The central research question and important background information are presented in the introduction. Because science is a process that builds on previous findings, relevant and established scientific knowledge is cited in this section and then listed in the References section at the end of the article. In many articles, a heading is used to set this and subsequent sections apart, but in the woodpecker article the introduction consists of the first three paragraphs, in which the history of the decline of the woodpecker and previous studies are cited. The introduction is intended to lead the reader to understand the authors' hypothesis and means of testing it. In addition, the introduction provides an opportunity for the authors to show that they are aware of the work that scientists have done before them and how their results fit in, explicitly building on existing knowledge.

Materials and methods: In this section, the authors describe the research methods they used (see The Practice of Science chapter for more information on these methods). All procedures, equipment, measurement parameters, etc., are described in detail sufficient for another researcher to evaluate and/or reproduce the research. In addition, authors explain the sources of error and procedures employed to reduce and measure the uncertainty in their data. The detail given here allows other scientists to evaluate the quality of the data collected. This section varies dramatically depending on the type of research done. In an experimental study, the experimental set-up and procedure would be described in detail, including the variables, controls, and treatment. The woodpecker study used a descriptive research approach, and the materials and methods section is quite short, including the means by which the bird was initially spotted (on a kayaking trip) and later photographed and video-taped.

Results: The data collected during the research are presented in this section, both in written form and using tables, graphs, and figures. In addition, all statistical and data analysis techniques used are presented. Importantly, the data should be presented separately from any interpretation by the authors. This separation of data from interpretation serves two purposes: first, it gives other scientists the opportunity to evaluate the quality of the data itself, and second, it allows others to develop their own interpretations of the findings based on their background knowledge and experience. In the woodpecker article, the data consists largely of photographs and videos (see Figure 3 for an example). The authors include both the raw data (the photograph) and their analysis (the measurement of the tree trunk and inferred length of the bird perched on the truck). The sketch of the bird on the right-hand side of the photograph is also a form of analysis, in which the authors have simplified the photograph to highlight the features of interest. Keeping the raw data (in the form of a photograph) facilitated reanalysis by other scientists: in early 2006, a team of researchers led by the American ornithologist David Sibley reanalyzed the photograph in Figure 3 and came to the conclusion that the bird was not an ivory-billed woodpecker after all (Sibley *et al.*, 2006).

Figure 3: An example of the data presented in the Ivory-billed woodpecker article (Fitzpatrick et al., 2005, Figure 1).

Discussion and conclusions: In this section, authors present their interpretation of the data, often including a model or idea they feel best explains their results. They also present the strengths and significance of their work. Naturally, this is the most subjective section of a scientific research article as it presents interpretation as opposed to strictly methods and data, but it is not speculation by the authors. Instead, this is where the authors combine their experience, background knowledge, and creativity to explain the data and use it as evidence in their interpretation. Often, the discussion section includes several possible explanations or interpretations of the data; the authors may then describe why they support one particular interpretation over the others. This is not just a process of hedging their bets – this is how scientists say to their peers that they have done their homework and that there is more than one possible explanation. In the woodpecker article, for example, the authors go to great lengths to describe why they believe the bird they saw is an ivory-billed woodpecker rather than a variant of the more common pileated woodpecker, knowing that this is a likely potential rebuttal to their initial findings. A final component of the conclusions involves placing the current work back into a larger context by discussing the implications of the work. The authors of the woodpecker article do so by discussing the nature of the woodpecker habitat and how it might be better preserved.

In many articles, the results and discussion sections are combined, but regardless, the data is initially presented without interpretation.

References: Scientific progress requires building on existing knowledge, and previous findings are recognized by directly citing them in any new work. The citations are collected in one list, commonly called "References," although the precise format for each journal varies considerably. The reference list may seem like something you don't actually read, but in fact, it can provide a wealth of information about whether the authors are citing the most recent work in their field or whether they are biased in their citations towards certain institutions or authors. In addition, the reference section provides readers of the article with more information about the particular research topic discussed. The reference list for the woodpecker article includes a wide variety of sources that includes books, other journal articles, and personal accounts of bird sightings.

Supporting material: Increasingly, journals make supporting material that does not fit into the article itself – like extensive data tables, detailed descriptions of methods, figures, and animations – available online. In this case, the video footage shot by the authors is available online, along with several other resources.

Reading the primary literature

The format of a scientific article may seem overly structured compared to many other things you read, but it serves a purpose by providing an archive of scientific research in the primary literature that we can build on. Though isolated examples of that archive go as far back as 600 BCE (see the Babylonian tablets in the Description chapter), the first consistently published scientific journal was the *Philosophical Transactions of the Royal Society of London*, edited by Henry Oldenburg for the Royal Society beginning in 1666 (see the Scientific Institutions chapter for more information). These early scientific writings include all of the components listed above, but the writing style is surprisingly different than a modern journal article. For example, Isaac Newton opened his 1672 article "New Theory About Light and Colours" with the following:

> I shall without further ceremony acquaint you, that in the beginning of the Year 1666... I procured me a Triangular glass-Prisme, to try therewith the celebrated Phenomena of Colours. And in order thereto having darkened my chamber, and made a small hole in my window-shuts, to let in a convenient quantity of the Suns light, I placed my Prisme at his entrance, that it might be thereby refracted to the opposite wall. It was at first a very pleasing divertissement, to view the vivid and intense colours produced thereby; but after a while applying my self to consider them more circumspectly, I became surprised to see them in an oblong form; which, according to the received laws of Refraction, I expected should have been circular. (Newton, 1672)

Newton describes his materials and methods in the first few sentences ("a small hole in my window-shuts"), he describes his results ("an oblong form"), refers to the work that has come before him ("the received laws of Refraction"), and highlights how his results differ from his expectations. Today, however, Newton's statement that the "colours" produced were a "very pleasing divertissement" would be out of place in a scientific article (Figure 4). Much more typically, modern scientific articles are written in an objective tone, typically without statements of personal opinion to avoid any appearance of bias in the interpretation of their results. Unfortunately this tone often results in overuse of the passive voice, with statements like, "a Triangular glass-Prisme was procured" instead of the wording Newton chose: "I procured me a Triangular glass-Prisme." The removal of the first person entirely from the articles reinforces the misconception that science is impersonal, boring and involves no creativity, lacking the enjoyment and

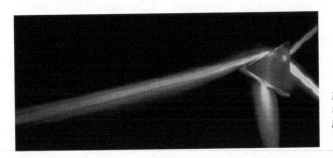

Figure 4: Sir Isaac Newton desribed the rainbow produced by a prism as a "pleasing divertissement."

surprise described by Newton. The tone can sometimes be misleading if the study involves many authors, making it unclear who did what work. The best scientific writers are able to both present their work in an objective tone and make their own contributions clear.

The scholarly vocabulary in scientific articles can be another obstacle to reading the primary literature. Materials and Methods sections often are highly technical in nature and can be confusing if you are not intimately familiar with the type of research being conducted. There is a reason for all of this vocabulary, however: an explicit, technical description of materials and methods provides a means for other scientists to evaluate the quality of the data presented and can often provide insight to scientists on how to replicate or extend the research described.

The tone and specialized vocabulary of the modern scientific article can make it hard to read, but understanding the purpose and requirements for each section can help you decipher the primary literature. Learning to read scientific articles is a skill, and like any other skill, it requires practice and experience to master. It is not, however, an impossible task. Strange as it seems, the most efficient way to tackle a new article may be through a piece-meal approach, reading some but not all the sections and not necessarily in their order of appearance. For example, the abstract of an article will summarize its key points, but this section can often be dense and difficult to understand. Sometimes the end of the article may be a better place to start reading. In many cases, authors present a model that fits their data in this last section of the article. The discussion section may emphasize some themes or ideas that tie the story together, giving the reader some foundation for reading the article from the beginning. Even experienced scientists read articles this way – skimming the figures first, perhaps, or reading the discussion and then going back to the results. Often, it takes a scientist multiple readings to truly understand the authors' work and incorporate it into their personal knowledge base in order to build on that knowledge.

Building knowledge and facilitating discussion

The process of science does not stop with the publication of the results of research in a scientific article. In fact, in some ways, publication is just the beginning. Scientific journals also provide a means for other scientists to respond to the work they publish; like many newspapers and magazines, most scientific journals publish letters from their readers. Unlike the common "Letters to the Editor" of a newspaper, however, the letters in scientific journals are usually critical responses to the authors of a research study in which alternative interpretations are outlined. When such a letter is received by a journal editor, it is typically given to the original authors so that they can respond, and both the letter and response are published together. Nine months after the original publication of the woodpecker article, Science published a letter (called a "Comment") from David Sibley and three of his colleagues, who reinterpreted the Fitzpatrick team's data and concluded that the bird in question was a more common pileated woodpecker, not an ivory-billed woodpecker (Sibley et al., 2006). The team from the Cornell lab wrote a response supporting their initial conclusions, and Sibley's team followed that up with a response of their own in 2007 (Fitzpatrick et al., 2006; Sibley et al., 2007). As expected, the research has generated significant scientific controversy and, in addition, has captured the attention of the public, spreading the story of the controversy into the popular media.

For more information about this story see our "The Case of the Ivory-Billed Woodpecker" article on the Visionlearning website.

Key Concepts for this module

► Scientists make their research available to the community by publishing it in scientific journals.

► In scientific papers, scientists explain the research that they are building on, their research methods, data and data analysis techniques, and their interpretation of the data.

► Understanding how to read scientific papers is a critical skill for scientists and students of science.

References

Fitzpatrick, J. W., Lammertink, M., Luneau, M. D., Jr., Gallagher, T. W., Harrison, B. R., Sparling, G. M., et al. (2005). Ivory-billed Woodpecker (Campephilus principalis) Persists in Continental North America. *Science*, 308(5727), 1460-1462.

Fitzpatrick, J. W., Lammertink, M., Luneau, M. D., Jr., Gallagher, T. W., & Rosenberg, K. V. (2006). Response to Comment on "Ivory-billed Woodpecker (Campephilus principalis) Persists in Continental North America". *Science*, 311(5767), 1555b-.

Kennedy, D. (2005). The Ivory-Bill Returns. *Science*, 308(5727), 1377.

Newton, I. (1672). New Theory about light and colors. *Philosophical Transactions*, 6, 3075-3087.

Sibley, D. A., Bevier, L. R., & Patten, M. A. (2007). Ivory-Billed or Pileated Woodpecker? *Science*, 315(5818), 1495.

Sibley, D. A., Bevier, L. R., Patten, M. A., & Elphick, C. S. (2006). Comment on "Ivory-billed Woodpecker (Campephilus principalis) Persists in Continental North America". *Science*, 311(5767), 1555a-.

Utilizing the Scientific Literature

"Science... has provided a record of ideas and has enabled man to manipulate and to make extracts from that record so that knowledge evolves and endures throughout the life of a race rather than that of an individual."

~ Vannevar Bush

Think about something you know and understand very well. Maybe you know everything about your favorite musical group, and when your friend asks you about them, you can list all of their songs and the band members' names and maybe even something about their history. Maybe you even predict when their next big hit will come out, based on what you know. Your friend asks how you know so much, and you admit that you read a book about them, and have all their albums, and you keep up on their tour dates on their web page. You've been to their concerts and seen them perform. You are referencing your sources, explaining how you know the facts, and why you are so comfortable making a prediction about them – and your friend trusts your knowledge and thus gives your opinion some weight.

Scientists use references in much the same way, drawing on available information to conduct their research. But unlike you, when expressing your opinion about your favorite band, scientists are, in fact, obligated to provide the details about where they got that information. The scientific literature is designed to be a reliable archive of scientific research, providing a growing, stable base for new research investigations. When scientists present their new ideas and results to the community, they are expected to support their ideas with knowledge of the scientific literature and the work that has come before them. If they don't show their understanding of the literature, it's like you telling your friend that you love everything a particular band has done, even though you've only heard one of their songs. In short, the scientific literature is of central importance to the growth and development of science as a whole.

A brief history of scientific literature

In its earliest stages, the scientific literature took the form of letters, books, and other writings produced and published by individuals for the purpose of sharing their research. For example, the Babylonians recorded significant astronomical events like lunar eclipses on clay tablets as early as the 6th century BCE (see the chapter on Description). The Persian scientist Alhazen hand-wrote a seven-volume treatise on his experiments in the field of optics while he was under house arrest in Cairo, Egypt between 1011 and 1021 CE (see the Experimentation chapter). Much of Galileo Galilei's groundbreaking work was published as a series of letters, such as his "Letters on sunspots" or the "Letter to Grand Duchess Christina." Isaac Newton's landmark *Philosophiæ Naturalis Principia Mathematica* was published as a series of books in 1686, largely paid for from the personal fortune of the English astronomer Edmund Halley.

Today, although scientists still publish books and letters, the vast majority of the scientific literature is published in the form of journal articles, a practice that started in the mid-1600s. In March 1665, the Royal Society of London began publishing *Philosophical Transactions of the Royal Society of London* (for more, see the Scientific Institutions and Societies chapter). The serial not only included a description of events that occurred at the weekly meetings of the Society, but it also included results from scientific investigations conducted outside of the Society meetings by its members. This publication was made available to other scientists as well as the general public, and thus it helped establish an archive of scientific research. Other journals in which scientists could publish their findings appeared around the same time. The French *Journal des sçavans* (translated as Journal of the savants – a "savant" is a member of a scholarly society) actually began publishing a

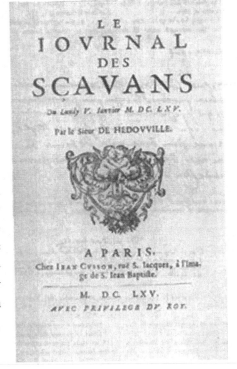

Figure 1: *Title page of the first issue of* le Journal des Sçavans.

few months before *Philosophical Transactions* but it did not carry scientific research reports until after (Figure 1). The Italian journal *Saggi di naturali esperienzi* (*Essays of natural experiments*) was first published in 1667 by the Accademia del Cimento in Florence. By the mid-18th century, most major European cities had their own scientific society, each with its own scientific publication.

As the number of scientific journals expanded, they helped promote the progress of science itself. Whereas Newton had to seek a wealthy donor to fund the publication of his research, it was no longer the wealthiest or best-known individuals who had the ability to publish their findings. As a result, many more individuals were encouraged to take up the study of science and publish their own research. This in turn led to an explosion in the number of scientific studies that were conducted and the resulting knowledge that was generated from this research.

However, the expansion of the scientific literature also created challenges. As the knowledge base of science grew, it became more difficult to keep track of the discoveries that were made. By the 18th century, many journals also included abstracts or short summaries of scientific research papers published in other journals so that their readers could stay current with the latest scientific advances.

In 1945, Vannevar Bush, an American scientist and statesman, highlighted the importance of the archive of research contained within the scientific literature when, in an essay first published in *The Atlantic Monthly*, he wrote, "A record if it is to be useful to science, must be continuously extended, it must be stored, and above all it must be consulted." Inspired by Bush's essay, Eugene Garfield, an American scientist, founded the Institute for Scientific Information (ISI). In 1960, ISI introduced Science Citation Index, the first citation index for scientific scholarly journals. Science Citation Index makes use of the inherent linking characteristics of scientific papers: a single scientific paper contains citations to any number of earlier studies on which that work builds, and eventually it too is cited by future research studies. Thus, each published manuscript is one node in a network of citations. In making these networks explicit, Science Citation Index emphasizes a key aspect of the scientific literature – the way that it is continuously extended and builds on itself. Evidence that scientists consult that continuously growing record is seen in the reference list that accompanies every scientific journal article. Understanding how scientists utilize the scientific literature is a key component to understanding how science works.

The scientific literature in practice

In a lecture discussing the connections between scientific writing and scientific discovery, Frederic Holmes, an American biologist and historian of science, has said:

> When scientists refer to the 'literature' of their fields, they have in mind something very different from what we mean when we talk of literature in general. The literature of a scientific specialty area is the accumulated corpus of research articles contained in the journals of the field, and it is regarded as the primary repository of the knowledge that defines the state of that field. (Holmes, 1987)

As Vannevar Bush noted, that literature is only useful if it is consulted, and scientists must make it clear in their own work when they have, in fact, consulted that "accumulated corpus of research articles." You are probably familiar with the notion of citing sources, the way that, for example, a journalist indicates the experts that he or she consulted to write a news article. When scientists cite sources in their scientific journal articles, they are doing more than just showing which experts they consulted, however. Scientists consult the literature to learn all they can about a specific area of study, and then cite those articles to both acknowledge the authors as the originators of the idea they are discussing and also to help readers understand their line of reasoning in coming to their own conclusions.

Using the literature is an ongoing, iterative process for all scientists. For example, when beginning to conduct a geologic field investigation in the Warner Range in northeastern California, Anne Egger first did a search in GeoRef, a geosciences-themed database of journal articles, to see if anyone had published geologic maps or other investigations in this region. She did not want to duplicate any work that had already been done, and also wanted to see what information was already available. She first came across a paper published in 1986 by two geologists from the U.S. Geological Survey, where they presented their work on determining the ages of volcanic rocks in the region (Duffield and McKee, 1986). These data would be very useful in understanding the volcanic history of the region. In addition, she used a technique that many scientists do when searching the literature: she consulted the reference list in this paper, as it provided a wealth of additional papers for her to search. One such paper was a publication entitled "Basin Range Structure and Stratigraphy of the Warner Range, Northeastern California," by Richard Joel Russell, published by the University of California Press in 1928 – this appeared to be the first published scientific investigation in this region (Russell, 1928). The USGS geologists had added more detail to Russell's work, but only in the southern part of the range. Therefore, these and other resources helped Egger and her colleagues decide to focus on the central and northern parts of the range, where less was known about the geology. In addition, they helped define where there were still unanswered questions.

Figure 2: *Sedimentary rocks in the Warner Range.*

One such unanswered question was the origin of the sedimentary rock layers in the Warner (see Figure 2). Several geologists had noted the presence of granite cobbles in these sedimentary rock layers. Cobbles in general indicate that the sediments were deposited by a large river, but the presence of granite cobbles indicates something else: although granite is common in other parts of California, there is none nearby, so they had to be carried a long distance by that ancient river. By looking at the age and chemical make-up of the granite cobbles, Egger and her colleagues could compare them to granite in other areas and try to determine where the cobbles came from. They collected data in the field and in the laboratory, eventually preparing a scientific journal article about the work they did entitled "Provenance and paleogeographic implications of Eocene-Oligocene sedimentary rocks in the northwestern Basin and Range" (Egger, Colgan, and York, 2009).

The authors recognized that a number of different names had been applied to the sedimentary rocks they were investigating, and they wanted to make it clear to others how the terminology they were using fit into what others had done. In the excerpt that follows, they explain the historical progression of work in the region starting with the first investigation in 1928, and referring to articles along the way in order to show how their new work utilizes the previously established names:

The Warner Range exposes a thick sequence of ... sedimentary and volcanic rocks... The base of this sequence is primarily sedimentary and volcaniclastic; it was originally called the Lower Cedarville Formation by Russell (1928). Based on detailed field mapping in a portion of the range between Cedarville and Lake City, Martz (1970) subdivided the Lower Cedarville Formation into five units and mapped at least one unconformity within it. In their mapping of the South Warner Wilderness area between Granger Canyon and Eagleville, Duffield et al. (1976) did not subdivide the sedimentary sequence, though they alluded to the presence of at least three recognizable units based on composition, color, and vegetation. Myers (1998) and (2006) retained the nomenclature of Martz (1970) in paleofloral analyses of fossil assemblages in this sequence (Myers, 1998; 2006). Our new mapping in 2004 and 2005 confirmed the formation boundaries suggested by Martz (1970) and extended these subdivisions to the south between Cedar Pass and the South Warner Wilderness, and thus here we use those formation names.

This explicit acknowledgement of other scientists' work shows that the authors examined the research archive in order to build on it, making use of the accumulated knowledge and understanding about the region in order to ask new questions about the sedimentary rocks. Later in the paper, the authors wanted to establish the age of the rocks they are describing. One kind of data that can help them make this determination is the fossils present in the rock, but this is not data they themselves collected. In this case, they cite papers where other scientists did look closely at the fossils:

The Steamboat Formation includes two fossiliferous layers... At its base north of Cedarville, a well-documented floral assemblage marks the transition from the latest Eocene to Oligocene (Myers, 2006). The fossils occur in a 1 m-thick ... siltstone that extends laterally (mainly to the south) approximately 7 km (Myers, 2006). ... [and] include ferns and conifers that occur throughout the sequence...

Myers' data about the fossils helped establish the age of the sedimentary rocks (Eocene to Oligocene, about 35 million years old). Building on this existing data, Egger and her co-authors could then show what the rivers were like in the region during that time. One of the kinds of data that they collected in the field is paleocurrent indicators, or measurements that show which direction the currents that deposited the sediments were flowing. In this case, they measured the orientation of granite cobbles in a channel, called imbrication (see Figure 3).

Figure 3: Joe Colgan measuring imbrication in cobbles in the field, and a close-up view of imbrications (right). The lines indicate the orientations that the authors measured.

> Imbrication directions were largely consistent within a single ... channel, but varied as much as 180 degrees between different channels. Data from Cottonwood Canyon exemplify this relationship: 17 measurements in a channel near the base of the exposure show a strong paleocurrent direction towards the NW, while 16 measurements in a bed approximately 30 m stratigraphically higher in the sequence show a bit more variability with an average paleocurrent to the ESE (Fig. 2). While braided rivers tend to display more consistency in their paleocurrent directions, a spread in paleocurrent directions of 180° is expected in a coarse alluvial fan or alluvial plain (e.g. Miall, 1977).

In the passage quoted above, the authors describe their own data (the measurements of the paleocurrent indicators), then suggest a possible reason or interpretation for this data – that this large variability in the orientation of the cobbles is typical of a river that is very broad and steep – an "alluvial plain." They cite Miall to indicate that he was the first person to describe the finding that a "spread in paleocurrent directions," or the fact that the cobbles were oriented in many directions, indicated the presence of a broad alluvial plain. Because he came to a similar conclusion in a different context, they are using the literature to find analogous situations and similar findings, to indicate that their interpretation is reasonable and show how it integrates into the existing research.

Throughout this paper and in scientific articles in general, the authors refer to the literature to do at least three key things: to indicate what other work has been done in the region or on the topic, to cite sources of data that they use, and to support their interpretation of the data (or show how their interpretation differs from previous interpretations). Citing these sources is an integral part of communicating research. Peer reviewers are usually familiar with the literature that authors are using, so one of their duties is to closely examine these references to see if the authors accurately describe their sources or if they missed any important sources (see the Peer Review chapter for more information about the peer review process).

The literature as a data source

In some cases, the literature itself can serve as source for data collection. This has been the case in paleontology, for example, where many investigations over the past several hundred years have involved publishing descriptions of fossil localities, including which species and genera are present in different rock layers. In 1982, John Sepkoski Jr. published a compilation of data of when individual species of marine fossils first appear in the rock record, and when they are no longer seen in rocks. These data came from thousands of published reports (Sepkoski, 1982). In several earlier papers, Sepkoski had analyzed these compiled data and, based on that analysis, developed new ideas about taxonomic diversity through time (for example Sepkoski, 1979). In 1984, Sepkoski and his colleague David Raup published a controversial paper on the apparent regular occurrence of mass extinction events through time (Raup and Sepkoski, 1984), based entirely on the collection of data from the published literature. This type of analysis – often called meta-analysis – could not be done without the reliable archive of research provided by the scientific literature. Meta-analysis is especially useful in fields like medicine and climate science, where the results of studies with disparate methods can be combined to yield more robust results.

Of course, our knowledge and understanding of the natural world continue to evolve, inevitably revealing some mistakes in interpretation in the existing literature, as well as causing some material and ideas to become out of date. Sepkoski recognized this likelihood, and in 1993, he published a paper entitled "Ten Years in the Library: New Data Confirm Paleontological Patterns" (Sepkoski, 1993). In that article, he notes:

> As soon as the manuscript for the 1982 Compendium went to press, I began discovering new and old paleontological literature that changed times of origination and extinction ... After publication..., the original data received special scrutiny from taxonomic experts, and embarrassing errors and promulgations of antiquated data were revealed.

Sepkoski collected the changes and reanalyzed the data. Interestingly, he found little difference in the conclusions about evolutionary patterns that he had published earlier (Sepkoski, 1993). For paleontology, this result has important implications – as Sepkoski states: "...the major patterns of ... evolution are rather insensitive to new fossil discoveries and changes in taxonomic interpretation, indicating that analyses of transitory data can be robust, so long as a large component of the biosphere is being considered." A similar conclusion can be drawn for the scientific literature as a whole, as well – though some mistakes get published, and our interpretations change, as a whole, the literature is robust and a reliable source of scientific data.

Accessing the scientific literature

Staying current with the literature in one's field is a challenge – far more research is being published every day than is possible to read. Many journals now send out email notices to subscribers when a new issue comes out, including the table of contents and links to each of the articles. This allows scientists to quickly browse a new issue and see if there is an article of relevance to their work. Very often, however, scientists have seen or heard preliminary versions of published articles through presentations at meetings or other interactions with colleagues at different institutions (see the chapter The Why and How of Scientific Meetings).

Having access to the scientific literature is critical to doing science. Today, digital and online databases make it easier for people to search the literature and sometimes to access scientific journals articles. Access to the vast majority of journals, however, even digital journals, is limited by subscription, which may run into the thousands of dollars. As a result, scientists at institutions without the resources to pay for these subscriptions are at a disadvantage (Evans and Reimer, 2009). More recently, many journals are providing open access to their content after a set time period, often a year (in the case of *Science* magazine), and some provide open access from the very beginning, such as the Public Library of Science. This change reflects awareness that a diversity of viewpoints improves our scientific understanding, and that everyone should have access to the scientific literature.

The reason why access to the literature is so important is because it is a reliable archive of scientific research. The fact that it is reliable does not mean that every published paper is correct, but it means that progress in our understanding can be tracked through time. When mistakes or even fraud are discovered, a paper can be retracted, which removes it from the literature and ensures that the record continues to be reliable. In this way, earlier ideas can be built upon or refuted, and multiple lines of evidence can accumulate that help scientists establish the "big ideas" of science – robust theories like plate tectonics, atomic theory, and evolution.

Key Concepts for this chapter

▶ The scientific literature provides an archive of research, which scientists make use of throughout the process of investigation.

▶ Scientists reference the literature to indicate what other work has been done on a research topic, to cite sources of data that they use, and to show how their interpretations integrate with the published knowledge base of science.

▶ New research questions can be investigated by reanalyzing or compiling data from the literature.

▶ While individual scientists can make errors, the knowledge-base of science as reflected in the scientific literature is self-correcting as new studies and new interpretations come to light.

References

Duffield, W. A., & McKee, E. H. (1986). Geochronology, structure, and basin-range tectonism of the Warner Range, northeastern California. *Geological Society of America Bulletin*, 97(2), 142-146.

Egger, A. E., Colgan, J. P., & York, C. (2009). Provenance and paleogeographic implications of Eocene-Oligocene sedimentary rocks in the northwestern Basin and Range. *International Geology Review*,51(9), 900-919

Evans, J. A., & Reimer, J. (2009). Open Access and Global Participation in Science. *Science*, 323(5917), 1025-.

Harmon, J.E., Gross, A. G. The Scientific Article: From Galileo's New Science to the Human Genome. *Fathom*, retrieved January 23, 2009, http://www.fathom.com/course/21722wd01730/index.html

Holmes, F. L. (1987). Scientific writing and scientific discovery. *Isis*, 220-235.

Raup, D. M., & Sepkoski, J. J. (1984). Periodicity of extinctions in the geologic past. *Proceedings of the National Academy of Sciences of the United States of America*, 81(3), 801-805.

Russell, R. J. (1928). Basin Range structure and stratigraphy of the Warner Range, northeastern California. *University of California Publications in Geological Sciences*, 17(11), 387-496.

Sepkoski, J. J. (1979). A kinetic model of Phanerozoic taxonomic diversity; II, Early Phanerozoic families and multiple equilibria. *Paleobiology*, 5(3), 222-251.

Sepkoski, J. J. (1982). A compendium of fossil marine families. *Contributions in Biology and Geology*, 51.

Sepkoski, J. J. (1993). Ten years in the library; new data confirm paleontological patterns. *Paleobiology*, 19(1), 43-51.

Peer Review

"Peer review is only a first, preliminary hurdle for a paper to cross; passing peer review and getting published does not mean that your work is right."

~ P.Z. Myers

When you go to see your doctor with a health complaint, he or she might make a preliminary diagnosis and then send you to a specialist to get a more detailed exam. For example, if you have foot pain, you might be sent to a podiatrist. A rash might be indicative of a skin disorder and merit examination by a dermatologist, or it may be due to some type of allergy, thus calling for an allergist's opinion. Patients complaining of chest pains might be sent to multiple specialists including a cardiologist, pulmonologist, gastroenterologist, or others depending on the nature of their pain. General practitioners know that there are far too many different and highly specific medical afflictions for one person to understand them all in detail, so they rely on a team of specialists to keep their patients healthy. Similarly, scientists rely on a team of other scientists, each with his or her own specialty, to review and comment on research before it is published, funded by grant agencies, presented at scientific meetings, or otherwise disseminated to the scientific community.

Scientific journal editors, funding program directors, and chairs of scientific meetings receive many highly diverse and detailed research submissions from scientists. For example, in just one issue of the journal *Science* (Figure 1), research articles can be found on subjects as diverse as the genetic factors that influence body size in dogs, the influence of changing climate on the fruiting patterns of fungi, the geomorphology of ice deposits on Mars, and new technology to generate small electrical currents using ultrasonic waves (*Science*, 2007). It would be impossible for one person to possess the background and experience necessary to review and evaluate these submis-

Figure 1: Scientific journals publish results from diverse research projects. Pictured: the April 6, 2007 cover from Science *magazine.*

sions. As a result, journal editors rely on the process of peer review in which they ask other scientists, who are specialists in those fields and are therefore likely to be familiar with methods presented in those papers, to review and comment on the research. Peer reviewers provide comments regarding the validity of the methods used, the reasonableness of the data analysis techniques, the logic of the interpretations drawn by the authors, and the quality of the writing and graphics. Peer reviewers commonly make recommendations regarding whether they feel a manuscript should be published or a research presentation should be made at a scientific meeting, or, in the case of a grant opportunity, whether a study should be funded. Peer review is also used by academic and other institutions to help provide feedback when a scientist is seeking to earn tenure or promotion to a higher rank.

History and development of peer review

The origin of peer review is closely tied to the development of scientific institutions and scientific journals. When the Royal Society of London began publishing its journal *Philosophical Transactions* in 1665 (Figure 2), the review process was solely the responsibility of the editor (at the time, Henry Oldenburg). The editor sometimes enlisted other scientists to provide opinions as necessary, but it was at his sole discretion whether works were reviewed by others or not. In 1752, the Society itself took over the editorial responsibilities for the journal and instituted a review policy wherein each manuscript was sent to a small group of experts in the field before being published (Spier, 2002). This practice was the beginning of the peer review process as we know it today. The process spread sporadically through the sciences in the 19th century, but became a standard for scientific review in the mid-20th century. Some have linked the spread of peer review in the 20th century to the popularization of Xerox® photocopying machines, which facilitated the replication and distribution of manuscripts to reviewers (Speir, 2002). Whatever the motivation, both *Science* and the *Journal of the American Medical*

Association implemented consistent peer review practices in the 1940s, and other scientific journals followed suit.

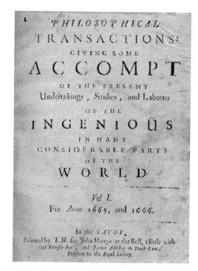

Today, more than 5,000 different scientific journals exist and each of them receives many manuscripts from scientists who feel their work should be published. The journal *Science* alone receives as many as 200 manuscripts per week. To evaluate the appropriateness of each manuscript for publication, journal editors identify two or three peer reviewers to read and comment on each submitted manuscript.

Peer reviewers are knowledgeable scientists who are not directly involved with the research being evaluated, but who are familiar with the field of study or the research methods used. The re-

Figure 2: *Cover of the first issue of* Philosophical Transactions *published by the Royal Society. The journal established one of the first peer review policies.*

viewers may not know the scientists who wrote the paper or grant proposal, they may be colleagues, or they may even be scientific competitors with the authors. So, in an attempt to remove bias from the review process, most manuscripts are independently considered by multiple reviewers and it is left to the journal editor to make the final decision regarding publication based on the reviewers' comments. Reviewers consider the relevance of the work to the journal or funding program being targeted, the validity of the methods and interpretations, the originality of the finding, and the clarity of the writing. Reviewers then provide feedback, generally in written form, on the work they have read. And these comments are commonly sent back to the authors so that the authors can use the reviewers' comments to refine and improve the text of their manuscript or their research. Reviewers can often choose whether they wish to remain anonymous to the authors or not. Journal editors and grant program directors rely on the reviewers' feedback to guide their decisions – they may choose to accept a work as is, they may ask the author(s) for revisions, or they may reject the work based on the peer review comments.

Peer review in practice

On January 22, 2007, Conrad Mauclair and colleagues submitted a manuscript entitled "Quantifying the effect of humic matter on the suppression of mercury emissions from artificial soil surfaces" for consideration to the journal *Applied Geochemistry*. The manuscript was sent out by the editor to two peer reviewers, who were given one to two months to complete the review. The reviewers sent comments to the editor, and after considering the reviewers' comments, the editor chose to accept the manuscript with revisions, and responded as such to the authors approximately five months after their initial submission. Excerpts from the letter the editor wrote to the authors detailing this decision are printed below.

27 May 2007

Dear Authors:

I have received two reviews of your manuscript entitled "Quantifying the effect of humic matter on the suppression of mercury emissions from artificial soil surfaces" submitted for publication in Applied Geochemistry. In addition I have read your paper and have some additional comments that are below. All reviewers including myself agree the paper after revisions is acceptable for publication.

I have attached both reviewers' comments to this email. Both reviewers raise some important issues that need to be clearly addressed in your revised paper. I agree with their concerns and below have added a few others that need to be addressed.

Sincerely,

Editor for Special Issue of *Applied Geochemistry*

Additional detailed comments from the Editor:

The mass balance needs to be considered [as detailed by reviewer 2]. My guess is your flow rate is producing an artificially high flux. The way to deal with this would be to use the actual concentration difference between the inlet and outlet instead of the flux to calculate the amount lost. Plot the difference between the outlet and inlet concentrations rather than flux.

The reviewers' comments were attached to the editor's letter with the names of the reviewers removed. In the case of journal manuscripts accepted with revision, the authors have the opportunity to read and respond to the reviewers' comments and make changes to the article in question. In the case of grant submissions, scientists read the reviewers comments and use these to strengthen their submission the next time they apply for a grant. For the article by Mauclair and colleagues, the reviewers had a number of recommendations for improving the article, as the excerpts provided below detail.

Excerpts of comments from Reviewer 1:

This research article reports a controlled laboratory experimental study to probe the role of humic matter in Hg emission from soils. The experiments appear to enjoy sound design and fine performance. The results are certainly very interesting and valuable; this study will stimulate more research to further the exploration.

The "suppression of mercury emission" [in the title] is an interpretation of the experimental observations, rather than an unequivocal conclusion. It might be better to use a [more] conservative title like "Quantifying the Effect of Humic Matter on Mercury Emissions from Artificial Soil Surfaces". I'd think the reader might come up with some different interpretations other than "suppression".

Would [additional experiments with] controls of humic matter plus Hg(II) salt only (without any sand) offer any more [information]?

Excerpts of comments from Reviewer 2:

In response to direct comments requested by the editor:

• Originality: This paper systematically tests the combined impact of humic matter content and light in synthetic soils. Very few studies have reported similar work.

• Importance: This work's main conclusion is that organic matter content alters Hg emissions from soils. This conclusion is of significant interest to mercury biogeochemists and may promote related field-based research, and help in the interpretation of current data sets.

• Manner of presentation: The paper is short, clear and to the point. More discussion of possible mechanisms and more details on related field studies (where fluxes and organic matter have been correlated) could be added.

• Quality of figures and tables: I do not think that the authors have reached an optimal design for the graphical presentation of their data. Figure 1, 2 & 3 could be easily combined, which would help the reader to compare the results taken at different intervals for the same experiments. In fact, these graphs could even be transformed in time series line graphs (instead of histograms). I am not sure of the most attractive final design, but the present design can be improved.

• Serious flaws or can [the paper] be improved by condensation or deletion of information: I have not found any serious flaws. I can say that I am not totally at ease with a study that reports only results from synthetic soils. It would have been nice to complement this data with some «real» soils. But I think that such a systematic, laboratory study is useful and pertinent.

• Does the title and abstract correspond to the content of the manuscript: Yes

• Would you be willing to re-review this paper after submission with revisions: Not necessary

Specific comments regarding the manuscript:

1. Can the authors comment on the realism of their approach? What are the limits of using synthetic soils and mixtures of inorganic Hg + humic acids? The fact that they tried different kinds of humic matter is comforting, but I would have like to see more info on potential limitations.

2. Page 9. Please clarify the design for the long term monitoring section. For instance, were the lights on for 14 days in the "light treatment"? Was this continuous flux sufficient to decrease the pool of Hg in the sample? The following back [of] the envelope calculations left me worried by the results presented here:

3. If we take an average flux of 2000 ng/m2/h for the light + sand treatment (see figures 1, 2 and 3), then we get over 14 days [and] 44 µg lost by evasion, whereas only 25 µg were added!!

Once comments are received regarding a manuscript, it is up to the authors to address those comments, or in cases where they disagree with a reviewer's comment, provide an explanation as to why they have not addressed the comment. In the above case, the authors addressed the majority of the reviewers' comments and sent a letter back to the editor on June 10, 2007 detailing the changes made to the article and discussing why some changes were not made:

July 10, 2007

Dear Editors,

Enclosed is our revised manuscript. We have addressed all of the comments returned to us in the reviews of our paper. In addition, at the suggestion of reviewer 1, we have conducted additional experiments with 100% humic acid and have added the results of this experiment to our paper to assure that we have adequately addressed the experimental design comments. A detailed list of all individual changes is included below.

All of the listed authors have read the revisions and agree with their conclusions.

Sincerely,

The Authors

Detailed list of manuscript revisions

Responses to comments raised by Reviewer 1:

• As directed, we have revised the title of the manuscript to "Quantifying the Effect of Humic Matter on the Emission of Mercury from Artificial Soil Surfaces."

• The reviewer raises an interesting question regarding the use of Hg-humic controls (without sand), these controls were not examined at the time of our study. However, to satisfy this question we have since conducted additional experiments with a 100% humic sample using 1g humic and $HgCl_2$ sample (no sand). The results from this sample were consistent with those presented for our 5% humic sample, confirming that the effect we saw was due to humics, and not the interaction of humics with the sand. We have added this data to the paper and to Figure 1.

Responses to specific comments raised by Reviewer 2:

• We have condensed the presentation of data in the Figures as suggested so that only one pair of graphs is now used (new Figure 1) instead of the three pairs that were used in the previous version of the manuscript (former Figures 1, 2, and 3). We have also edited Figures 2 and 3 (formerly Figures 4 and 5) as recommended.

1. We have better qualified the limitations of the artificial soil system in the discussion.

2. Regarding the manner in which samples were stored between measurements, we had detailed this in the version of the manuscript submitted for review, our Methods section states "All samples were stored in the dark at constant temperature (~23°C) between measurements and monitored in both dark and light for mercury flux at regular intervals." We have tried to emphasize this statement in the results section of the rewritten manuscript and we have added a statement that all flux measurements were taken over a 1.5-2 hr sampling period.

3. The mass balance calculated by the reviewer overestimates Hg loss from the samples as he/she assumes that the samples were exposed to light continuously (see point #2 above). We conservatively estimate that the maximum Hg loss from the sample exhibiting the highest emission rate (sand-Hg only) was 30% of the mercury added. Humic-containing samples showed much lower Hg losses.

4. As the reviewer states, the samples were not under light continuously and this has been clarified as per the two points above.

Responses to specific comments raised by the Editor:

• While turnover rate is a significant issue, our work represents the relative comparison of samples that were all measured at a constant turnover rate, thus the effect of chamber turnover rate on our conclusions is negated. A discussion of this has been added to the manuscript. In an effort to guide future research, we have added mention of more recent personal communication regarding chamber turnover rate, to our knowledge new data regarding turnover rate is not published. A suggestion was made to report the difference between chamber inlet and outlet Hg concentrations rather than fluxes. As described above, the mass balance of Hg in the samples is not problematic. Further, because all Co-Ci differences are multiplied by a constant turnover rate in the flux equation, this would simply have the effect of changing the magnitude of the numbers (and graph axes) reported, not the relative difference between numbers - which is the basis of all conclusions of the work. Also, because the majority of researchers report results as fluxes, we feel that reporting our results as concentration differences would make this work inaccessible to mercury researchers. Our methodology and flux measurements are all based on peer-reviewed, published literature (Lindberg et al., 2002) and follow standard protocols. We believe discussing the limitations of the method is therefore sufficient in this context.

The comments from Reviewer 2 highlight the fact that peer review helps the scientific publishing system to assure that manuscripts meet certain minimal standards. Reviewer 2 commented on the originality of the submission, the perceived importance of the work in the field of science, the manner of presentation of the writing in the text, the quality of the figures and tables and data analysis in general, whether he/she found any serious flaws in the work, and specifically the appropriateness of the manuscript title and abstract since these are the parts of the paper that will be cataloged by literature databases and thus widely read. Reviewers may recommend that authors clarify the text or add certain references that they had not previously considered; they might suggest changes because they feel that the authors' interpretations are not supported by their data; they may recommend additional research to clarify questionable points in the study; or they may recommend that a manuscript be rejected completely because of questions about the research methods, data collection, or interpretation. Similarly, grant proposal reviewers may make specific recommendations for improving a study and recommend that the authors resubmit their proposal in another grant cycle after it has been improved. Grant reviewers might also recommend that more background research be conducted before the authors submit their proposal again, that another scientist with a different expertise be included on the research team, or that the scope of the research be broadened (or narrowed).

Mauclair and colleagues made the majority of the changes requested by the reviewers to their manuscript; they revised the title, added additional explanation to the text, and even conducted additional experiments to satisfy a question raised by Reviewer 1. In the reviews, Reviewer 2 calculated a mass balance of mercury in the experiments and concluded that the samples lost more mercury than was added to the system; the editor then followed this comment with a suggestion as to why this might have occurred and suggested reporting the data in a different manner. The authors address this comment by correcting an erroneous assumption of the reviewer, and explain why they have chosen not to report the data in a different manner as suggested by the editor. Thus, while they did

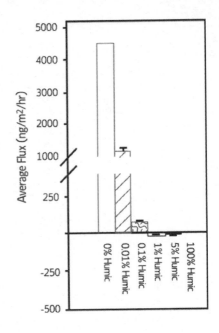

Figure 3: Part of Figure 1 from Mauclair et al. (2008). Data indicated as "100% Humic" are from new experiments run in response to the peer review comments.

not follow the suggestion made in the review, they provide a detailed explanation as to why. Once a revised manuscript is resubmitted, the editor reads the authors' response, and if satisfied that the authors adequately addressed all of the issues raised, moves the manuscript forward in the journal's publishing cycle. In some cases, where major revisions are required, the editor may redistribute the manuscript to the peer reviewers a second time before accepting it as complete. The Mauclair manuscript was accepted for publication in August 2007, it was first published on the journal's website in January 2008, and finally published in the March 2008 issue of the printed version of the journal (Mauclair *et al.*, 2008).

Implications of peer review

It is worth noting the lengthy timescale involved in publishing scientific articles. From the initial submission to the final printing, the described article took 14 months, which does not even include the time spent doing the initial work that led to the publication. The sluggishness of the peer review process is often criticized, but it reflects the understanding that published work enters the scientific literature permanently, as work that can be built upon by other scientists, and thus should be carefully considered.

Additionally, journals and funding agencies vary in their selectivity and research focus. Consequently, scientists choose where to submit their manuscript based on the perceived impact of the research, the likelihood of acceptance, and the size of the audience they wish to reach. In turn, reviewers consider the appropriateness of the research to the journal's audience. For example, while the journal *Applied Geochemistry* focuses on research articles that discuss chemical transformations and process that take place in the environment, the journal *Cell* publishes articles focused on biological process related to cell function. The article by Mauclair and colleagues was published in *Applied Geochemistry*; however, it would likely have been rejected by *Cell*.

As part of the scientific process, reviewers are expected to keep the information in a manuscript confidential until it is published, but it is rare that the work comes as a complete surprise to the entire scientific community. This is because peer review is integrated into almost every step of science, including requests for public funding for research. Funding decisions are made by a committee of peer review scientists who debate each proposal's likelihood of success, the validity of its approach, and the importance of the question being asked. The research methods and ideas published by Mauclair and colleagues in 2008 were reviewed as part of a grant submitted to the Research Foundation of the City University of New York, which was funded in 2005 (Carpi and Frei, 2005). Once funded, the research begins, and preliminary data may be presented at scientific meetings. This allows the findings to be described and debated with colleagues prior to publication. Data that were eventually used in the manuscript were presented to the scientific community in August 2006 at a large international conference on the pollutant mercury (Mauclair *et al.*, 2006), and thus the final publication was anticipated by some scientists in the field.

Peer-reviewed publications and funded research proposals carry significance for the individual scientist beyond simply doing science. In many cases, hiring, promotion, and award decisions are made on the basis of the number and quality of peer-reviewed publications or grants authored by an individual. Scientists also benefit in many ways from serving as peer reviewers – being asked to review a manuscript or proposal is an acknowledgement of one's expertise in an area. All scientists both receive reviews from their peers and review the work of others, and this process comes with a cost. A recent report by the Research Information Network estimated the cost of volunteered time provided by scientists for peer review at $3.7 billion (Research Information Network, 2008). So why do scientists volunteer so much time to this process? Because it is one of the obligations of their profession and one factor that helps build the community of science (see the chapter on Scientists and the Scientific Community).

Peer review is just one of several mechanisms embedded within the process of science that help validate the work of scientists. While it helps to validate journal and grant submissions, it is not a fool-proof filter that assures quality in scientific publishing, especially when the authors of a study are engaged in fraud or deception (see the Scientific Ethics chapter). For example, between 2000 and 2003, Jan Hendrick Schön and colleagues published over 25 papers on superconductivity, all of which passed through the peer review process. After several of the papers were published, Professor Lydia Sohn and Professor Paul McEuen noticed that different experiments carried out under very different conditions and published in different papers displayed the same background error (Figure 4). When confronted with the problem, Schön first claimed that a graph had been mistakenly reproduced in several papers. Shortly thereafter, Bell Labs, the research institute where Schön worked, conducted an investigation; they found numerous instances

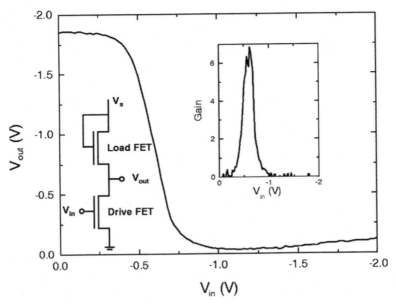

Figure 4: A figure from Schön et al. (2001B) - retracted. Scientists first noted problems with the publication when background noise in the curve (top left and bottom right) appeared identical to that published in a different paper (Schön at al., 2001A)

of misconduct and fraud and consequently fired Schön. At least sixteen of his papers have since been declared to be false, and the journal *Science* has withdrawn eight of his papers (Bao *et al.*, 2002).

While cases of scientific misconduct can be embarrassing because of the publicity they receive, they highlight the self-correcting nature of science. A key aspect of science is that research results must be reproducible and well-documented. Instances of scientific misconduct that have gotten through the peer review system are often quickly exposed when other scientists scrutinize the data and attempt to reproduce the results. To keep this system working, scientific articles include detailed descriptions of research protocols that enable others to reproduce experiments, and they include tabular or graphical presentations of data so that they can be scrutinized by the community at large (see the chapter Understanding Scientific Journals and Articles). One of the first pieces of evidence that raised suspicion over Schön's work was the fact that other scientists had trouble reproducing his experiments with similar results. As occurred with most of Schön's publications, scientific research articles can be retracted if they are found to be in error (whether or not that error is a result of misconduct), thus removing them from the literature of science.

The truth is that retractions are rare, and retractions due to scientific misconduct are even rarer. In an analysis of the scientific literature cataloged in the MEDLINE database maintained by the National Library of Medicine, Sara Nath and colleagues identified 395 articles that were retracted in the two decades from 1982 to 2002 out of over 8.5 million citations listed in the MEDLINE database for that same period (Nath *et al.*, 2006). Of those articles retracted, only 27% were found to be cases of scientific misconduct, 62% were identified as unintentional errors, and 11% of retractions could not be categorized. Nash and colleagues also found that an addition 2,772 errata were published during this same period, which are simple corrections of small mistakes in published manuscripts.

Consequences of peer review

One of the consequences of the peer review system is that it can influence the dissemination and progress of scientific research. It is the peer reviewers that make recommendations as to what research is published in what journals. And it is the peer reviewers that influence the types of research studies that receive funding. This is generally a positive effect as it opens the process to the scientific community at large. But bias among reviewers can negatively impact this process. For example, some researchers have suggested that peer reviewers can be biased in favor of research that reports positive effects (i.e. that drug x has an effect) over research reports that report a no effect (i.e. drug y has no significant effect) (Callaham *et al.*, 1998). Thus, published studies showing positive effects far outnumber ones showing none. Another complication that affects the peer review process is that in a closed review system, where reviewers are kept anonymous from the authors, it is possible for reviewers to pass unnecessarily harsh judgment – or unworthy praise – on a manuscript or application for funding, simply because they have personal differences or friendships with authors.

The widespread use of electronic publishing has prompted a recent re-evaluation of the peer review process as a whole. While scientists still largely agree on the value of peer review, they are sometimes discouraged by the length of time involved from submission of a manuscript, through review, revision, and resubmission, which may take a year or more – as in the case of the article described here. As a result, some authors have suggested that the time-consuming and closed pre-publication peer review process be abandoned entirely in favor of open access, online publishing that allows for constant reviews and updates. A number of scientific publishing media are adapting to the changing nature of publishing. For example, the Public Library of Science (PLoS) project publishes a number of journals in the PLoS family that make their formal peer reviews available to the public and then they further provide a mechanism for additional public comment and review of published articles on their website. Even the journal *Nature*, which has published for over 130 years, has recently experimented with open access peer review for submitted manuscripts.

Publications without peer review

There are publications in the sciences that are not peer-reviewed. For example, many journals, including *Science* and *Nature*, publish news and commentary sections in which they provide weekly updates on major scientific events or issues. A number of journals also publish "letters." Letters to journals include commentary on previously printed articles, but they may also report new, preliminary and intriguing scientific results that have not yet been tested and replicated enough to pass full peer review.

Scientists also write material specifically for non-peer reviewed publication. For example, the evolutionary biologist Steven J. Gould was a prodigious writer and became well known for his books and magazine articles on topics ranging from evolution to baseball. The theoretical physicist Stephen Hawking is well known for his books aimed at explaining cosmology, which include such popular titles like *A Brief History of Time* and *The Universe in a Nutshell*. And the astronomer Carl Sagan not only wrote numerous popular magazine articles, but also authored the best-selling book *Contact*, which was turned into a blockbuster film. The articles and books that scientists write for sources other than peer-reviewed journals have an important, but very different, purpose than the peer-reviewed literature. These pieces are often directed at explaining science in more common language to non-scientists and thus serve a crucial role in describing the impact of science to the general public. As such, they are generally, but not always, based on the peer-reviewed literature that forms the basis of our scientific knowledge.

Key Concepts for this chapter

▶ Scientific manuscripts and funding proposals are reviewed by several peer scientists who are familiar with the field of research and who make recommendations on whether or not the work should be published and/or funded.

▶ Peer review works on many levels and is a fundamental component of the process of science.

▶ After publication, scientific papers and other forms of research dissemination are further scrutinized by the scientific community when scientists read or try to reproduce the research.

▶ Scientists conduct peer review as part of their responsibility to the scientific community, and are themselves evaluated by the peer review process.

References

Bao, Z., Batlogg, B., Berg, S., Dodabalapur, A., Haddon, R.C., Hwang, H., Kloc, C., Meng, H., Schön, J.H. (2002). Retraction of Schön et al., *Science* 294 (5549) 2138-2140. Retraction of Schön et al., *Science* 293 (5539) 2432-2434. Retraction of Schön et al., *Science* 292 (5515) 252-254. Retraction of Schön et al., *Science* 290 (5493) 963-965. Retraction of Schön et al., *Science* 289 (5479) 599-601. Retraction of Schön et al., *Science* 288 (5475) 2338-2340. Retraction of Schön et al., *Science* 288 (5466) 656-658. Retraction of Schön et al., *Science* 287 (5455) 1022-1023. *Science*, 298(5595):961.

Callaham, M.L., Wears, R.L., Weber, E.J., Barton, C., Young, G. (1998). Positive-Outcome Bias and Other Limitations in the Outcome of Research Abstracts Submitted to a Scientific Meeting. *Journal of the American Medical Association*, 280: 254-257.

Carpi, A., Frei, A. (2005). The Terrestrial Mercury Cycle and Climate: Measuring and Modeling the Impact of Global Change. Grant funded by the Research Foundation of CUNY, Collaborative Research Incentive Award program, funding period, August 2005 – September 2008.

Hixson, J. (1976). *The Patchwork Mouse*. Anchor Press/Doubleday Garden City, New York.

Langfeldt, L. (2001). The Decision-Making Constraints and Processes of Grant Peer Review, and Their Effects on the Review Outcome. *Social Studies of Science*, 31(6):820-841.

Mauclair, C., Layshock, J., Carpi, A. (2008). Quantifying the effect of humic matter on the emission of mercury from artificial soil surfaces. *Applied Geochemistry*, 23(3):594-601.

Mauclair, C., Layshock, J., Carpi, A. (2006). The Effect of Humic Matter on Soil Mercury Emissions, presented at the 8th International Conference on Mercury as a Global Pollutant, Madison, Wisconsin, August 5-11, 2006.

Nath, S., Marcus, S.C., Druss, B.G. (2006). Retractions in the research literature: misconduct or mistakes? *Medical Journal of Australia*, 185(3):152-154.

Nature (2006). Nature peer review trial and debate. Retrieved January 7, 2008 from Nature http://www.nature.com/nature/peerreview/.

PLoS (2008). Public Library of Science. Retrieved January 7, 2008 from http://www.plos.org/.

Research Information Network (2008). *Activities, costs and funding flows in the scholarly communications system in the UK.* Research Information Network, London.

Schön, J. H., Meng, H., Bao, Z. (2001A). Self-assembled monolayer organic field-effect transistors. *Nature*, 413(6857): 713-716.

Schön, J. H., Meng, H., Bao, Z. (2001B). Field-Effect Modulation of the Conductance of Single Molecules. *Science* 294 (5549), 2138.

Science (2007). *Science Magazine.* 316(5821), April 6, 2007, The American Association for the Advancement of Science, Washington, DC.

Spier, R. (2002). The history of the peer-review process. *Trends in Biotechnology,* 20(8), 357-358.

van Rooyen, S., Godlee, F., Evans, S., Black, N., & Smith, R. (1999). Effect of open peer review on quality of reviews and on reviewers' recommendations: a randomised trial. *BMJ*, 318(7175), 23-27.

The How and Why of Scientific Meetings

"Free and constant intellectual communication between scientists is essential for the health of science, and frequent personal contact is very desirable."

~ Francis Crick and others, in a letter to *Nature*

On April 20, 2010, the Horizon Deepwater drilling rig exploded off the coast of Louisiana, starting an unprecedented oil spill that continued for 3 months. The details of that event were chronicled extensively in the popular media: the *New York Times* alone lists 775 articles about the spill (New York Times, 2010), and thousands of journalists were on the scene to report the day-to-day progression of the spill.

Scientists were on the scene, too (see Figure 1). Scientific agencies including the National Science Foundation (NSF) and the National Oceanographic and Atmospheric Administration (NOAA) funded rapid response teams of scientists to collect data, perform experiments, monitor water and air quality, and model the spread of the oil plume in the critical days after the explosion. But while the journalists got their stories out immediately, the scientists had more work to do. Data collection might happen quickly, but processing, analyzing, and understanding the implications of those data and then submitting findings to be peer reviewed prior to publication can take much longer. As a result, some early findings from these rapid response studies were presented first at scientific meetings, such as the fall meeting of the American Geophysical Union (AGU) held in San Francisco in December of 2010. In a series of sessions entitled "Lessons Learned from the Deepwater Horizon Oil Spill," dozens of scientists reported on the results of their research on the spread of the oil, the effects of the chemical dispersants on the oil and marine life, the effects of the spill on the coastal ecosystems, the amount of methane released into the air above the Gulf of Mexico, and much

Figure 1: Scientists examining tar balls on Timablier Island, Louisiana

more. The meeting provided an ideal opportunity to present these new findings to a broad community, both to inform the community of exciting new research and to get feedback quickly.

Scientific meetings are one of the primary venues for scientists to present their new work to their colleagues with the purpose of receiving feedback at an early stage of their research and get feedback on it, and thus they are an integral part of the process of science. They serve as an informal peer-review that can help researchers to develop, clarify and refine their work as they proceed to write it up and submit it for formal review and final publication. In addition, meetings allow researchers to hear about what others in their field and related disciplines are doing, talk with colleagues from different institutions around the world, and learn about new research, tools, and techniques that might be relevant to their work. Some meetings are small and narrowly focused on a specific topic or theme, others are meant to bring many thousands of scientists together annually and are very broad. Regardless of the size of the meeting, the main goal is to bring a community of scientists together and provide opportunities for them to interact.

The development of the modern scientific meeting

Groups of men (and they were, in fact, all men) interested in discussing science met as early as 1640 in London; eventually, these meetings led to the establishment of the Royal Society of London in 1660 (Gribbin, 2007) (see Scientific Institutions and Societies). Since then, scientific societies and meetings have grown together. Early meetings remained small and local for about 200 years, since transportation was difficult and costly, but larger meetings began to proliferate (along with scientific societies) in the mid-1800s.

For example, a group of scientists gathered in Philadelphia, Pennsylvania, on September 20, 1848, with the goal of establishing a new national-scale organization: the American Association for the Advancement of Science (AAAS). They held six days of talks and presentations by prospective members and, by the end of the meeting, had 461 registered members on the books (Kohlstedt *et al.*, 1999). Louis Agassiz, one of the founders, worked with two other scientists to draft the "Rules and Objectives of the Association," which stated that one of the fundamental goals of the new society was, "By periodical and migratory meetings, to promote intercourse between those who are cultivating science in different parts of the United States" (as quoted in Kohlstedt *et al.*, 1999). In other words, they recognized that scientists were at work all over the country, and they hoped to overcome geographic barriers that kept scientists apart by holding regular meetings that moved around the country.

Another goal of the new society was "to give a stronger and... more systematic direction to scientific research in our country" (as quoted in Kohlstedt *et al.*, 1999). The new society, therefore, would not only provide an opportunity to bring the community together through meetings, but would guide research through consensus of the membership. At the first AAAS meeting in 1848, a group of new members – still all men – wrote three resolutions to influence research directions in the United States. One of these resolutions was to establish a committee to address "the Secretary of the Navy, requesting his further aid in procuring for Lieut. Maury the use of the observations of European and other foreign navigators, for the extension and perfecting of his charts of winds and currents" (AAAS, 2010). The support of a wide group of scientists may have eventually helped Lieutenant Maury hold an international meeting in 1853 to establish standards for weather measurements (see Data: Analysis and Interpretation). In many cases, meetings still provide the opportunity to bring the membership of a society together to vote on resolutions or position statements and to give direction to future research.

AAAS is a broad society, and its meetings include presentations from all disciplines in science, including the social sciences. Throughout the late

1800s and early 1900s, groups of scientists organized into more discipline-specific societies as well, which hosted their own meetings to bring their members together. For example, the American Chemical Society (ACS) was established in 1876; the founding of the Ecological Society of America was discussed proposed at a meeting of ecologists in 1914 and officially formed in 1915 at its inaugural meeting; the American Geophysical Union held its first meeting in 1919. All four of these societies continue to hold annual meetings open to their large and diverse memberships (ACS, for example, now has over 163,000 members), which also are now much more diverse than their original membership of largely white males. Today, there are hundreds of scientific conferences every year hosted by a wide variety of organizations.

As membership in these disciplinary organizations and attendance at annual meetings grew, scientists recognized another need for communication: smaller, more focused meetings that addressed a specific theme or topic. In 1931, Neil Gordon (see Figure 2), a chemist at Johns Hopkins University, brought together a small group of scientists working at the "frontiers of research" to give them the opportunity to work together intensely for five days (Daemmrich, Gray, and Shaper, 2006). Over time, these meetings evolved to the Gordon Research Conferences, a non-profit organization that runs over 200 meetings a year. Each of these meetings is proposed by a group of scientists that wish to focus on a topic, so new, topical meetings are held every year. These meetings average about 140 attendees, where an annual meeting of the American Geophysical Union might have as many as 16,000 attendees.

Figure 2: Neil Gordon, founder of the Gordon Research Conferences

Why scientists go to meetings

Going to and presenting at meetings is a common component of most scientists' lives, especially those who work at universities and research laboratories. They go to scientific meetings in order to present new work and get feedback from their peers, make connections with other scientists, learn new things, and get together with friends and colleagues.

For example, at the 2010 Annual Meeting of the Geological Society of America, Anne Egger presented the results of using some of the Visionlearning modules, like the one you are reading now, in college science classrooms. One of her goals was to get feedback on her work teaching students about the nature of scientific theories in preparation for publishing her results. A comment she received in response to the talk was particularly helpful, pointing out that the meaning of "theory" in the social sciences is different from both the scientific and colloquial definitions – an interesting and relevant point that had been overlooked in analysis. This useful feedback can be incorporated into future publications. Several weeks later, Egger received an email from a scientist and university professor who had been at the meeting: he had seen her presentation, and was wondering if he could use the materials she had discussed. This is one example of what many scientists call "dissemination" – presenting their work to a broad audience in hopes that it will get used and incorporated into others' work. During that same meeting, Egger walked through several poster sessions and came across someone who had done new geologic mapping in Mesa Verde National Park, where she teaches a class. She talked to the scientist and was able to download his new map, which she can now incorporate into her teaching.

Sometimes, meeting attendees seek out particular presentations or scientists in order to make new connections. After a presentation he made at the 2008 Ocean Sciences meeting, Kevin Arrigo, a biological oceanographer at Stanford University, was approached by a scientist in charge of a funding program at NASA. She wanted to work with him to develop a new funding program to study biological oceanography in the Arctic (see our research profile of Kevin Arrigo online for more information). In this case, dissemination of results at a meeting catalyzed the development of a whole new research area. As Arrigo said, "You never know who's going to be in the audience."

On the other hand, meetings are also an opportunity for students and beginning scientists to meet other people in their field and to begin to establish professional relationships. For example, when Anthony Carpi had completed his MS thesis at Cornell University and was seeking a PhD project, he began searching for someone to serve as his dissertation advisor, but was coming up empty handed. His MS advisor offered to fund his travel to a 1994 conference on Mercury as a Global Pollutant to present his masters work and to search for dissertation projects/advisors. At the conference, he approached a scientist whose work he had read, Steve Lindberg at the Oak Ridge National Laboratory in Tennessee. Lindberg listened to his ideas, gave him some quick feedback, suggested some additional literature to read, and asked him to follow up after the conference. Carpi did so, and applied for scholarships that fund students (or scientists) to go to national labs to do research. As a result of that brief encounter at a meeting, Carpi spent 8 months working with Lindberg at Oak Ridge National Lab, research that allowed him to complete his PhD and publish three journal articles.

These individual stories are not unique. In a 2004 survey of over 1000 scientific conference attendees, 66% of respondents reported learning something that changed the direction of their research (Aiken, 2006). Just over half indicated that something they had learned at the meeting had saved them time and money in their own work. Sixty percent reported that their meeting attendance led to a new collaboration. All of these are common gains from attending meetings.

Beyond allowing scientists to get together to share their work, scientific meetings are also important social events. After the first meeting of AAAS in 1848, one of the founders, William Barton Rogers, wrote,

> For us, such reunions of the scientific brethren… are of precious value and form the best compensation we can enjoy for the prolonged restraints of our vocation. What new impulses to exertion, what encouragement and guidance do they not give? … how many cheering and delightful social recollections?

Meetings are full of formal and informal times to interact with friends and colleagues, and these often prove to be both socially and professionally productive. Many scientific meetings have planned social events such as dinners or receptions, but the halls of scientific meetings are usually filled with scientists talking in pairs or groups (see Figure 3). The conversations range from catching up with friends to discussing a new collaborative research project or debating the interpretation of results in the talk they just heard. Despite the proliferation of web-based communication, scientists still place value on attending meetings, in part because of the informal opportunities to interact with other scientists (O'Brien, 2006).

At large meetings, such as the annual American Geophysical Union meeting described earlier, the media are in attendance, and their job is to disseminate these new scientific findings to the general public. Science journalists, freelance science writers, and public information officers at scientific institutions can get press passes in order to attend the sessions without having to pay the registration fee. Blogs are now also a common part of scientific meetings, with frequent posts by the organization hosting the meeting, and links to scientists' and journalists' blogs that are focused on the meeting pro-

Figure 3: *Scientists chatting it up between sessions at a scientific meeting.*

ceedings. All of the media involvement helps spread the word about new scientific findings beyond the community of science and out to the general public.

Attending a meeting

Spending a day or two at a meeting held by a scientific society like AAAS or AGU offers a glimpse into how the scientific community functions. At most meetings, there are both oral and poster presentations. In an oral presentation, presenters generally have 15-20 minutes to present their research and take a few questions. Usually, there are also longer keynote addresses that are given by prominent scientists and present a major theme of the meeting. Talks are grouped into topical sessions that last 1-2 hours, and there are usually multiple concurrent topical sessions. People who give oral presentations are usually at or near the culmination of their research, because the time allowed for questions is not enough to get detailed feedback. In a poster presentation, presenters make a poster displaying their research and stand with their poster for an hour or two (or perhaps more), explaining their work, answering questions, and talking with others. Posters are grouped together in large sessions, often with hundreds of posters up at once, and people wander through long rows (see Figure 4). Because this type of presentation allows a lot more time to interact with people, this is a good way to get feedback on work in progress.

When attending a scientific meeting, it is a good idea to look at the program in advance and plan a strategy. Read abstracts to choose which talks and posters to see. Because they have only a short amount of time, oral presenters tend to talk fast and use a lot of jargon, so it helps to be familiar with the subject. There is usually more time to get explanations from people at their posters – ask questions and find out more about the work. If you are a student, meetings are also a great place to find out more about graduate schools. In addition to asking people questions about their research, ask them about the institution where they study or teach. Often, there are areas at the meeting where schools set up information booths about their graduate programs.

Attending a scientific meeting is invigorating, though it can also be exhausting and overwhelming for even experienced scientists. Time spent at a meeting results in new ideas and new collaborations as well as recognition of research accomplishments, all of which help generate the energy, creativity, and enthusiasm that helps drive the process of science.

Figure 4: Poster session at American Geophysical Union meeting in 2007.

Key Concepts for this chapter

▶ Scientific meetings bring scientists from all over the world together to communicate the results of new research.

▶ The growth of scientific meetings is closely tied to the growth and development of scientific societies since the 1800s.

▶ Individual scientists attend meetings in order to get feedback and disseminate their work, make connections with scientists in their field and beyond, and learn about new research, tools, and ideas.

References

AAAS, 2010, About AAAS: *History & Archives*, Volume 2010.

Daemmrich, A.A., Gray, N.R. and Shaper, L., 2006, (eds.) *Reflections from the Frontiers: 75 Years at the Frontiers of Science with Gordon Research Conferences, 1931-2006*, Volume 2010.

Gribbin, J., 2007, *The Fellowship: Gilbert, Bacon, Harvey, Wren, Newton, and the Story of a Scientific Revolution*: London, Overlook Hardcover, 352 p.

Kohlstedt, S.G., Sokal, M.M., and Lewenstein, B.V., 1999, *The Establishment of Science in America*: New Brunswock, NJ, Rutgers University Press, 236 p.

New York Times, 2010, Gulf of Mexico Oil Spill (2010), *Times Topics*, Volume 2011.

Afterword

Scientists do not generally think of themselves as belonging to a "culture of science," and yet there are customs and ways of thinking that unite us across disciplines, nationalities, and ethnicities. If you are a professional scientist who is reading this, we hope you feel that we have portrayed your culture accurately and effectively. And we hope that you have learned something new about science, as we did in writing these chapters.

If you are not someone who already spends their days (and, often, nights) engaged in doing science, we hope that you have found these pages interesting, informative, and perhaps even inspiring. Science plays a critical role in our world, and you can't get away with ignoring it. Frankly, it's far too interesting to ignore.

As scientists, we are always seeking feedback on our work. If you would like to get in touch, please visit our website (www.visionlearning.com) and click the "Contact Us" link.

Anthony Carpi, PhD (Cornell University)

Anthony is a Professor of Environmental Toxicology and Chemistry and Director of the undergraduate research program in science at John Jay College of the City University of New York. He has created and teaches a host of courses at both the undergraduate and graduate level to educate students in the methodologies of science. These include science in society, research methods, and scientific writing. He has also developed a variety of online and physical resources to support diverse audiences of students as they learn about the content and process of science. In addition to his work in science education, Anthony's scientific research focuses on the detection, transport, and chemistry of trace atmospheric pollutants toward understanding the effect that climate change may have on their biogeochemical cycles and potential toxicity. In 2011, Anthony was presented with a Presidential Award for Excellence in Science, Math, and Engineering Mentoring by Barack Obama.

Anne E. Egger, PhD (Stanford University)

Anne is an Assistant Professor in Geological Sciences and Science Education at Central Washington University. From 2004 to 2011, she was the Undergraduate Program Coordinator and director of the undergraduate research program in the School of Earth Sciences at Stanford University. She teaches a variety of courses where she integrates the process of science, including introductory physical geology, science methods for education majors, research preparation, and science writing. Anne also leads workshops for faculty to help them integrate the process of science into their teaching. In her research, she combines geology and geophysics to better understand the geologic setting and faulting history of regions such as the Basin and Range, lending insight into the study of seismic hazards and potential for geothermal energy exploration.

Index

Made in the USA
Middletown, DE
31 December 2015